D0166369

The Making of Sporting Cultures

The Making of Sporting Cultures presents an analysis of western sport by examining how the collective passions and feelings of people have contributed to the making of sport as a 'way of life'. The popularity of sport is so pronounced in some cases that we speak of certain sports as 'national pastimes'. Baseball in the United States, soccer in Britain and cricket in the Caribbean are among the relevant examples discussed.

Rather than regarding the historical development of sport as the outcome of passive spectator reception, this work is interested in how sporting cultures have been made and developed over time through the active engagement of its enthusiasts. This is to study the history of sport not only 'from below', but also 'from within', as a means to understanding the 'deep relationship' between sport and people within class contexts – the middle class as well as the working class. Contestation over the making of sport along axes of race, gender and class are discussed where relevant. A range of cultural writers and theorists are examined in regard to both how their writing can help us understand the making of sport and as to how sport might be located within an overall cultural context – in different places and times.

The book will appeal to students and academics within humanities disciplines such as cultural studies, history and sociology and to those in sport studies programmes interested in the historical, cultural and social aspects of sport.

This book was published as a special issue of *Sport in Society*.

John Hughson is Professor of Sport and Cultural Studies at the University of Central Lancashire, England.

The Making of Sporting Cultures

John Hughson

Routledge
Taylor & Francis Group

LONDON AND NEW YORK

First published 2009 by Routledge
2 Park Square, Milton Park, Abingdon, Oxfordshire OX14 4RN

Simultaneously published in the USA and Canada
by Routledge
711 Third Avenue, New York, NY 10017

Routledge is an imprint of the Taylor & Francis Group, an informa business

© 2009 Taylor & Francis

First issued in paperback 2011

Typeset in Times by Value Chain, India

All rights reserved. No part of this book may be reprinted or reproduced or utilised in any form or by any electronic, mechanical, or other means, now known or hereafter invented, including photocopying and recording, or in any information storage or retrieval system, without permission in writing from the publishers.

British Library Cataloguing in Publication Data
A catalogue record for this book is available from the British Library

ISBN13: 978-0-415-46836-7 (hbk)
ISBN13: 978-0-415-67585-7 (pbk)

CONTENTS

SERIES EDITORS' FOREWORD

SPORT IN THE GLOBAL SOCIETY was launched in the late nineties. It now has over one hundred volumes. Until recently an odd myopia characterised academia with regard to sport. The global *groves of academe* remained essentially Cartesian in inclination. They favoured a mind/body dichotomy: thus the study of ideas was acceptable; the study of sport was not. All that has now changed. Sport is now incorporated, intelligently, within debate about *inter alia* ideologies, power, stratification, mobility and inequality. The reason is simple. In the modern world sport is everywhere: it is as ubiquitous as war. E.J. Hobsbawm, the Marxist historian, once called it the one of the most significant of the new manifestations of late nineteenth century Europe. Today it is one of the most significant manifestations of the twenty-first century world. Such is its power, politically, culturally, economically, spiritually and aesthetically, that sport beckons the academic more persuasively than ever – to borrow, and refocus, an expression of the radical historian Peter Gay – 'to explore its familiar terrain and to wrest new interpretations from its inexhaustible materials'. As a subject for inquiry, it is replete, as he remarked of history, with profound 'questions unanswered and for that matter questions unasked'.

Sport seduces the teeming 'global village'; it is the new opiate of the masses; it is one of the great modern experiences; its attraction astonishes only the recluse; its appeal spans the globe. Without exaggeration, sport is a mirror in which nations, communities, men and women now see themselves. That reflection is sometimes bright, sometimes dark, sometimes distorted, sometimes magnified. This metaphorical mirror is a source of mass exhilaration and depression, security and insecurity, pride and humiliation, bonding and alienation. Sport, for many, has replaced religion as a source of emotional catharsis and spiritual passion, and for many, since it is among the earliest of memorable childhood experiences, it infiltrates memory, shapes enthusiasms, serves fantasies. To co-opt Gay again: it blends memory and desire.

Sport, in addition, can be a lens through which to scrutinise major themes in the political and social sciences: democracy and despotism and the great associated movements of socialism, fascism, communism and capitalism as well as political cohesion and confrontation, social reform and social stability.

The story of modern sport is the story of the modern world – in microcosm; a modern global tapestry permanently being woven. Furthermore, nationalist and imperialist, philosopher and politician, radical and conservative have all sought in sport a manifestation of national identity, status and superiority.

Finally, for countless millions sport is the personal pursuit of ambition, assertion, well-being and enjoyment.

For all the above reasons, sport demands the attention of the academic. *Sport in the Global Society* is a response.

J.A.Mangan, Boria Majumdar
and Mark Dyreson – Series Editors

Sport in the Global Society

Sport in the Global Society

Series Editors: J.A. Mangan, Boria Majumdar and Mark Dyreson

The Making of Sporting Cultures

Sport in the Global Society

Series Editors: J.A. Mangan, Boria Majumdar and Mark Dyreson

As Robert Hands in *The Times* recently observed the growth of sports studies in recent years has been considerable. This unique series with over one hundred volumes in the last decade has played its part. Politically, culturally, emotionally and aesthetically, sport is a major force in the modern world. Its impact will grow as the world embraces ever more tightly the contemporary secular trinity: the English language, technology and sport. *Sport in the Global Society* will continue to record sport's phenomenal progress across the world stage.

Other Titles in the Series

Sport and American Society
Exceptionalism, Insularity, 'Imperialism'
Edited by Mark Dyreson and J.A. Mangan

Sport and Foreign Policy in a Globalizing World
Edited by Steven J. Jackson and Stephen Haigh

Sport and International Relations
An Emerging Relationship
Edited by Roger Levermore and Adrian Budd

Sport and Memory in North America
Edited by Steven Wieting

Sport, Civil Liberties and Human Rights
Edited by Richard Giulianotti and David McArdle

Sport, Culture and History
Region, Nation and Globe
Brian Stoddart

Sport in Asian Society
Past and Present
Edited by Fan Hong and J.A. Mangan

Sport in Australasian Society
Past and Present
Edited by J.A. Mangan and John Nauright

Sport in Europe
Politics, Class, Gender
Edited by J.A. Mangan

Sport in Films
Edited by Emma Poulton and Martin Roderick

Sport in Latin American Society
Past and Present
Edited by Lamartine DaCosta and J.A. Mangan

Sport in South Asian Society
Past and Present

Edited by Boria Majumdar and J.A. Mangan

Sport in the City
Cultural Connections
Edited by Michael Sam and John E. Hughson

Sport in the Cultures of the Ancient World
New Perspectives
Edited by Zinon Papakonstantinou

Sport in the Pacific
Colonial and Postcolonial Consequencies
Edited by C. Richard King

Sport, Media, Culture
Global and Local Dimensions
Edited by Alina Bernstein and Neil Blain

Sport, Nationalism and Orientalism
The Asian Games
Edited by Fan Hong

Sport Past and Present in South Africa
(Trans)forming the Nation
Edited by Scarlet Cornelissen and Albert Grundlingh

Sport Tourism
Edited by Heather J. Gibson

Sporting Cultures
Hispanic Perspectives on Sport, Text and the Body
Edited by David Wood and P. Louise Johnson

Sporting Nationalisms
Identity, Ethnicity, Immigration and Assimilation
Edited by Mike Cronin and David Mayall

Superman Supreme
Fascist Body as Political Icon – Global Fascism
Edited by J.A. Mangan

The making of sporting cultures: introduction

'I love baseball. You know it doesn't have to mean anything, it's just beautiful to watch.' So declares Woody Allen in his 1983 film *Zelig*. Of course, much has been written on the meaning of baseball. A recent book by the political scientist Michael Mandelbaum bearing the title *The Meaning of Sports* carries chapters on the importance of baseball, American football and basketball to people in the United States.[1] But to write on the meaning of sport to people's lives is not to take issue with Allen's heralding of baseball's pure aesthetic quality. Indeed, such questioning may well find some people believe baseball to be an art form and it is in this capacity that it means a great deal to them.

The aesthetic appreciation of sport and its expression in collective contexts is of central interest to the present volume. The volume, as the title suggests, is especially concerned with how communal passions and feelings of people have been so strongly invested as to make possible a discussion of the *making* of sporting cultures. Such discussion implies dissatisfaction with the historical tendency within cultural and social criticism to regard sport as an element of mass-produced popular culture, handed down to, and passively consumed by, a compliant and indiscriminate audience. This view is raised and challenged at various points throughout the volume.

Discussion throughout the volume is marked by explicit reference to cultural history. While the terms cultural history and social history are becoming increasingly interchangeable within contemporary scholarship, I believe there is reason to discuss these approaches to history as related yet distinct. The case for a cultural history approach to the study of sport is set out in the opening essay and need not be rehearsed in these introductory comments. The volume proceeds with thematic rather than chronological essays and an early essay on sporting customs within ancient Greece and Rome is included in such vein. As the rock music historian Greil Marcus has noted, 'history without myth is surely a wasteland; but myths are compelling only when they are at odds with history'.[2] Such has been and continues to be the legacy of ancient sport; its myths in various retellings pervade the histories of modern sport. And with modern sport, as with ancient, investigating the propensity of myth rather than debunking it tends to be the more fruitful historical undertaking.

The Making of Sporting Cultures forms part of an ongoing project on sport and modernity. The volume is not offered as my final word on, let alone a thoroughgoing coverage of, the topic. More central is the concern with a cultural historical approach to the study of sport than a presumption to present a comprehensive cultural history of sport over the years. Accordingly, the volume focuses on a number of key sports that have provoked collective passions to the extent that such sports have been popularly referred to as 'national pastimes' and may therefore be discussed as elements within what Raymond Williams identified as the 'common culture' of particular countries. Baseball in the United States and association football (soccer)

John Hughson, Professor of Sport and Cultural Studies, International Football Institute, University of Central Lancashire, Preston, UK. Correspondence to: jehughson@uclan.ac.uk in Great Britain bear focus throughout much of the volume with excursions into other sports and national contexts occurring along the way, for example, cricket in the Caribbean islands.

In the opening essay it is contended that via a cultural history approach we can best understand how particular sports, in particular places, have, over time, been appreciated aesthetically in collective contexts and may thus be regarded as forms of popular art. This essay is intended to provoke readers' thoughts on, and further historical study into, sensuous experiences of sporting appreciation that have resulted in the *making of sporting cultures*. Relevant reflection is offered in subsequent essays upon empirical examples, as indicated, soccer in Britain and baseball in the United States being at the fore. In what might be regarded as a merging of intellectual history and cultural history a number of writers – some of whom wrote very little, if anything, about sport – are discussed throughout the volume. The reason for this is to locate the consideration of sport as a form of culture within a relevant and historically pertinent framework of enquiry. Sometimes unexpected sources of cultural commentary are able to provide new angles to look at the empirical circumstances of collective sporting passions.

Following the opening essay outlining the case for a cultural history of sport, and a second essay on the sporting culture of the Greeks and Romans – including the emergence of the 'negative classicism' that has developed in modern times in antipathy to so-called mass culture – *The Making of Sporting Cultures* proceeds with essays on physical culture and the sporting body, the making of sporting culture within contexts of class, the making of sporting culture within contexts of colonialism, the cultural significance of sport heroes, the cultural significance of sport within the modern city and the significance of documentary and feature film to an understanding of the relationship between sport and cultural history. The volume concludes – borrowing a term from John MacAloon – by considering the 'global triumph' of sport.

A number of colleagues and friends within the area of sport scholarship are to be thanked for various forms of advice and support over the years. Some of these acknowledgements are long overdue. Thank you to Wray Vamplew, Philip Mosely, Richard Cashman, Richard Giulianotti, Chris Hallinan, David Rowe, Jim McKay, Tara Magdalinski, Eric Dunning, Emma Poulton and Boria Majumdar. Thank you also to Frederic Roberts and Frank Ardolino for generously supplying hard copies of papers difficult to obtain in New Zealand.

The Making of Sporting Cultures was written during my time at the University of Otago and I must thank students in my second year undergraduate course on the history of sport for their attentiveness to some of the material that has found its way into the volume. Discussions with my doctoral student Christin Tapsell on the history of the mind/body dichotomy were especially helpful to the preparation of the essay on physical culture. I am enormously grateful to my lecturing assistants at Otago, Fiona McLachlan and Geoffery Zain Kohe. Their ability to put up with the cranky 'old man' is testimony to the strength of human spirit that I attempt to invoke at points throughout the volume. It has been my pleasure to work with them.

Notes

[1] Mandelbaum, *The Meaning of Sports*.
[2] Marcus, *Mystery Train*, 123.

References

Mandelbaum, Michael. *The Meaning of Sports: Why Americans Watch Baseball, Football, and Basketball and What They See When They Do*. New York: Public Affairs, 2004.
Marcus, G. *Mystery Train: Images of America in Rock'n'Roll Music*. 4th rev ed. New York: Plume, 1997.

Cultural history and the study of sport

This essay sets out to make the case for cultural history to be used as a particular form of historical study, distinct from other approaches. Imperative to the essay, therefore, is the setting out of what is meant by cultural history. An immediate difficulty arises in that there is no one accepted definition of cultural history held by those who regard themselves as cultural historians, let alone by writers who find themselves categorized, in one way or another, as scholarly contributors to the field of cultural history. Whatever differences may exist between cultural historians, and those sometimes described as such, there must be some commonality of enterprise if we can speak meaningfully of cultural history. In his *What is Cultural History*, Peter Burke proposes that 'the common ground of cultural historians might be described as a concern with the symbolic and its interpretation'.[1] This basic understanding of the project of cultural history permeates the essays in the present volume. Accordingly, focus is placed on the symbolic importance of sport to people. The meanings people in western countries give to engagements with sport – both as participants and spectators – evince a life passion not generally observable in other cultural domains.

A fundamental point of enquiry is, therefore, in the symbolic meaning sport has to people's lives, not in the symbolism of sport in an objectified textual sense. Furthermore, the focus is on peoples' collective – rather than individual – emotional investment in sport. Inspirational to this interest is the cultural historical scholarship that became associated with the emergence of the academic area of cultural studies in Britain in the early 1960s. The so-called founding figures of cultural studies, Richard Hoggart, Raymond Williams and E.P. Thompson, each concentrated on the symbolic significance of cultural activities to the working class. In doing so they moved the academic study of culture beyond the formal arts to make the study of culture an intrinsic dimension of the historical study of the common people in Britain. The importance of Hoggart and Williams to the cultural study of sport – in relation to the theme 'common culture' – has been discussed at length by the author elsewhere.[2] E.P. Thompson is especially inspirational to the understanding of cultural history being concerned with how culture is 'made' within collective contexts, although, I go on to argue, the related focus need not be confined to the working class. Thompson's account of the classed nature of cultural history is taken up in a subsequent essay in this volume. Towards the conclusion of the present essay, Thompson's grievance with overly theoretical interpretations of culture is discussed in relation to the intellectual project of cultural history. The essay commences with a reconsideration of the work of Raymond Williams. Williams is especially pertinent here as he explicitly ties a definitional understanding of culture into an analytical outline of cultural history.

Locating culture

In his enquiry into the meaning of *Keywords* Williams – as often cited – declared, 'culture is of the two or three most complicated words in the English language'.[3] The main reason for this complication, according to Williams, is that the word culture, over time, became muddled within 'several distinct intellectual disciplines' and 'incompatible systems of thought'. Williams's own attempt at conceptual clarification is evident in his early landmark studies, *Culture and Society* and *The Long Revolution*. In the latter Williams identifies three 'general categories in the definition of culture'.[4] Firstly, the 'ideal' where culture is associated with a 'state of human perfection'. The second category is the 'documentary', in which culture is recorded within 'intellectual and imaginative work'. These two categories are closely related, the second consisting of a body of works that give inspiration to fulfilment of the ideal. The spirit of Matthew Arnold (nineteenth-century educator, poet and cultural critic) pervades both categories: culture according to Arnold involved 'the best which has been thought and said in the world'.[5] His view of culture – contrary to his caricaturing within cultural studies – was dynamic; he believed that perpetuating human awareness of perfection (the ideal culture) required the regeneration of great works in art and literature (documentary culture).

To the ideal and documentary categories of culture, Williams added a third – the 'social' definition of culture. It is worth quoting Williams's explanation of the social category of culture at length as his linkage between this category and the other two is insightful to an understanding of cultural history:

> culture is a description of a particular way of life, which expresses certain meanings and values not only in art and learning but also in institutions and ordinary behaviour. The analysis of culture, from such a definition, is the clarification of the meanings and values implicit and explicit in a particular way of life, a particular culture. Such analysis will include the historical criticism already referred to, in which intellectual and imaginative works are analysed in relation to particular traditions and societies, but will also include analysis of elements in the way of life that to followers of the other definitions are not 'culture' at all.[6]

This outlining of the 'social' definition of culture reiterates Williams's well-known earlier claim that 'culture is ordinary'.[7] Williams clearly suggests that human activities unlikely to be recognized as culture under the first two categories are, according to a social definition, 'elements' of culture within 'a particular way of life'. Williams did not, at this point, identify 'elements' of culture that exist beyond the realm of 'intellectual and imaginative works', but a later comment towards the conclusion of *The Long Revolution* where Williams rhetorically questions, 'can we agree, perhaps ... that football is indeed a wonderful game', indicates his recognition of sport as an example of such an element.[8] Importantly, by broadening the definition of culture to include 'elements' of popular culture such as associational football (soccer), Williams is not proposing a shift to cultural relativism, but rather, promoting a genuinely humanistic view of culture in which elements traditionally not considered part of the cultural domain must be given due acknowledgement to the extent that they contribute to the enrichment of life.[9] Williams's insistence that sport 'is as real as the need for art' is not about a cultural levelling down, but about the elevation of sport to recognize its significance within 'particular way(s) of life'.[10] Williams does not suggest that all forms of sport are of equivalent cultural worth and he would accept that, as with the arts, cultural distinctions should be made in regard to sport.[11] Sport, like the arts, embodies values intrinsic to the lived expression of the 'universal human condition'. Sport thus provides a useful means for seeing the connections between Williams's categories of culture, certainly the ideal and the social. Sport as documentary culture, in the manner of Williams, is discussed in various essays of the volume as illustration of the connection at work.

Williams was acutely aware of the difficulties facing the cultural historian. While recognizing the importance of studying particular cultural aspects of historical periods, he warned against compartmentalizing the particular in cultural study. Williams's focus was panoramic and he adopted, albeit in modified way, the conservative dictum of culture involving a 'whole way of life'.[12] According to Williams, 'Cultural history must be more than the sum of the particular histories, for it is with the relations between them, the particular forms of the whole organization, that it is especially concerned'.[13]

While Williams recommended a wide-framed analysis of the culture within a period, he believed the temporal breadth of historical study to be limited and subject to qualification. Specifically he maintained:

> It is only ... our own time and place that we can expect to know, in any substantial way. We can learn a great deal of the life of other places and times, but certain elements, it seems to me, will always be irrecoverable ... The most difficult thing to get hold of, in studying any past period, is this felt sense of the quality of life at a particular place and time: a sense of the ways in which the particular activities combined into a way of thinking and living.[14]

Learning and retelling the past, from Williams's perspective, can never be done completely and adequately. It is necessarily a subjective business because cultural history is ultimately not about presenting a precise picture of a time but getting to know, as closely as possible, how a particular time was experienced by particular groups of people. To know of the cultural experience of one group of people in a period it is important to know of the experience of others, and Williams – influenced by the anthropologist Ruth Benedict – describes the social relationships that form around and between cultural 'interests and activities' as the 'pattern of culture'. However, Williams sought a 'firmer' and more 'definite' term to explain how the 'pattern of culture' held together to constitute the 'culture of a period'. He thus referred to the 'structure of feeling'.[15]

Although applicable to particular periods Williams's 'structure of feeling' is a historically dynamic term. The structure of feeling changes from one period to the next, but is, nevertheless, inherited in 'certain ways' across generations. It is not 'learnt' but, as Williams's reference to feeling suggests, passed on through collective sensual engagement with elements of culture, for example, generations of familial support of a football team based in identification with locality. According to Williams, 'the new generation responds in its own ways to the unique world it is inheriting ... shaping its creative response into a new structure of feeling'.[16]

The historical nature of culture is further explained by Williams with reference to 'levels' of culture. The 'lived culture' of the current period (level one) is connected to the past 'period cultures' (level two) by the 'culture of the selective tradition' (level three).[17] The cultural relevance of past periods – often temporally marked by decades – to the lived culture of the present is carried by the selective tradition comprising aspects and items of culture. Many aspects and items of culture will be forgotten and only some will leave a mark over time. It is thus the *selective* tradition that denotes contemporary remembrance of culture from the past. The establishment of cultural tradition, for Williams, involves active and ongoing engagement with the 'selective tradition':

> Cultural tradition can be seen as a continual selection and reselection of ancestors. Particular lines will be drawn, often for as long as a century, and then suddenly with some new stage in growth these will be cancelled or weakened, and new lines drawn ... We tend to underestimate the extent to which the cultural tradition is not only a selection but also an interpretation. We see most past work through our own experience, without even making the effort to see it in something like its original terms.[18]

'Spirit of the age' and 'special histories'

Cultural history is thus concerned with understanding cultural tradition as it is formed and redeveloped in one period and passed on to the next. Rather than merely looking back, cultural historians, such as Williams, seek to gain perspective from within a particular historical period and look forward to the cultural developments in subsequent periods. In this way cultural historians make sense of the ongoing inheritance of cultural or selective tradition. Studying the cultural connections within particular historical periods is usually traced to the philosopher

Hegel's interest in the notion *Zeitgeist* or 'spirit of the age'.[19] Williams does not use this actual phrase but at one point does use a related terminology associated with Hegel, 'spirit of the nation'. The notion of *Zeitgeist* was explicitly brought into British cultural study by Matthew Arnold and has been reflected in some historical works, notably G.M. Young's *Portrait of an Age: Victorian England*.[20]

Jacob Burckhardt (1818–97), a founding figure of academic cultural history, advocated studying the 'spirit of the age', but in a way removed from Hegel's determinism – i.e. Hegel's belief that history follows an inevitable path of progression. Burckhardt made no claim toward viewing the march of history but was interested in the cultural 'cross-sections' that make up the 'unity of an age'.[21] Related to this understanding, Burckhardt was not interested in explaining the causes of particular events but in the interrelationships between what we have been referring to thus far as cultural elements. Similar to subsequent cultural historians, including Williams, Burckhardt did not invest greatly in the idea of historical truth but focussed on what people believed and how they interpreted historical moments.[22] In keeping with his historical view, Burckhardt was a product of his time and his account of culture was limited to the cultural activities associated with the social elites in the periods he examined. Nevertheless, as Oswyn Murray points out, 'the study of gestures, customs and behaviour patterns, festivals and other forms of popular expression' – the everyday life of contemporary cultural studies – was all to be found in the work of Burckhardt, and his intellectual legacy to the study of quotidian ways should thus be acknowledged.

Burckhardt's focus on 'high culture' did not preclude sport, this being particularly the case with his discussion of the Olympic Games within the cultural life of ancient Greece. Indeed, Burckhardt provides much fuller discussion of sport and physical activity within this age than Williams, Hoggart and Thompson do in their respective accounts of working-class life in Britain. Of course, it can be said that one could hardly provide an historical account of ancient Greece without discussing the Olympic Games and such activities as wrestling, yet one might also say that it is surprising that the aforementioned writers wrote so little about sport in their cultural histories of the British working class given the prominence of sport, particularly association football, within that class's collective lifestyle.

While sport has not been particularly well accounted for within broader cultural historical studies, cultural history has rarely been specifically addressed within the sub-field of sport academe known as sport history.[23] An interesting exception is an essay published by Roberta J. Park in 1983. Park, following Mandelbaum, distinguishes between 'special' and 'general' histories.[24] She indicates that special histories are firmly focused on their particular subject matters and reference to other aspects of culture remains tangential rather than integral to the study. Mandelbaum's distinction rests on a definitional axis between culture and society, 'special histories (which deal with culture) trace various aspects of culture as they arise or change in a society, or as they cross the boundaries separating societies, whereas general history (which deals with societies) is concerned with the nature of and the changes in particular societies'. However, Park's discussion suggests that culture can be accounted for in both special and general histories. Relatedly, it is useful to see a *cultural history* involving the infusion of the general into the special. Accordingly, a project dedicated to the cultural historical study of sport simultaneously signifies speciality and evinces generality. It achieves the latter by highlighting the connections between sport and other forms of culture within a particular time and place. Conversely, Park contends that sport is as important to general studies of culture as the general study of culture is to the specialist study of sport:

> When *culture* is conceived of as a set of shared conventions by which human beings orient themselves to the world and to each other, give *meaning* to their existence, and engage

in a whole range of symbolic interactions, the importance of studying games and sports in historical contexts becomes apparent.[25]

The omission of sport from generalist cultural histories will, therefore, say more about the biases of particular historians than about the cultural significance of sport during any given historical time and place.

The *style* of cultural history

There is a tendency within contemporary history to use the terms cultural history and social history interchangeably. For example an editorial in the first issue (2004) of the journal *Cultural and Social History* assumes 'that "the cultural" and "the social" are mutually constitutive and inextricably linked … "culture" is understood not as an entity distinct from "society", but as a product of social practice'. Culture and society are thus regarded as hermeneutic equivalents. However, although the word culture has been opened to social interpretation, particularly since its systematic redefining by Raymond Williams, this need not result in a terminological conflation that closes off distinct lines of enquiry. Thus we continue to speak of works in cultural history and works in social history. Both forms of enquiry might appear in an overarching historical study; thus, in his textbook *The New Nature of History*, Arthur Marwick argues for a *total history*. Total history 'endeavours to integrate together all aspects of human society, aesthetic and cultural, as well as social, economic and political, private as well as public'.[26]

The case for a distinctive cultural history need not be at odds with Marwick's ambition. A cultural history is undoubtedly interested in the social, economic and political dimensions of life during a period; a lack of interest in these dimensions would inhibit an understanding of the cultural realm. Cultural history is interested in the social patterns of cultural activity and in the economic dimensions of culture and related questions of cultural production. Without such an interest cultural history will have no understanding of how cultural items are produced at particular points in time within changing economic contexts. Cultural history must also be cognizant of the political climate of a time or remain naive to political issues that come to bear on cultural life. The overlapping interest is mutual as social, economic and political histories often address points of articulation with culture.

However, although culture may well be embraced within a 'total history', the cultural aspects of historical study are distinct in character from the social, economic and political aspects of historical study. To understand the distinct character of cultural history we can recall from the opening paragraph, reference to the 'symbolic meaning' of culture to people's lives. Sociologists are also interested in 'symbolic meaning', especially those who work according to theoretical constructs generically called interpretivism. However, the sociologist's interest is in 'symbolic meaning' as a social process that gives rise to patterns of social interaction. They are certainly interested in the collective meanings of cultural items and practices but in a secondary way. The cultural historian, by contrast, is *primarily* interested in the symbolic meanings that people give to cultural forms. Cultural history thus resides in the disciplinary domain of the humanities with a direct concern in understanding lived human experience, whereas sociology, and to some extent the related area of social history, is more appropriately located in the domain of social sciences, where the emphasis is on the systematic study of social phenomena whether in terms of social structures or social interactions.

With specific regard to the respective forms of historical study, it can be said that cultural history is interested in the humanizing effects of culture whereas social history is interested in the social outcomes of meanings and related usages of culture. Social history is interested in what happens after interpretations and engagements with culture, whereas cultural history is interested in the very interpretations and engagements. Cultural history is concerned in the sensory dimension of these interpretations and engagements and, therefore, recognizes the sensuousness of 'lived experience'. The poet John Milton, who was dissatisfied with the sexual connotation carried by the existing word sensual, reputedly brought the word *sensuous* into the English language in the mid 1600s. Milton sought a word to define a state of heightened sensory awareness that was not merely associable with carnal gratification. Milton needed such terminological clarification to make a morally acceptable case for poetry to become more 'simple, sensuous and passionate'.[27] Studying the sensuous experience of culture is the hallmark of cultural history and is its ultimate distinction from social science-inspired historical enquiry.

This point is not explicitly made within the writing of keynote cultural historians but is clearly alluded to in such work. For example, Johan Huizinga (1872–1945), often cited as the indirect heir to Burckhardt, contends that the cultural historian studies particular cultural activities as 'expressions of spirit' within a particular time.[28] According to Jacques Barzun (b. 1907) in his essay *Cultural History: A Synthesis* (1954), 'cultural life is both intricate and emotionally complex' and the cultural historian's realization of this duality results in a connection between fact and emotion. Cultural history is thus unlike other forms of history which are high on detail but 'emotionally simple'.[29] The connection between fact and emotion is, Barzun maintains, established by the cultural historian's interest in *style*. Style, pertaining to the cultural forms of a period, is 'a pose, a stance', which is indicative of peoples' sensuous attachment to and usage of material items of culture.[30] Importantly, style 'means a good deal more than outward marks of fashion', it embraces the idea of 'cultural effort that is ... creative from that which is given, a product or resultant of anonymous forces'. Style is the 'common feel and texture' of culture, clearly for Barzun; it is a matter not of intellect but of the senses.[31]

Thomas Babington Macaulay makes reference to 'popular style' in his monumental *History of England*, written in the mid 1800s.[32] However, this popular style is a form of speech used by theologians in the 1600s to make religious debate comprehensible to the general public. Macaulay's foremost awareness is not of the common peoples' cultural interests. Although Macaulay incorporated discussion of popular activities into his *History* he overwhelmingly presents an historical account 'from above'. As such, as with other historians of his time, he was not able to grasp the sensuous significance of cultural life to sections of society outside of the elite. Writing in 1976, Peter Burke declared the history of *popular* culture to be a new and exciting development within academe.[33] Burke was writing at a time when the historical study of popular culture had emerged in both undergraduate and postgraduate programmes in Britain, for example at the Open University in regard to the former and the Centre for Contemporary Cultural Studies at the University of Birmingham the latter. Burke's alternative naming of this history of popular culture as the 'history of the inarticulate' lends agreement to the view that popular culture is experienced sensuously. Certainly, popular and common cultural interests are today widely discussed by the people who enjoy them. Modern communication has ensured the articulation of all forms of culture. However, the more important point here is that once it is accepted that culture is primarily a matter of sensuous experience rather than intellect, the task for cultural historians is how the sensuous experience of culture in its different forms (whether popular or so-called elite) across time and place can be recorded, studied and reported. If culture is primarily sensuous its historical articulation is necessarily problematic.

Coming to know: 'How they go on'

More generally, recognition of the historian's difficulty in representing common voices has led to growing interest in the method known as oral history. A leading work in this area is Paul Thompson's *The Voice of the Past*, originally published in 1978. How the voice of the past is studied depends on the temporal focus of particular projects. A historian can study voices of the past long gone by locating materials that would not appear in official recordings of the opinion of a period. Oral history is also concerned with recording the living voices of the past, the key rationale being to capture the reflections of older people on life in previous decades, before they pass away. Historical writing on communities and townships is increasingly based on this approach.[34] At a third level, one not readily recognized as historical work, academics record the voices of the present, which over time become voices of the past. Exemplary in this regard, and especially pertinent to cultural history, is the work of Paul Willis. In his 1978 book *Profane Culture* Willis studies the contemporaneous subcultures of the early 1970s, bikers and hippies, and notes a homological fit between the music enjoyed by the respective groups and their collective cultural values – viz. the hippies liked mellow popular music and favoured a tranquil life existence, while the bikers liked loud rock music and favoured aggressive non-conformity to social rules. Willis thus notes that 'particular items parallel and reflect the … style … attitudes and feelings of the social group'.[35] Willis's work now stands as a cultural history of the recent past, focussing on the sensuous cultural experience of distinct groupings of young people in their time.

Willis's favoured methodology is ethnography, a research mode related to oral history and used chiefly by anthropologists in the direct observation of members of particular social groups. Influential to ethnographers, such as Willis, is anthropologist Clifford Geertz's recommended practice of 'thick description'. Geertz believed that mere description of actions gives little insight into their meaning. He suggests that understanding the cultural significance of group dynamics requires a research technique whereby the researcher can gain insight into embedded cultural meanings.[36] Willis believes this to be best done by researchers immersing themselves into the cultural lifestyle of groups being studied:

> The ethnographic impulse is to … go and look for yourself, to see 'what's going on' as bound up with 'how they go on'. Physical and sensuous presence then allows observation and witness and the use of the five-sense channels for recording data relating to social atmosphere, emotional colour and unspoken assumptions. You can sense for yourself important aspects of context and of the material and institutional features of the enclosures and regimes through which subjects pass, seeing for yourself how they use and manipulate surrounding resources in their cultural practices … how subjects symbolically inhabit their worlds.[37]

Willis thus recognizes culture as involving sensuous collective experience and that optimal research understanding of this experience will come through sensuous field engagement by the researcher. In Harper Lee's novel *To Kill a Mockingbird* Atticus Finch advises his daughter Scout, 'you never really understand a person until you consider things from his [*sic*] point of view … until you climb into his skin and walk around in it'.[38] This notion of corporeal inhabitation captures simply Willis's thoughts on how to study lived cultural experience. Importantly, though, Willis is not a historian, he is an ethnographer and cultural studies academic whose work on contemporary youth culture has become a matter of cultural history with the passing of time. The cultural historian, by the very nature of his/her work cannot have the immediate type of ethnographic engagement discussed by Willis. The research engagement of the cultural historian is vicarious, usually occurring via the usage of source materials – whether documentary or some form of artefact – and, as discussed above, via oral history through discussion with people of senior age about a past period. However, the cultural historian does well to maintain an ethnographic interest in the sensuousness of culture and to bring out, to the best of their capability, not only the voice of the past but the vision and feel as well. The obvious limitations of this endeavour should not be a deterrent. As van Maanen suggests, ethnographic scholarship is excusably impressionistic[39] and this is particularly so in work accounting for the sensuous significance of cultural practices – the staple of cultural history as argued here.

Sport and the 'common people'

The historical bias within cultural history towards high culture has resulted in firmly established links with art history. Indeed, prominent historians in this field, such as Erwin Panofsky (1892–1968), Ernst Gombrich (1909–2002), and Bernard Smith (b. 1916) are referred to interchangeably as either cultural historians or art historians. However, with the expansion of academic interest into popular culture, cultural history has become more inclusive and eclectic. This includes recognition of the history of sport within the sphere of cultural history.[40] Sport is, of course, connected to the broader theme of leisure and, although not declared as cultural histories, a number of works within the history of leisure have tellingly located sport within an overview of the popular pastimes of a particular period. For example, R.W. Malcolmson's *Popular Recreations in English Society 1700–1850* draws on a range of primary and secondary sources with the intention of mapping out the neglected history of the recreational activities of the 'common people'.[41] Malcolmson's work is particularly insightful in revealing overlapping sporting interests of gentlemen and labourers. An example is his retrieval of eloquent first-hand reports describing how both groups would gather in the public house to enthusiastically watch and exchange bets over cock-fights.

Leisure in the Industrial Revolution by Hugh Cunningham is an especially interesting book to consider in terms of cultural history as discussed in this essay. Cunningham explicitly applies E.P. Thompson's idea of the making of culture to leisure and sport. This results in Cunningham contending that leisure and sporting activities were not started 'from high up the social scale and ... diffused downwards',[42] but, to some extent, emerged from the creative cultural life of the common people. The interpretation is most apt for sports with strong working-class roots, such as association football. According to Cunningham, 'middle-class claims for their own impact on the game have had more influence on the historiography of football than they have had on its practice'.[43] In a related point, Cunningham warns historians against overstating the role of macro trends in economic history, such as modernization and urbanization, to explain socio-cultural developments in leisure and sport. To do so, Cunningham believes, risks overlooking the significance of active human engagement in cultural life.

Cunningham's account strikes a chord with Barzun's discussion of culture being creatively made by people and thus having a 'common feel and texture'. Intellectuals of opposing political persuasion hold different versions of this understanding of cultural engagement. Barzun's downplaying of the 'anonymous forces' of cultural production is a conservative rendering of Raymond Williams's later claim in *Marxism and Literature* – a book quoted by Cunningham – that the 'productive forces' of capitalism do not necessarily result in 'negative effects' in the uses of culture by ordinary people.[44] Williams's 'cultural materialism' has proven inspirational to subsequent work in cultural studies by scholars wanting to retain the legacy of Marx without the pessimistic interpretation of popular culture that had become associated with leading Marxist cultural theorists such as Althusser and Adorno. Paul Willis's work is an example of such scholarship, but he has been subsequently criticized for straying so far from the foundations of Marxist political economy that he indulges in 'cultural populism', whereby capitalist production processes are divorced from the analysis of cultural consumption.[45]

Cultural history has itself developed from a pessimistic tradition of cultural analysis. Significantly, Burckhardt was branded as a 'prophet of doom' in Jacques Barzun's essay *Cultural History* and is described in Murray's authoritative biographical notes as a 'pessimistic conservative ... standing against the tide of history'.[46] Burckhardt's pessimism no doubt is tied to his cultural elitism and the seemingly inevitable historical concern that the cultural standards of a given period are threatened by emergent cultural trends. His particular fear about cultural decline subsequent to the high point of Greek civilization is not so different to the fear expressed within British cultural criticism – from Matthew Arnold to F.R. Leavis (1895–1978) – whereby standards of excellence within the English literary tradition are threatened by a morally void, American driven, mass culture. The moral vacuity of sport was explicitly attacked by the English liberals L.T. Hobhouse and C.F.G. Masterman, the latter of whom incorporated sport into his updating of Carlyle's 'question on the condition of England' in 1909. Although liberals such as Hobhouse and Masterman were genuinely concerned with seeing improvement in the living conditions of the working class, their intolerance to sport betrayed both cultural elitism and a total lack of appreciation of the cultural significance of sport to that class.[47]

Beyond pessimism and elitism, Cunningham identifies himself, if somewhat guardedly, as being in the 'embrace of the optimist school of historians'.[48] Cunningham's application of Thompson's making of culture thesis to leisure in Britain between 1780–1880 distances him from the more common historical description of this period, being one of unrelieved gloom. However, Cunningham's contrasting interpretation of the period, as one featuring 'vigorous growth of popular leisure', should not be characterized as celebration. Indeed, Cunningham's analysis of the period incorporates implicit criticism of inhumane leisure activities such as bearbaiting and cockfighting.[49] In their attuning of historical study to the sensuousness of cultural life, cultural historians investigate activities that might be deemed either positively or negatively from both moral and social standpoints. A number of studies within the history of sport allow for evaluation in these terms, thus reflecting the interrelationship, yet not inextricableness, of cultural and social history. Let us take some examples from British scholarship.

Best of British

Exemplary is Richard Holt's *Sport and the British*, published in 1989. Holt's book, focussing on the sporting life of the common people, spans the period from 1800 to the present.[50] Its chapters are ordered in the manner of cultural history according to particular themes, rather than an unbroken chronology. Seemingly positive outcomes of the cultural life of sport are tainted by historically engrained bias and exclusion, no more so than in the case of gender. Holt notes in his introduction:

> Sport has always been a male preserve with its own language, its initiation rites, and models of true masculinity, its clubbable, jokey cosiness. Building male friendships and sustaining large and small communities of men have been the prime purpose of sport. Women have been banished to the sidelines both literally and metaphorically, except for a minority of public schoolgirls.[51]

Accordingly, Holt's later reference to the bolstering of 'civic pride' through sport is qualified by an awareness of the male chauvinism prevalent in working-class sporting culture. Holt claims that working-class men achieved a sense of 'symbolic citizenship' through passionate support of local association football teams, the communal bond sealed in a mutually shared aesthetic experience:

> Bound together with the sense of urban community there was the sheer excitement and beauty of the thing – the perfect pass that suddenly switches the play from end to end, the shuffle and swerve that turns a defence and sends a winger away with the time to cross to a centre-forward tearing past his marker, the sudden reflex movement of a goalkeeper twisting and diving full-length to save a fierce shot. In the end these moments are instinctive and aesthetic, beyond social and historical analysis.[52]

This passage from Holt clearly reveals the sensuous attachment that supporters have to football through aesthetic appreciation. The final sentence implicitly sounds the cultural historian's recognition of the inability of conventional social and historical analysis to grasp the deeply sensory experience of football as physical culture. Holt also recognizes that the cultural experience of football developed within an exclusive masculine domain, claimed by men as 'their' space outside of the home. Holt – again in keeping with cultural history – draws on a literary source, J.B. Priestley's *The Good Companions*, to highlight the male communal affair that football had become by the 1920s:

> It turned you into a member of a new community, all brothers together for an hour and a half, for not only had you escaped from the clanking machinery of this lesser life, from work, wages, rent, doles, sick-pay, insurance-cards, *nagging wives* [emphasis added], ailing children, bad bosses, idle workmen, but you had escaped with most of your mates and your neighbours … cheering together, thumping one another on the shoulders … having pushed your way through a turnstile into another and altogether more splendid kind of life.[53]

Richard Hoggart, in *The Uses of Literacy: Aspects of Working-class Life with Special Reference to Publications and Entertainments*, his classic study that led to the emergence of cultural studies as a field of academic enquiry, noted the communal appeal of rugby league football to young men in his Yorkshire home town. When the Hunslet team returned with the Cup won in the national final at Wembley Stadium they were greeted as 'our lads' and many young male supporters were 'prepared to risk staying out hours after their bedtime for the excitement of seeing their local champions'.[54] For Hoggart, rugby league in the local area became the leisure time focal point of a masculinised 'us', a demarcation point not only from the drudgery of work hours, but also the 'authoritarianism' of the general 'public life' associated with 'them', the bosses and their cohorts in civic officialdom. In an insightful study on the origins of rugby league, Tony Collins notes the complex relationship between the common people and civic leaders in the formation of rugby league clubs. The popularity of rugby league was no doubt manipulated as part of the local bureaucracy's 'quest for civic pride' in towns such as Bradford, Huddersfield and Wakefield, but in a way that did not wrench the *culture* of sport away from the people.[55] The sensuous investment that ordinary men retained in rugby league support fostered a sense of community that existed, at best, on the margins of municipal life. Again, though, the sense of community remained within the realms of masculinity, and, as Collins notes, this was seen as a strong point of rugby league by some of its early leading advocates. The president of the Salford club commented in 1891, 'it was perhaps the only game that was absolutely masculine in the country. Women took part in cricket and other pastimes but he had never heard of them playing football'.[56]

The stubborn masculine roots of football that remain intact today were undoubtedly planted long ago, and, as shown by Collins, are revealed in the cultural historical study of particular codes such as rugby league. Collins, in another study with prominent sport historian Wray Vamplew, examines the enduring historical link between sport and alcohol consumption. The multifaceted cultural connections traced by Collins and Vamplew between these potentially unrelated dimensions of popular leisure – given that the former is customarily associated with health, the latter ill-health – justifies the subtitling of the study as 'a cultural history'.[57] With regard to themes of civic identity and gender, Collins and Vamplew note a direct relationship between alcohol and sport in cases where the local brewery and its product was associated with the football club, 'loyalty to a local beer was often as strong as loyalty to the local team'.[58] In the north of England the local ales were presumed stronger and became a status marker of tough masculinity against a comparatively inferior and insipid beer from the southern counties. This simplistic binary view of strength and weakness extended to football and even cricket as northerners believed their teams to be tougher and therefore in possession of greater competitive spirit. The emergent symbiosis between supporting sport and consuming alcohol further entrenched the masculinity of sporting culture and the exclusion of women from that culture. Sport undoubtedly provides sensuous cultural engagement for devoted enthusiasts, but the attendant cultural life will often be parochial and discriminatory. Studying the sensuousness of culture is a warts and all matter, certainly so in the study of sport. A cultural history is concerned with revealing the various dimensions of sporting passions, rather than celebrating and selectively interpreting the sensuousness of sporting experience.

The *experience* of cultural history

Cunningham concludes *Leisure in the Industrial Revolution* with a brief discussion of 'theoretical perspectives' pertinent to his book. However, perhaps more interesting than Cunningham's actual discussion of theory is his decision to place theory at the end of the book – and only briefly at that – and his reason for so doing. His declaration, 'like many historians I am most comfortable when my feet are firmly planted on empirical ground', gives a clue to the uneasiness that has long existed in the relationship between theory and observation within academic history.[59] Cultural history has a strong empirical tradition, exemplified by the work of Burckhardt and Huizinga. However this tradition has been challenged, significantly since the 1980s. The turn to theory, inspired by the work of Foucault and other theorists of post-structural bent, has resulted in the descriptor 'new cultural history'. Academic work of this kind has been criticized by some historians as a fashionable yet unhelpful development that, in its worst manifestations, risks 'the killing of history'.[60]

Empiricism and theory need not be at odds, the work of Raymond Williams being one of the greatest testaments to this claim. Williams's work became progressively theoretical as he engaged with and adapted the ideas of Marx to contemporary and historical cultural life. However, he was not interested in theory detached from a commitment to understanding and explaining human experience. Williams's faith in theory was that it could enhance this understanding and explanation. Williams's contemporary, the historian E.P. Thompson, was less favourably disposed to theory. Thompson, already famous for his book, *The Making of the English Working Class*, became a key figure in a heated debate at the end of the 1970s in Britain over the roles of theory and empiricism in historical work. Thompson sided decisively with the latter; his lengthy essay *The Poverty of Theory* savagely, yet wittily, attacked the Marxist 'structuralism' of Althusser, the dominant theoretical trend of the time. Thompson regarded structuralism as theory for the sake of theory, with tenuous links to meaningful historical enquiry interested in human cultural experience. Thompson was a Marxist activist as well as an academic and he believed structuralism to be overly deterministic in its emphasis on people being manipulated by the ideology of capitalist society. This view offended Thompson's own that humans are active agents in the shaping of their cultural lives.[61]

Thompson was particularly dismissive of the disjuncture in Althusserian theory between consciousness and experience. He accepted Marx's dictum that the working class needed to become aware of its conditions of exploitation but did not accept that the experience of living under capitalism blighted this awareness. Furthermore, he certainly did not accept the cultural activities and pastimes of the working class to be an extension of their exploited work conditions and a failure of collective class consciousness. Thompson regarded the Marxist intellectual suspicion of human experience as nothing more than lofty supposition 'that ordinary mortals are stupid'.[62] On the contrary, he accepts experience as 'valid and effective but within determined limits: the farmer "knows" his seasons, the sailor "knows" his seas, but both remain mystified by kingship and cosmology'. Thompson's understanding of experience here is supported by Williams in *Keywords*, where experience is discussed in direct relationship to consciousness: 'experience ... is ... the fullest, most open, most active kind of consciousness, and it includes feeling as well as thought'.[63] Similarly, Thompson maintained that there is constant dialogue going on between 'social being' and 'social consciousness' and that intellectuals must appreciate this if they are to understand the 'real world' that goes on 'outside their offices'.[64]

Thompson's attack on theory, as indicated above, in turn drew criticism from theoretically inspired Marxist historians. Of most pertinence to our discussion of cultural history, Thompson is accused of 'romanticism' and 'culturalism'. Believing scientific critique of modern history to be dry and passionless in the neglect of human agency, Thompson turned to the Romantic critique of industrial capitalism, associated with prominent literary figures such as Wordsworth and non-Marxist socialists, principally William Morris.[65] This resultant 'stress on culture' was criticized as a retreat from political economy; Thompson's chief antagonist on the academic left, Richard Johnson, referred to him 'vacating the ground of economic relations'.[66] In related criticism, Perry Anderson accuses Thompson of introducing a 'creeping culturalism' into historical analysis, the emphasis on lived cultural experience being pronounced strongly enough to disqualify *The Poverty of Theory* as a Marxist tract.[67] However, while Thompson's position caused major rumblings within the academic left, this need not be the case for historians without such political disposition. Cultural history can be mindful of the production processes that impinge upon experiential engagement with culture without professing to political partisanship.

Raphael Samuel has noted that 'the Left can make no proprietorial claim' to 'people's history'.[68] The same can be said for cultural histories recounting popular leisure and pastimes. Thompson would no doubt object to his work being detached from Marxist moorings, yet his (and Williams's) interpretation of experience benefits cultural historians wary of the shackles of theoreticism. His contention that, 'people do not only experience their own experience as ideas, within thought and its procedures ... they also experience their own experience as *feeling*, and they handle their feelings within their culture ... as reciprocities, as values or within art', is as significant to the 'whole project' of cultural history as it is to that of socialism – as believed by Thompson.[69] To the extent that we can say that the farmer knows his seasons and the sailor his seas, we may say that the sport enthusiast *knows* his/her game. The cultural history of sport thus takes interest in how sports have been *sensuously known* by people; in how sport has embraced and reflected cultural values and with the symbolic and aesthetic relevance that sport has had to peoples' lives.[70]

Notes

[1] Burke, *What is Cultural History*, 3.
[2] Hughson, Inglis, and Free, *Uses of Sport*, 30–50.
[3] Williams, *Keywords*, 87.
[4] Williams, *The Long Revolution*, 57.
[5] Arnold, *Culture and Anarchy*, 6.
[6] Williams, *The Long Revolution*, 57–8.
[7] Williams, 'Culture is Ordinary'.
[8] Williams, *The Long Revolution*, 364.
[9] Ibid., 59.
[10] Ibid., 364.
[11] The argument for the retention of value distinction within popular culture is well made by Stuart Hall and Paddy Whannel in *The Popular Arts* and by Richard Hoggart in 'Culture: Dead and Alive'.
[12] The conservative position can be found in the cultural commentary of Samuel Taylor Coleridge and T.S. Eliot. Discussed in Hughson, Inglis, and Free, *Uses of Sport*, 9–14.
[13] Williams, *The Long Revolution*, 63.
[14] Ibid.
[15] Ibid., 64.
[16] Ibid., 65.
[17] Ibid., 66.

18 Ibid., 69.

19 Burke, *What is Cultural History*, 7.

20 Williams, *Culture and Society*, 30; Arnold, 'Address to the Wordsworth Society', Young, *Portrait of an Age*.

21 Burke, *Culture and Society in Renaissance Italy*, 8. For the original source see Burckhardt, *The Civilization of the Renaissance*. An excellent critique of Burckhardt's position is set out by Gombrich in *In Search of Cultural History*.

22 Murray, 'Introduction', xvii.

23 Discussion of the institutional origins of academic sport history appears in Struna, 'Sport History'.

24 Park, 'Research and Scholarship'; Mandelbaum, *The Anatomy of Historical Knowledge*, 12, 13.

25 Park, 'Research and Scholarship', 99.

26 Marwick, *The New Nature of History*, 295. A related discussion appears in Burke, 'People's History or Total History'.

27 *The Oxford English Dictionary*, vol.xiv, 989.

28 Huizinga, 'The Task of Cultural History'.

29 Barzun, 'Cultural History', 394.

30 Ibid., 400.

31 Ibid., 399.

32 Macaulay, *History of England*, 606.

33 Burke, 'Oblique Approaches', 71.

34 Thompson, *The Voice of the Past*.

35 Willis, *Profane Culture*, 191.

36 Geertz, *The Interpretation of Cultures*.

37 Willis, *The Ethnographic Imagination*, xiii.

38 Lee, *To Kill a Mockingbird*, 31.

39 van Maanen, *Tales of the Field*.

40 Burke, *What is Cultural History*, 58.

41 Malcolmson, *Popular Recreations in English Society*.

42 Cunningham, *Leisure in the Industrial Revolution*, 10.

43 Ibid., 128.

44 Williams, *Marxism and Literature*, 90–4.

45 A defence of Willis's position on cultural commodities pertaining to sport appears in Hughson and Free, 'Paul Willis'.

46 Murray, 'Introduction', xiii.

47 Hobhouse, *Democracy and Reaction*; Masterman, *The Condition of England*. A useful summary of Hobhouse and Masterman's comments on sport is provided by Peatling, 'Rethinking the History of Criticism of Organised Sport', 363–5.

48 Cunningham, *Leisure in the Industrial Revolution*, 9.

49 Ibid., 45.

50 Holt, *Sport and the British*.

51 Ibid., 8.

52 Ibid., 172.

53 Ibid., 168. The passage is from Priestley, *The Good Companions*, 5–6. The socialist-minded Priestley was well aware of the cultural importance of association football and other sports to the working class. This is made clear in his non-fiction writing in a chapter titled 'The Uncommon Common People' in which he comments: 'we can make a distinction between *the arts* ... and *art*. We can find art of a varying sort in many different activities and places ... it can be discovered in sports and games, and that is where so many of the English common people – certainly the male half of them – have found it and loved it'. Priestley, *The English*, 134.

54 Hoggart, *The Uses of Literacy*, 92. It can be deduced that Hoggart is referring to Hunslet's 11-5 victory over Widnes in the 1934 Challenge Cup final.

[55] Collins, *Rugby's Great Split*, 16.

[56] Ibid., 128.

[57] Collins and Vamplew, *Mud, Sweat and Beers*. One of the authors has indicated in personal correspondence that the use of 'cultural history' in the subtitle was proposed by the publisher.

[58] Ibid., 73.

[59] Cunningham, *Leisure in the Industrial Revolution*, 192.

[60] Windschuttle, *The Killing of History*. See especially the discussion of the 'anti-humanism' of Michel Foucault, 121–57.

[61] Thompson, 'The Poverty of Theory'. A brief discussion of Thompson's antagonism with other British intellectuals is provided by Turner, *British Cultural Studies*, 64–6; a thoroughgoing account by Dworkin, *Cultural Marxism in Postwar Britain*, 225–45.

[62] Thompson, 'The Poverty of Theory', 199.

[63] Williams, *Keywords*, 127.

[64] Thompson, 'The Poverty of Theory', 201.

[65] See also Thompson, *The Romantics* and Thompson, *William Morris*.

[66] Johnson, 'Three Problematics', 221.

[67] Anderson, *Arguments within English Marxism*, 82–3.

[68] Samuel, 'People's History', xx.

[69] Thompson, 'The Poverty of Theory', 363.

[70] Thompson's position on the sensuousness of knowledge bears similarity to Bourdieu's idea of *habitus* – an 'embedded history' which is 'internalised' by an individual and lived out as 'second nature'. Bourdieu, *The Logic of Practice*, 56.

References

Anderson, P. *Arguments within English Marxism*. London: Verso, 1980.

Arnold, M. *Culture and Anarchy*, edited by J. Dover Wilson. Cambridge: Cambridge University Press, 1932.

Arnold, M. 'Address to the Wordsworth Society'. In *Philistinism in England and America (The Complete Works of Matthew Arnold)*, edited by R. Super, vol. x, 131–4. Ann Arbor, MI: University of Michigan Press, 1974.

Barzun, J. 'Cultural History: A Synthesis'. In *The Varieties of History: From Voltaire to the Present*, edited by F. Stern, 387–402. New York: Meridian, 1956.

Bourdieu, P. *The Logic of Practice*. Cambridge: Polity, 1990.

Burckhardt, J. *The Civilization of the Renaissance: An Essay*. Trans. S.G.C. Middlemore. Oxford: Phaidon, 1945.

Burke, P. *Culture and Society in Renaissance Italy 1420–1540*. London: Batsford, 1972.

Burke, P. 'Oblique Approaches to the History of Popular Culture'. In *Approaches to Popular Culture*, edited by C.W.E. Bigsby, 69–84. London: Edward Arnold, 1976.

Burke, P. 'People's History or Total History'. In *People's History and Socialist Theory*, edited by R. Samuel, 4–8. London: Routledge and Kegan Paul, 1981.

Burke, P. *What is Cultural History*. Cambridge: Polity, 2004.

Collins, T. *Rugby's Great Split: Class, Culture and the Origins of Rugby League Football*. London: Frank Cass, 1998.

Collins, T., and W. Vamplew. *Mud, Sweat and Beers: A Cultural History of Sport and Alcohol*. Oxford: Berg, 2002.

Cunningham, H. *Leisure in the Industrial Revolution*. London: Croom Helm, 1980.

Dworkin, D. *Cultural Marxism in Postwar Britain: History, the New Left, and the Origins of Cultural Studies*. Durham, NC: Duke University Press, 1997.

Geertz, C. *The Interpretation of Cultures*. New York: Basic Books, 1973.

Gombrich, E.H. *In Search of Cultural History*. Oxford: Clarendon Press, 1969.

Hall, S., and P. Whannel. *The Popular Arts*. London: Hutchinson, 1964.

Hobhouse, L.T. *Democracy and Reaction*. London: T. Fisher Unwin, 1904.

Hoggart, R. *The Uses of Literacy: Aspects of Working-class Life with Special Reference to Publications and Entertainments*. London: Chatto and Windus, 1957.

Hoggart, R. 'Culture: Dead and Alive'. In *Speaking To Each Other – Volume One: About Society*, 129–32. Harmondsworth: Penguin, 1973.

Holt, R. *Sport and the British: A Modern History*. Oxford: Clarendon Press, 1992.

Hughson, J., and M. Free. 'Paul Willis, Cultural Commodities and Collective Sport Fandom'. *Sociology of Sport Journal* 23, no. 1 (2006): 72–85.

Hughson, J., D. Inglis, and M. Free. *The Uses of Sport: A Critical Study*. London: Routledge, 2005.

Huizinga, J. 'The Task of Cultural History'. In *Men and Ideas: History, the Middle Ages, the Renaissance*, 17–76. London: J.H. Spottiswood, 1960.

Johnson, R. 'Three Problematics: Elements of a Theory of Working-class Culture'. In *Working Class Culture: Studies in History and Theory*, edited by J. Clarke, C. Critcher, and R. Johnson, 201–37. London: Hutchinson, 1979.

Lee, H. *To Kill a Mockingbird*. London: Heinemann, 1960.

Macaulay, T.B. *History of England: To the Death of William III*, chapter VI (volume I of this edition). London: Heron Books, 1967.

Malcolmson, R.W. *Popular Recreations in English Society 1700–1850*. Cambridge: Cambridge University Press, 1973.

Mandelbaum, Maurice. *The Anatomy of Historical Knowledge*. Baltimore, MD: Johns Hopkins University Press, 1977.

Marwick, A. *The New Nature of History: Knowledge, Evidence, Language*. Basingstoke, Hampshire: Palgrave, 2001.

Masterman, C.F.G. *The Condition of England*. London: Methuen, 1909.

Murray, O. 'Introduction', to *Greeks and Greek Civilization*, by Jacob Burckhardt (trans. by S. Stern). London: Fontana, 1998.

Park, R.J. 'Research and Scholarship in the History of Physical Education and Sport: the Current State of Affairs'. *Research Quarterly for Exercise and Sport* 54, no. 2 (1983): 93–103.

Peatling, G.K. 'Rethinking the History of Criticism of Organised Sport'. *Cultural and Social History* 2, no. 3 (2005): 353–71.

Priestley, J.B. *The English*. London: Heinemann, 1973.

Priestley, J.B. *The Good Companions*. London: Heinemann, 1980.

Samuel, R. 'People's History' (Editorial Preface). In *People's History and Socialist Theory*, edited by R. Samuel, xv–xxxix. London: Routledge and Kegan Paul, 1981.

Struna, N. 'Sport History'. In *The History of Exercise and Sport Science*, edited by J.D. Massengale and R.A. Swanson, 143–79. Champaign IL: Human Kinetics, 1997.

The Oxford English Dictionary, 2nd ed., prepared by J.A. Simpson and E.S.C. Weiner. Oxford: Clarendon Press, 1989.

Thompson, E.P. *William Morris: Romantic to Revolutionary*. New York: Pantheon, 1976.

Thompson, E.P. 'The Poverty of Theory: or an Orrery of Errors'. In *The Poverty of Theory and Other Essays*, 193–397. London: Merlin, 1978.

Thompson, E.P. *The Romantics: England in a Revolutionary Age* (essays assembled by Dorothy Thompson). Rendlesham Woodbridge, Suffolk: Merlin Press, 1997.

Thompson, Paul. *The Voice of the Past: Oral History*. Oxford: Oxford University Press, 1978.

Turner, G. *British Cultural Studies: An Introduction*. 2nd ed. London: Routledge, 1996.

van Maanen, J. *Tales of the Field: On Writing Ethnography*. Chicago, IL: Chicago University Press, 1988.

Williams, R. *Culture and Society 1780–1950*. Harmondsworth: Penguin, 1961.

Williams, R. *The Long Revolution*. Harmondsworth: Penguin, 1965.

Williams, R. *Marxism and Literature*. Oxford: Oxford University Press, 1977.

Williams, R. *Keywords*, rev. ed. London: Fontana, 1988.

Williams, R. 'Culture is Ordinary'. In *Resources of Hope: Culture, Democracy, Socialism*, edited by R. Gable, 3–18. London: Verso, 1989.

Willis, P. *Profane Culture*. London: Routledge and Kegan Paul, 1978.

Willis, P. *The Ethnographic Imagination*. Cambridge: Polity, 2000.

Windschuttle, K. *The Killing of History: How a Discipline is Being Murdered by Literary Critics and Social Theorists*. Sydney: Macleay, 1994.

Young, G.M. *Portrait of an Age: Victorian England*. 2nd ed. Oxford: Oxford University Press, 1953.

The ancient sporting legacy: between myth and spectacle

As indicated in the introduction, *The Making of Sporting Cultures* is primarily concerned with sport in modern times, from the latter part of the nineteenth century until the present day. However, given the volume's focus on the development of sport within western society, it is appropriate to give attention to the historical antecedents of modern western sporting cultures. In this regard, the influence of the ancient Greeks is often believed paramount. Of particular interest is how a sporting ethos derived from the ancient Greeks has presumably transpired into modern sport, remaining relevant to the current day. A Greek sporting ethos cannot be considered in isolation from the broader cultural influence of the Greeks and, therefore, sport finds itself enmeshed within a discussion of, *inter alia*, art and social philosophy. Furthermore, the influence of an ancient sporting past to the west needs to incorporate a consideration of the Romans along with that of the Greeks. The Romans are often unfavourably regarded in discussions of sport. Inheritors themselves of the Greek sporting culture, they have been deemed responsible for instituting degenerative sporting festivals that undermined the Greek tradition of organized games, including the Olympic Games. The sporting spectacle – a pejorative term of currency within contemporary debates about sport – is usually attributed to the carryings on within the Roman coliseum and circus. While not advancing a facile moral dichotomy between the Greeks (good) and the Romans (bad) this essay is dedicated to examining the symbolic legacy of ancient sporting culture in its presumed positive and negative manifestations.

Sport and the gods

The very discussion of *sport* in the ancient world reflects the modern fascination for making the Greek and Roman civilizations either relevant to the present, or comprehendible to the contemporary mind. The Greeks and Romans did not speak of sport in the way that it is understood today, yet books about sport in ancient Greece and/or Rome abound on university library bookshelves. Sport entered modern English usage as a descriptor of the activities we now recognize as sports, following the codification of games such as cricket, baseball and association football and the establishment of organizations to administer the conduct of these sports. *Sport* was earlier defined by Dr Johnson, in his *A Dictionary of the English Language* (1755), to mean 'divert, frolic, game, trifle'.[1] It is listed as synonymous to the word *disport* (of French derivation), meaning 'play, pastime, merriment'. Johnson also lists the words *sportful*, meaning 'merry, ludicrous, done in jest, and *sportive*, meaning 'gay, merry, playful, and wanton'. *Sportsman* is defined as 'one who loves hunting', and, relatedly, entries for *falcon* and *spaniel* refer to sport. This association is not surprising as at the time Johnson's dictionary was published the practical application of the term sport was to activities of English country life, principally hunting and racing. Towards a broader understanding, Johnson defined *game* to mean 'sport of any kind' as well as 'animals pursued in the field', and, most interestingly in regard to the later modern understanding of sport arising from ancient influence, as 'contests exhibited to the people'.

The impression that the word sport was used in ancient Greece may be gleaned from English translations of Homer's pre-classical period epics *The Iliad* and *The Odyssey*. E.V. Rieu, respected Homerian scholar and editor of Penguin Classics, refers to sport in his translations of these works.[2] The penultimate book of *The Iliad* tells of the funeral games hosted by Achilles in honour of his fallen friend Patroclus. Achilles prevented the Achaean troops from disassembling following Patroclus' funeral by telling them 'all to sit down in a wide ring where the sports were to be held'. He announced that prizes, including 'women in their girdled gowns' as well as the belongings of Patroclus, would be awarded to victors.[3] Too old to compete in the events, the boastful Nestor declares that in his youth there was not 'a man to match' him at various 'funereal sports'.[4] A sequence of events is held, commencing with a chariot race, followed by boxing, all-in wrestling, running, one-on-one gladiatorial combat with weaponry, discus throwing, archery and javelin throwing.

Book VIII of *The Odyssey* recounts Odysseus' meeting with the Phaeacians. Following a banquet in Odysseus' honour, King Alcinous addresses his Lords and Counsellors, 'let us go out of doors now and try our hands at various sports, so that when our guest has reached his home he can tell his friends that at boxing, wrestling, jumping, and running there is no one who could beat us'.[5] Exhausted from his travels and emotionally fraught, following a performance by a bard singing of his quarrel with Achilles, Odysseus is happy to let the Phaeacians have their moment of glory and to look on as a spectator. However, he is challenged by Alcinous' son Laodamas to 'take a hand with us in our games, if you're good at any sport'.[6] Laodamas continues, 'You must surely be an athlete, for nothing makes a man so famous for life as what he can do with his hands and feet'. Upon rejecting the invitation to compete he is openly insulted by the former Argonaut Euryalus, who facetiously states, 'You are quite right sir, I should never have taken you for an athlete such as one is accustomed to meet in the world...No; one can see you are no sportsman.'[7] Infuriated by this impertinence Odysseus retorts, 'I'd have you realise that I am no novice at sport, but consider myself to have been in the first rank so long as I was able to rely on the strength of my youth'. Despite his present weariness, Odysseus is stung into action by Euryalus' words. He leaps to his feet and takes hold of a massive discus, clearly larger than those normally used in contest, and hurls it to a distance far in advance of the throws of the Phaeacian competitors. Odysseus then throws down the challenge to his hosts to reach the length he has achieved if they are so able. He also invites challenges in boxing, wrestling and running or 'any kind of manly sport'.[8] Stunned by his awesome display with the discus, no Phaeacian stepped forward to take on Odysseus in any form of sporting event. At this point Alcinous intercedes and declares the games closed in favour of entertainment in dance and song.

H.A. Harris warns against exaggerating the link between sporting festivals and religion in ancient Greece.[9] Indeed, the accounts from Homer's *The Iliad* and *The Odyssey* indicate the worldly nature of such affairs. However, this caveat to scholarship is not intended to detract from the reverence that the Greeks intended such occasions to afford their gods. They believed that the victors in sport were blessed by the gods, particularly the King of Gods, Zeus. Accordingly, locked in stalemate with Odysseus during their wrestling match at Patroclus' funeral games, Aias requests of his rival that each man be allowed to try a throw on the other: 'What happens afterwards is Zeus's business'.[10] Neither man is able to gain the upper hand, Achilles – whose sea nymph mother Thetis had been sought by Zeus until he heard sage advice from Prometheus that she would bear a son greater than his father – eventually intervenes declaring the bout a draw and awarding the two combatants equal prizes. In *The Odyssey*, Alcinous intimates that Odysseus' sporting prowess is bestowed by Zeus but asks his visitor to note and report upon returning home that the Phaeacians have been looked upon favourably by the King of Gods for their running – yet not feats of strength – and in the performing arts of dance and song.[11] The latter part of his entreaty reveals how, from an early point of their civilization, the Greeks regarded all aspects of physical culture highly.

The symbolic connection between Zeus and sport was especially strong in the early period of Greek athleticism. The warrior-like image of Zeus casting thunderbolts from the heavens found earthly similarity in athletes throwing the javelin.[12] Javelin became one of the pentathlon events reputedly introduced to the Olympic Games in 708 BC.[13] Conjecture surrounds the origins of competitive games at Olympia but 776 BC is the generally accepted date of the first Olympic Games, featuring a sole event, the 200 metres footrace.[14] The choice of Mount Olympus, the legendary home of Zeus, as the established site for the Games, left no doubt as to which of the gods the predominant occasion of athletic celebration was meant to honour. Furthermore, as Guttmann notes, Zeus' temple, built around 460 BC to the design of Libon of Elis, became the largest structure at Olympia.[15] From circa 432 BC the temple contained the massive ivory and gold plated Statue of Zeus by the sculptor Phidias. Later in the fifth century BC, the statue was designated one of the Seven Wonders of the Ancient World, by Herodotus and fellow scholars. This honouring, so soon after its construction, lends credence to David C. Young's claim that by the time it was built the Statue of Zeus 'was already the relic of another age'.[16] The power of Zeus within worldly affairs, sport as in politics, had declined by the sixth century BC under the secular style of leadership of the Athenian statesman Solon, discussed further below.[17]

The athletic desire to receive favour from Zeus was inextricably tied to the concept of *arête*. While no equivalent exists in English a definitional approximation, according to Miller, may be found in an amalgam of the following words: 'virtue, skill, prowess, pride, excellence, valour, and nobility'.[18] Overall, *arête* 'imbued ancient athletics with an aura of the quest of man for perfection'. The best-known Greek commentator on the athletic ideal of the ancient games is the fifth-century poet Pindar who, often on the basis of commission, wrote numerous odes (*epinician*) to victors at the Pythian, Isthmian, Nemean and Olympic games. It was the games of Olympia that Pindar held in 'highest esteem', declaring that festival 'the peak of contests'.[19] Pindar's writing confirmed the idea that great athletes are blessed by the gods, but he also stressed the importance of needing to strive for excellence rather than relying on natural ability. As noted by E.N. Gardiner, this idea is well exemplified in Pindar's eleventh *Olympian Ode* in honour of the winner of the boys' boxing event at the Olympic Games of 476 BC.[20] The opening stanza, taken from a recent translation, captures Pindar's message:

> There is a time when it is for winds that men have greatest need;
> there is a time when it is for heavenly waters,
> the drenching children of the cloud;
> but if through toil someone should succeed,
> honey-sounding hymns are a beginning for later words of renown,
> and faithful pledge of great achievements.[21]

Pindar then implies, 'with help from god a man flourishes', but that 'praise dedicated to Olympic victors' is earned by human deed. Accordingly, and without losing his own reverence for the gods, he keeps athletic success within secular perspective. As noted by Young, in the fifth *Olympian Ode* (and similar message can be found in other odes) Pindar warns the Olympic victor against seeking to be like a god.[22] Like many artists over time Pindar was in somewhat of an invidious position. As a commissioned writer, on the one hand, he needed to deliver a poetic offering to meet suitably the patron's expectation. On the other hand, he would not compromise his artistic reputation by stifling his own beliefs. Indeed, Pindar felt so strongly about organized games being an ultimate test of humanness, he believed it his duty to report so in lyric form.[23] The heroic feats of athletes may well place them in an intermediate position between gods and men, but the glory they attain from athletic victory should not lead to the delusion of immortality.[24] Pindar acknowledged an Olympic victory would bring 'glory, happiness, fame, an extended sense of being and some kind of survival in remembrance after death'.[25] But readiness to accept the last mentioned of these rewards must also serve as a reminder to the great athlete of his own mortality.

Sport and the city-state

Unsurprisingly, Pindar was writing for the society of his own time and his humanistic position on the worthiness of individual aspiration and achievement was not out of step with ideas acceptable in fifth-century Greece.[26] By that time something of a 'cultural revolution' had occurred under the impetus of the poet and statesman Solon, who became the *Archon* (political leader) of Athens in circa 594 BC.[27] Although a religious man well versed in, and respectful of, Greek mythology, Solon shifted Greek thought onto a decidedly philosophical terrain. Solon's conviction for civic affairs was backed up by an elementary theorizing on the city contained in a preamble to the laws he set out for the governance of Athens. According, to Lewis Mumford, 'Athens [under Solon] became a symbol for all that was veritably human'.[28] While Solon was hardly a democrat in the modern understanding of the term, he instituted democratic reforms that set in train the long history towards the forms of representative democracy known to western nations. Solon broke down the existing system of aristocratic privilege in Athens and overhauled the franchise to favour wealthy citizens (timocracy). Slavery was maintained, slaves and women alike were not afforded political rights. Yet, within the context of his time, Solon was regarded as a great reformer, a moderate rather than a tyrant, a leader concerned with the welfare of the citizenry at large. His ultimate concern for *Eunomie* ('good order') in Athens is described by one historian as the highpoint of the Greek classical 'spirit'.[29]

Sport assumed a place of importance within Solon's programme which was aimed at achieving good order.[30] Solon recognized the unifying potential of games (festivals incorporating athletic and performing arts) and it is no coincidence that the aforementioned Pythian, Isthmian and Nemean Games commenced in the early decades of the sixth century under Solon's archonship. Solon was also the inspiration for the Panathenaic Games, organised by his protégé Pisistratus in 566 BC. These games had an especial social significance, which 'helped Athens move from private to civically oriented and administered games'.[31] These games featured a procession to the Parthenon, which was extremely popular with the citizenry. The Panathenaic Games also saw the introduction of prizes in the form of *amphora* (vases) containing sacred olive oil. These prizes were of considerable material value and seemingly held in high public regard as a mark of honour for the recipient.[32] The awarding of prizes for athletic victory is also traceable to Solon. Best-known is his instituting of monetary prizes for the winners of athletic events at the Olympic (500 drachmas) and Isthmian Games (100 drachmas).[33] Young contends that such payment was astronomical for the time and suggests it can be seen as an ancient forerunner to the mega prize money and salaries paid to sportspeople – if not directly to Olympic athletes – today.[34]

The awarding of significant prize money may appear to be at odds with the Olympic ideal of amateurism as it is popularly imagined in association with the Greeks, but the case is not clear cut. Some historians of ancient sport, chiefly Kyle and Young, contend that the amateurism of Greek athletics is a myth peddled by earlier and influential historians, such as J.P. Mahaffy and E.N. Gardiner.[35] According to Young, it is oxymoronic to speak of amateur athleticism in regard to the ancient Greeks because the very term athletics implies competing for a prize.[36] There is no indication that the greater substantiation of prize lessened the Greek athletes' intrinsic quest for honour. For his part, Solon appears to have been motivated by a concern for just rewards rather than bowing to the avarice of elite athletes. Indeed, his comments as recorded by Diogenes Laertius indicate that he was anything but a panderer to athletes. If Diogenes is to be believed, Solon personally held athletes in 'scant respect'.[37] However, Solon openly promoted Athens as a competitive society, and the athletic games, as well as the rewards that went with them, were regarded as positively symbolic of competition being conducted in a regulated and fair manner.[38] Solon was thus able to reconcile the concept of *agon* (contest) with his classical humanism symbolically via athletic festivals.

In an entertaining fictional dialogue written by the satirist Lucian, Solon explains the merits of athleticism to a puzzled Anacharsis (a Scythian philosopher who reputedly visited Athens circa 589 BC). Watching a wrestling match, Anacharsis asks Solon why the young men tangle around one another 'in the mud, wallowing around like pigs'.[39] He is especially bemused by what he sees as a disjuncture between preparation and enactment. The young men commence the athletic ritual by disrobing then peacefully oiling each other down, before launching into a violent physical confrontation. Anacharsis concludes that the behaviour of these young men could have them deemed insane. Solon calmly, perhaps condescendingly, explains that such behaviour looks odd to Anacharsis because he is culturally unaccustomed to it. He suggests that should Anacharsis spend greater time in Greece he will come to regard wrestling as 'very pleasant as well as useful'. There is hint here to Solon being appreciative of both the aesthetic and utilitarian benefits of wrestling. Solon is able to explain in impressive detail the skill and agility involved in the bodily movement of the wrestlers. And, respectful or otherwise of athletes, Solon invites Anacharsis to view a wrestler hosed down and free of mud, and then adjudge whether he would not want to resemble such a fine physical specimen.[40] This comment also gives a clue to Solon's view of the practical benefits of physical exercise that came to the fore in his programme for the education of boys. The point, as Thompson suggests, is not to look for the inconsistency in Solon's views, but to recognize the uniformly positive place of sport within his schema for the well ordered polis.[41]

The demonstration of agon in Athenian festival ranged from the sublime to the ridiculous. Drama and comedy were written and performed for prizes, while contests were held, *inter alia*, for eating, drinking, beauty and kissing.[42] However, as indicated by Anacharsis' consternation, wrestling seems to have been the most agonistic of all physical performances. One form of wrestling to which Anacharsis was witness was the particularly brutal *pankration*, literally meaning 'complete victory'.[43] Pankration was close to an anything-goes brawl, with punching, kicking and strangling being permitted along with conventional wrestling holds. Victory came not through the throwing of an opponent or the pinning of his shoulders, but upon a competitor signalling submission. Only biting and gouging were prohibited from the Athenian pankration, and even these tactics were allowed in the Spartan version of the sport. During Anacharsis' visit to a *gymnasium*, Solon stood with his guest and specifically drew attention to young men practising for the pankration.[44] Again, Solon's views can only be guessed at. On the one hand the serious injury, if not death, that could result from the pankration, rendered defence on physical exercise grounds tenuous. Indeed, pankration was eventually condemned for such reason by the Greek physician Galen in the second century AD.[45] Solon's recorded word on the connection between wrestling and military preparation is ambiguous. His enthusiasm for pankration may, perhaps, best be understood for its enhancement of spectacle within the games.

Greek sport and spectacle

As well as attempting to have Anacharsis see the merits of Greek athletics for the participant, Solon impressed upon him the magnificence of the spectacle for the gathered crowd. Anacharsis' visit to Athens did not coincide with an occasion of games, but had it done so Solon assures him of the 'pleasure' it would have brought:

> you would learn for yourself, sitting in the middle of the crowd, watching the arête of men and physical beauty, amazing conditioning and great skill and irresistible force and daring and pride and unbeatable determination and indescribable passion for victory. I know that you would not stop praising and cheering and applauding.[46]

It is hardly surprising that a further popularized version of this quote has been used by journalist Tony Perrottet in preface to his general readership book *The Naked Olympics*.[47] The substance of Solon's statement would do a contemporary sports promoter proud. His words also give clear indication that the Olympics and other Greek games must be considered as popular sporting spectacles. The dominant modern perception is of an historical hiatus whereby spectacle is associated with the Romans in remove from the purer sporting occasions of the Greeks. However, as Kyle suggests, this is an embellishment as the Olympics and other games were the province of 'impassioned crowds' enjoying 'bloody violence' as were the later Roman sporting carnivals.[48] But was there something qualitatively different about the games of which Solon spoke from those later in time? Again, the issue of amateurism raises its head. In the manner of his mentor E.N. Gardiner, H.A. Harris contends that a decline in Greek sporting culture occurred between the fourth and second centuries BC as professionalism and commercialization took hold. His oft-quoted comparison of the decline of ancient and modern sport – 'when money comes in at the door, sport flies out the window, and the Greek athletic scene thereafter exhibits the same abuses that are becoming only too familiar to us in our big business world of so-called "sport"' – has been referred to as an 'inadmissible though common fiction'.[49]

Harris's blaming of professionalism for the decline of the Greek games is a form of cultural elitism, which evinces what Brantlinger refers to as 'negative classicism'.[50] The Greek games were at their best for Harris when 'athletics was at first the leisure occupation of the classes wealthy enough to afford the time for such activities'.[51] The problem arises as the games become 'the greatest spectator attractions in the Greek world commanding the same enthusiastic following as chariot-racing among Romans or football in our own day'. According to Harris, the mass interest in the games, as with football in modern times, led to an exaggerated professionalism whereby participants are driven by money rather than honour. Harris's elitism through amateurism has important implications for modern sport as it implicitly denies the appropriateness of lower status social groupings having a hand in the making of sporting cultures. It is an essentially anti-democratic view that fails to recognize the synchronicity of developments in ancient Greece in culture and politics.

Solon's words provide an interesting counterpoint. His remark to Anacharsis on spectatorship emphasizes the pleasure of being at one with the crowd, the collective appreciation of athletic performance. Furthermore, although Solon no doubt recognized the practical benefits of a citizenry harmoniously joined in the spectacle of games, he is at odds with Anacharsis' completely utilitarian outlook – any usage of time is wasted unless it serves an identifiable purpose and definable end. Anacharsis appears to have no conception of leisure. This was not the case with Solon, indeed, his positive view of sports spectatorship is, no doubt, at least partly explained by his recognition of the importance of leisure. Like Aristotle after him, Solon viewed leisure (*schole*) as an important dimension of life which provides much needed relief and relaxation from the ardours of work (*ascholia*). Solon has been referred to as a 'glutton for work', a reflection of his own indefatigable labours as a statesman and also his expectation of all good citizens of Athens.[52] But in a just society people cannot be worked into the ground; they are afforded free time in which work should be put aside. In the Greek sense, connected with the notion of democracy, 'leisure is freedom from the necessity of being occupied'.[53] Leisure thus understood applied only to those enfranchised by Solon's democratic reforms, so it is not surprising that subsequent philosophical discussions of leisure focussed on activities considered noble. Aristotle, for example, was insistent upon the pre-eminent importance of music within leisure as it can touch and sooth the soul like no other art form can.[54]

Sport is difficult to place within this Greek binary of work and leisure. Sport resembles a form of work *ponos*, manual work involving toil, sweating, fatigue and, possibly, pain.[55] But unlike manual work sport can be enjoyed. It is at once, though, purposive when aimed at victory and thus of complicated leisure status when conducted in a competitive context. Gardiner suggests that sport in ancient Greece was work rather than leisure because it was intrinsically agonistic.[56] Conversely, Roman sport was leisure as it was based in the play principle (*ludi*). But, again, a false dichotomy is apparent. This distinction focuses Greek games on participants, Roman games on spectators. In regard to the latter, Gardiner advises 'Roman games are *ludi*, amusements, entertainments, and the performers are slaves or hirelings; they exist for the spectators'.[57] This is very much a top-down view of history, which asks us to regard the ancient games in Greece and Rome as they were regarded by those who instituted and administered them (at least in terms of Gardiner's perception of such regard). Without complicating the disputation it can be said that Gardiner's position implies the foreclosure of analysis of participants in Roman games and spectators in Greek games. Regarding spectatorship, this foreclosure potentially serves an interesting ideological function. In keeping with the notion of 'negative classicism', subsequent forms of collective sport spectatorship in western society have been necessarily at risk of pejorative interpretation, because sport spectatorship has carried the historical burden of an association built on spuriously assumed origins with the (non) culture of Roman games.

When referring to sport as leisure, Solon appears more likely to have been thinking of participation than spectatorship. His reference to the 'possession of horses for racing and dogs for the hunt' foresaw the view of sporting leisure that was to emerge in Europe and Britain some centuries later.[58] Yet his comment to Anacharsis gives glimpse as to how sport spectatorship might be given reconsideration as a form of leisure within ancient Greece, not in terms of a gratuitous bloodlust, but as a collective form of aesthetic appreciation of athletic endeavour and performance. This is not to say that Greek spectators behaved with decorum. Evidence suggests they were a proto form of what I have referred to elsewhere as 'expressive fans'.[59] Legend has it that during the Olympic Games of 212 BC the boxer Clitomachus of Thebes rallied the spectators to such supportive passion, after initially being out of favour with them, that he was able to vanquish his opponent, 'more by the temper of the crowd' than his own doing. Accordingly, Finley and Pleket maintain, 'crowds at ancient Games were as partisan, as volatile and as excitable as at any other period of time'.[60] Describing a painting in his collection *Imagines*, the third-century AD art historian Philostratus tells of the death, during the Olympic Games, of the wrestler Arrichion who fought so momentously as a crowd favourite that he not only defeated his opponent but died at the end of the bout.[61] Philostratus observes the image of this occasion not morosely but in celebration of the passion evoked by the crowd for their victorious yet fallen hero, as in death he is crowned by the Judge of the Games:

> the spectators jump up from their seats and shout, some wave their hands, some their garments, some leap from the ground, and some grapple with their neighbours for joy; for these really amazing deeds make it impossible for the spectators to contain themselves. Is anyone so without feeling not to applaud this athlete? For after he had already achieved a great deed by winning two victories in the Olympic Games, a yet greater deed is here depicted, in that, having won his victory at the cost of his life, he is being conducted to the realms of the blessed with the very dust of victory still upon him.

Roman sport and spectacle

Also writing in the third century AD the early Christian moralist Tertullian wrote far less favourably of the contemporary sport crowd within the Roman Empire. His essay De Spectaculis (Concerning Spectacles) attacked the civic displays, including those sportive, which occurred within the amphitheatre.[62] He referred to the amphitheatre as 'that dreadful place ... the temple of all demons', its 'spectacles involve idolatry'.[63] Tertullian was particularly damning of wrestling, which he referred to as 'the devil's own trade'.[64] Its combatants he found totally unworthy of adoration, accusing them of developing their physiques in an 'unnatural way (outdoing God's handiwork)'. The carryings on of wrestlers – 'all the recklessness of the fist, any and every disfigurement of the human face' – Tertullian believed unfit for a decent human audience. Yet the audience approached such carnage with frenzy, a populace gone mad with 'shouts for the charioteer'.[65] The gathering in the stadium tacitly embraced an unholy pact: 'That sharing of emotions, that agreement, or disagreement in backing their favourites, makes an intercourse that fans the sparks of lust'. Tertullian did, though, hold on to one hope, this being that pity and fair mindedness would come to the fore on occasion as individuals protest, 'that blow is forbidden!' or that bear is being treated cruelly in battle with the armed gladiator.[66] When this awareness hits, the person will stop 'cheer[ing] for the gladiator' and realize the waywardness of his false communion. Importantly, though, Tertullian suggests that such recognition involves an awakening of individual consciousness from the mob mentality of spectatorship.

Roland Auguet, in his study of the Roman Games, notes an historical shift in gladiatorial combat from 'rite' to 'spectacle'.[67] Whereas the comparably violent contestations in Greek games were originally conducted to honour the gods, Roman gladiators fought to honour the dead.[68] Such funerary rite was initially the preserve of aristocrats who pitted their slaves against each other in fatal combat as a mark of respect to the bereaved: 'the blood of gladiators was thus shed for the dead'.[69] However, even before the Roman Republic transformed into the Empire the gladiatorial contest diminished as a 'sacred ceremony' to become a secularized festivity of widespread public appeal.[70] Such contests became increasingly used by those wealthy enough to sponsor them as a means of currying political favour with the plebeian class.[71] An increase in the frequency of gladiatorial festivals led to greater public expectation of entertainment value: 'they must be dazzled, their pride flattered by splendours'.[72] Juvenal's famous aphorism – 'the Roman people which once dispensed power ... now sits on its hands and anxiously waits for just two things: bread and circuses' – is relevant here.[73] The paradox is apparent enough; the people are depoliticized but not disempowered by the gladiatorial occasion.[74] In the most utilitarian of political circumstances, subsequent Emperors enjoyed popular rule by being seen to give the people what they wanted.

However, the modern opprobrium for Roman gladiatorial combat was not so apparent in writings of the day. Even Cicero, renowned for his humanism, was at best ambivalent in his attitude towards the contests. His criticism appeared to be levelled at gladiatorial fighting when conducted as sheer spectacle rather than at gladiatorial combat as such. Divorced from 'schooling against pain and death' the fights were merely 'cruel and brutal', emblematic of the social malaise into which Rome had descended.[75] In earlier form, the gladiatorial contest, for Cicero, was a showcase of discipline in which the combatants displayed loyalty to their masters and gave their audience a view of the old Roman soldier spirit.[76] Criticism tended to be made of the intellectual vacuity rather than moral debasement of the sporting spectacle. Although speaking of the chariot race in this instance, Pliny the Younger held similar view of the gladiatorial contest:

> I'm always amazed that so many thousands of men so childishly love to watch the horses run and the men standing in chariots ... When I think about people like that, who so insatiably long for something empty, cold, and impermanent, I take certain pleasure in never having been taken by this pleasure.[77]

Explicit moral criticism of spectatorship at gladiatorial battles is mainly associated with the philosopher and statesman Seneca the younger. According to Seneca:

> You cannot yet trust yourself to be safe in a crowd . . . I never bring back the same morals as I brought out. And nothing is so damaging to good morals as to hang around at some spectacle. There, through pleasure, vices sneak in more easily. I come back more greedy, more desirous of honour, more dissolute, even more unfeeling and cruel, because I have been among people. By chance I happened to be at the spectacle at noontime, expecting some witty entertainment and relaxation, to rest men's eyes from the gore. It was the opposite. Whatever fighting there was before was comparative mercy. Now there was pure murder, no more fooling around. They have nothing to shield them, and with the whole body exposed to the blow, no one ever misses.[78]

The noontime show, to which Seneca refers, was not a gladiatorial bout in the real sense but an execution staged as gladiatorial combat.[79] These 'contests' featured criminals, unskilled in fighting, who were given swords but no protective armour and then forced to fight to the death. But Seneca does not so much question the morality of killing men who may well deserve such fate. His objection is to those 'wretched' enough to believe they 'deserve to watch'.[80] Kyle contends that Seneca's wilful confusion of the execution-type battles in the amphitheatre with gladiatorism – Seneca's view is well rehearsed within historical literature on ancient Rome – is responsible for a popular misconception of the latter involving 'indiscriminate slaughter' and being a 'mass melee in which chaos reigned and death abounded'.[81] On the contrary, Kyle argues, gladiatorial contests were 'well orchestrated', fought under the watchful eyes of two referees.[82] Gladiators were willing combatants who wanted to face top calibre opponents in what he interestingly refers to as 'Roman extreme sports'. Importantly, for Kyle, unlike the popular misconception that permeates modern cinematic and other media representations, these contests were governed by conventions, rules and fair play. Similarly, the spectators at the amphitheatre were not the baying mob as familiarly depicted. Rather, according to Kyle, spectators were 'knowledgeable and discerning consumers of gladiatorial entertainment', interested in 'skilled swordsmanship' rather than gratuitous gore.

Academic experts within the field will no doubt have some differences with Kyle over this interpretation and it will be interesting to read the ensuing debate. Yet, however the debate might unfold, Kyle's argument is an important interruption as it unsettles the common assumption about Roman spectatorship being barbaric. An implication of this unsettling is that further scrutiny must be given to the facile acceptance of the Romans corrupting the culture of sport spectatorship they supposedly inherited from the Greeks. A reconsideration of Roman sport spectatorship also challenges the established history that puts the Romans towards the beginning of a story of cultural decline whereby the sport crowd, extending into modern times, is little more than an unruly mob. The image of the Roman sporting audience as mob has been emblazoned on the contemporary mind by popular cinema. From *Ben-Hur* (1959) and *Spartacus* (1960) through to *Gladiator* (2000) Roman spectators are seen as a 'shouting, jostling, sweaty . . . crowd gone wild'.[83] Connolly contends that the Roman crowd has worked symbolically to mirror the modern audience whether in duped and passive form in the cinema or in the worryingly active form of the boisterous sports crowd. On the other hand the cinematic (viz. Hollywood) Roman crowd has served an ideological function by servicing 'the American fantasy of popular republican will'.[84]

Matthew Arnold and 'Victorian Hellenism'

Such ambivalence has not existed in the English context and here the name Mathew Arnold looms large. Arnold's father Thomas Arnold, famously headmaster of Rugby School, was a passionate admirer of the Roman Republic, and Matthew likewise became a Romanist. However, as his biographer Stefan Collini notes, Arnold 'was a republican but not a democratic'.[85] In *Culture and Anarchy* – first published as a book from Arnold's essays in 1869 and thoroughly revised by Arnold in 1875 – Arnold denounced the socially and culturally deleterious nature of mass democracy.[86] Arnold's notion of republicanism was in keeping with Cicero's civic humanism, which in practical terms meant that the running of political affairs are best left to a public-minded elite. In Arnold's view the most dangerous manifestation of democracy, one that penetrated from the political realm into the cultural, was in the United States. Accordingly, he warned in Britain against the encroachment of 'Americanization'.[87]

Arnold was no parochial Englishman, he believed England to be in a state of cultural decline in the 1800s, but believed America to be in a worse condition. To retrieve the situation in England he turned to the influence of the Greeks, rather than the Romans, presumably because the Greeks had fostered a non-utilitarian spirit of individualism in the form of arête. Arnold thus became a significant intellectual figure within what has been referred to as 'Victorian Humanistic Hellenism'.[88] Arnold claimed that under the influence of Christianity England had developed a Hebraist culture of obedience, which was sceptical of human quests for excellence. Accordingly, he believed Hebraism should be balanced with a good dose of Hellenism.[89] Arnold maintained that Hellenism, a simple and charming ideal, is naturally spontaneous and 'full of what we call sweetness and light'.[90] The term 'sweetness and light' is somewhat overused in detachment from Arnold, a pity because, as Collini claims, in remove from Hellenism the words sound 'unctuous . . . genteel, even anaemic', the words of a 'do-gooder who never seems to have felt the pull of any real human appetites'.[91] This was not Arnold's intention; although using an airy metaphor he meant it to have earthy connotation. Indeed, Arnold's 'sweetness and light' was anything but anaemic. Its quest, and thus that for human perfection, demanded bodily health and vigour.[92]

Arnold worked as an inspector of schools and it is interesting to note his recommendations on physical education. In short, Arnold favoured a programme of gymnastics being slotted into the busy school schedule for the purpose of maintaining bodily health.[93] That organized sport did not feature in his recommendation is not surprising given the flippancy of his reference to sporting activity in *Culture and Anarchy*. Arnold alludes to field-sports as a key marker of the cultural barbarianism he believed characteristic of the English aristocracy: 'I never take a gun or a fishing-rod in my hands without feeling that I have in the ground of my nature the self-same seeds which . . . do so much to make the Barbarian'.[94] Arnold's disinterest in sport reflects his particular version of Hellenism – more Plato than Solon. For Arnold physical exercise is not autotelic. Indeed, Arnold quotes favourably the 'utilitarian [Benjamin] Franklin' to assert that bodily health is necessary but secondary to mental and spiritual health. Arnold is quite clear that physical activity should not be undertaken for its own sake or as an end in itself. Disconnected from the 'idea of a perfect spiritual condition' physical activity becomes an 'unintelligent and vulgarising' form of worship.[95] That Arnold was opposed to utilitarianism in culture but prepared to use the term explicitly as the governing principle for his endorsement of physical exercise, shows undoubtedly that he did not countenance sport as a form of culture.

The likeness of Arnold's position on physical exercise to that of Plato is well exemplified by the latter's prescription for 'physical culture' in the schooling of children set out in his last dialogue *The Laws of Plato* (circa 360–348 BC).[96] Plato notes that instruction for 'physical culture' should consist of two practices, wrestling and dance.[97] In a wonderful precursor to criticism of modern professional wrestling, Plato dismisses the use of gimmickry and tricky manoeuvres as 'vain-glory' and 'unworthy of celebration'. However, according to Plato, 'anything which comes under "stand-up wrestling", exercises in the disengaging of the neck, arms and ribs which can be practised with spirit and gallant bearing to the benefit of strength and health, is serviceable for all occasions and may not be neglected'.[98] The well-rehearsed rumour that Plato was himself a wrestler is under challenge within contemporary scholarship.[99] But Plato certainly gave more consideration to wrestling and other sportive practices than Arnold. He did so not with thought of the well-rounded person, but as an occupation for men of able body who, for whatever reason, were unable to find remunerative work of other kind.[100] Plato encouraged such men to prepare themselves as competitors for either the Olympic or Pythian Games. He insisted that such athleticism must be treated as a fulltime job, as the requisite 'provision of needful exercises and regimen for the body' demanded such dedication.[101] He also advocated the holding of athletic contests for soldiers as training in anticipation of war service.[102] Thus, although Plato spoke of the worthiness of athletics and games he did so in practical terms, explicitly as work rather than leisure, as means to ends rather than as activities of intrinsic value.[103]

Walter Pater and 'muscular paganism'

Plato's position on sport pertains directly to his view on the relationship of the mind/soul to the body – the latter needing to be subservient to the former. Plato was an ancient forbear to the ongoing debate over this dualism, which is taken up as a key theme within the next essay. The present essay concludes with a discussion of the ideas of the Victorian art critic Walter Pater, a Hellenist of different temperament to Matthew Arnold.[104] Curiously Pater championed Plato for providing 'vindication of the dignity of the body'. He cited Plato's educational programme involving gymnastics to music as evidence of the body being given 'utmost fairness' in relation to the 'fair soul'.[105] While Plato saw the body working in concert with the mind/soul, Pater went much further, explicitly promoting the body, most interestingly in his essay 'The Age of Athletic Prizemen'.[106] Pater was especially interested in the iconography of youth within Greek art, tellingly displayed in the sculptural representation of athletes. Such art, claimed Pater, gave clear view of how youthfulness was respectively valued in ancient Greece and in modern Britain. In Greece young men engaged in games ('voluntary labours'), in England their physicality became 'habitual and measured discipline', physicality conducted for the sake of work. Furthermore, modern physical activity done for leisure, in the name of sport, while earning prizes for winners, is not 'heroically' honoured in the manner of the Greeks. Conducted beyond the time of war and apart from military training, athletics was for the Greeks, according to Pater, 'peaceful combat as fine art'.[107] Here we have the earliest explicit recognition within modern scholarship of sport – removed from social debates about amateurism and related issues – as being intrinsically aesthetic. From Pater's interpretation the Greeks, therefore, leave a legacy of sport *as* culture.

Although Pater believed sport not to be generally valued as culture within the England of his time, he believed this to be merely a limitation of vision. The bodily aesthetic of sport is there to be witnessed by the appreciative eye. To make this point Pater claimed that the natural bodily disposition observable in Myron's famous statue *Discobulus* could also be seen in 'any passable representation of the English cricketer'.[108] The essential beauty of sport, from Pater's perspective, is the transitional moment between rest and motion, and he regarded sculpture as the ultimate artistic means of representing such grace.[109] William Shuter notes that sculpture, as an art form located in place rather than time, cannot actually represent bodily movement. However, sculpture does have the capacity to imitate bodily movement and this is keenly recognized by Pater.[110] Accordingly, Pater spoke of the gifted sculptor's ability to unlock the 'mystery of combined motion and rest' or 'rest in motion'.[111] While regarding motion and rest as inseparable within the conception of the living body, Pater selected examples of ancient Greek sculpture that are readily identifiable more with one transition than the other – the aforementioned *Discobulus* by Myron (motion) and *Diadumenus* by Polycleitus (rest).[112]

The magnificence of these sculptures, adduced from Pater's discussion, is in their secret revelation of the counter ideal to that which they typify. Thus, while Myron's *Discobulus* typifies the '*beau ideal* of athletic motion',[113] between the athlete's imagined '*backward* swing of the right arm' and his '*movement forwards* on which the left foot is in the very act of starting' is 'that moment of rest which lies between [the] two opposed motions'.[114] In imagining this moment of rest between those of motion we can appreciate the essential 'artistic form' of *Discobulus*. Conversely, while *Diadumenus* typifies the '*beau ideal* of athletic repose', the victor in 'rest after toil', it at once anticipates the athlete's resumption of movement: 'the moment of the perfecting of restful form, before the mere consciousness of technical mastery in delineation urges forward the art of sculpture to a bewildering infinitude of motion'.[115] Complementarily, *Discobulus* and *Diadumenus* represent physical excellence not in godlike form but with view to the living splendour yet mortality of youth. The athletic figures of these sculptures may be 'befitting messengers from the gods', but, for Pater, gods they are not.[116]

While 'muscular Christianity' prevailed in Victorian England Pater's evocations of Greek athleticism were muscularly pagan.[117] This mention flags an important difference between the Hellenism of Arnold and Pater. Arnold's association with muscular Christianity is at best indirect, but his insistence upon the balancing of Hellenism and Hebraism clearly indicates his concern to reconcile Christianity with his advocacy of Greek culture. Although Pater was a deep, albeit idiosyncratic, Christian thinker he did not share Arnold's anxiety for the need to find compatibility between Hellenism and Hebraism. He was chiefly concerned that art be left to stand alone – of English writers, he is known for using the term 'art for art's sake'[118] – without having to be interpreted in relation to Christian notions of moral goodness.[119] Pater's predilection to aesthetic primacy has been variously interpreted. The Arnold enthusiast Basil Willey refers to Pater as being 'effete' and 'precious'.[120] Alternatively, Geoffrey Tillotson argues that although 'beauty remained one of Pater's favourite words' it was often given 'footing in the concrete'. He thus refers to Pater's 'vigorousness as an aesthete'.[121] This opinion is interestingly matched with that of Graham Hough, who sees Pater leaving behind the 'longing for certitude' of Arnold in preference for the 'flux' of the dawning modernity.[122] Using this view to inform the present discussion, Arnold's embrace of the Greeks in the Victorian age is revealed as nervous and nostalgic, Pater's confident and forward looking.

History on its head or what the Greeks still do for us

But why was Pater looking to the very distant past as a guide to the present, if not the future? After all, he was well aware of the implications of George Grote's contention in his voluminous study *A History of Greece* (originally published between 1846 and 1856) that there is little of which we can be sure given the basis of Greek history in myth and legend. However, Pater took inspiration rather than dissuasion from Grote's attendant claim about the purpose of history to the Greeks:

> Neither discrepancies nor want of evidence, in reference to alleged antiquities, shocked the faith of a non-historical public. What they wanted was a picture of the past, impressive to their feelings and plausible to their imagination ... *a past which never was present*.[123] (emphasis added)

Pater indirectly embraced Grote's view of Greek history to turn it on its head.[124] He agreed that a history steeped in mythology served a purpose within ancient times, but rejected Grote's suggestion that myth has no place within modern history. This theme appears in a number of essays in Pater's *Greek Studies*, the following line being most typical: 'myth[s] ... having no link on historical fact, yet, because they arose naturally out of the spirit of man, and embodied, in adequate symbols, his deepest thoughts concerning the conditions of his physical and spiritual life, maintained their hold through many changes, and are still not without a solemnising power even for the modern mind'.[125] Pater thus challenged the modern view that knowing history is an exclusively rational exercise. History is also about the felt experience of the past and for such ways of knowing, via myth, we can always turn to the Greeks. Pater's view on historical knowledge can be seen here to mesh with his position on aesthetics, which he derived from the influence of the English Romantic poets. Wordsworth, Coleridge and others believed Greek myths, which inspired thought on eternal beauty, to be entirely relevant to modern times.[126] From Pater's essay on Wordsworth we get a sense of aesthetic appreciation – in keeping with Pater's interpretation of the Greeks – relevant to an understanding of sport as culture in the purest form:

> To treat life in the spirit of art, is to make life a thing in which means and ends are identified…to withdraw the thoughts for a little while from the mere machinery of life, to fix them, with appropriate emotions, on the spectacle of those great facts in man's existence which no machinery affects…is the aim of all culture.[127]

Pater is here speaking of contemplation as associated with art and culture as traditionally perceived. However, we may have little doubt when we recall his discussion of *Discobulus* and *Diadumenus*, Pater would not spin in the grave at the suggestion that as we may talk of art for art's sake, so may we talk of sport for sport's sake. Otherwise he would not have seen the modern cricketer as one with Myron's discus-throwing athlete.

Pater's mention of the spectacle of culture also provides grounds for retrieving the notion of spectatorship. While he was talking of an individual experience of artistic appreciation he objected to art being used for utilitarian purposes not to it being collectively enjoyed. The logic of Pater would hold that a gathering of modern sport fans at the cricket are as capable in essence of exhibiting athletic appreciation as were the Greek spectators at the ancient Olympic Games. The popularized view of the Roman mob has serviced an anti-collectivist ideology of modern sport spectatorship. Turning back to the Greeks – with the above discussion on historical myth in mind – as an 'exemplar' of sport spectatorship, via Pater, provides a useful starting point for the consideration of collective examples of modern sport fandom to be taken up in subsequent essays. We cannot interpret the present via the past and, therefore, as Finley and Pleket note, 'sport in the modern world…has to be worked out and defended from modern values and modern conditions'.[128] But just as we enquire into how the Greeks *made* their sporting culture free from the judgemental gaze of modernity, we should be prepared to approach inquiry into the sport of more recent times at a remove from jaundiced presumptions about the baseness of mass spectatorship.

Notes

1 Hamilton, *Johnson's Dictionary*.
2 Homer, *The Iliad*; Homer, *The Odyssey*.
3 Homer, *The Iliad*, 417.
4 Ibid., 429.
5 Homer, *The Odyssey*, 124.
6 Ibid., 126.
7 Ibid.
8 Ibid., 127.
9 Harris, *Sport in Greece and Rome*, 16–17.
10 Homer, *The Iliad*, 431.
11 Homer, *The Odyssey*, 128–9.
12 Baker, *Sports in the Western World*, 15.
13 Guttmann, *Sports*, 21.
14 Baker, *Sports in the Western World*, 16.

15 Guttmann, *Sports*, 19.

16 Young, *A Brief History of the Olympic Games*, 65.

17 Lewis, *Solon the Thinker*, 16.

18 Miller, *Arête* (2nd ed.), vii.

19 Bowra, *Pindar*, 162.

20 Gardiner, *Athletics of the Ancient World*, 69.

21 Pindar, 'Olympian Ode XI', 177.

22 Young, *A Brief History of the Olympic Games*, 73; Pindar, 'Olympic Ode V', 95.

23 Bowra, *Pindar*, 179.

24 Bowra refers to heroes occupying an 'intermediate class' between gods and men in 'Pindar's world', but does not directly relate this classification to athleticism; Bowra, *Pindar*, 89.

25 Ibid., 191.

26 Livingstone, *The Greek Genius and Its Meaning to Us*, 140.

27 Lewis, *Solon the Thinker*, 12.

28 Mumford, *The City in History*, 159.

29 Ehrenberg, *Society and Civilisation in Greece and Rome*, 45–6.

30 Kyle, *Sport and Spectacle in the Ancient World*, 152.

31 Ibid.

32 Ibid., 153.

33 As reported by Plutarch in his *Parallel Lives*. See Freeman, *The Work and Life of Solon*, 129.

34 Young, *A Brief History of the Olympic Games*, 98.

35 Kyle, 'E. Norman Gardiner and the Decline of Greek Sport'; Young, *The Olympic Myth of Greek Amateur Athletics*.

36 Young, *A Brief History of the Olympic Games*, 93.

37 Diogenes Laertius, *Lives of Eminent Philosophers*, vol.1, 57.

38 This is not to say that the conduct of ancient games was beyond reproach and free of corruption. See Finley and Pleket, *The Olympic Games*, 131.

39 The account of Lucian provided here is taken from Miller, *Arête* (2nd ed.), 28–31 (28).

40 Ibid., 31.

41 Thompson, 'Solon on Athletics'.

42 Poliakoff, *Combat Sports in the Ancient World*, 104.

43 Ibid., 54.

44 Miller, *Arête* (2nd ed.), 30.

45 Poliakoff, *Combat Sports in the Ancient World*, 56–7.

46 From Lucian in Miller, *Arête* (3rd and expanded ed.), 78.

47 Perrottet, *The Naked Olympics*, ix.

48 Kyle, *Sport and Spectacle in the Ancient World*, 128.

49 Harris, *Sport in Greece and Rome*, 40; Poliakoff, *Combat Sports in the Ancient World*, 19.

50 Brantlinger, *Bread and Circuses*.

51 Harris, *Sport in Greece and Rome*, 39.

52 Balme, 'Attitudes to Work and Leisure in Ancient Greece', 143.

53 de Grazia, *Of Time, Work and Leisure*, 14.

54 Barker, *The Political Thought of Plato and Aristotle*, 436-441.

55 de Grazia, *Of Time, Work and Leisure*.

56 Gardiner, *Athletics of the Ancient World*, 119.

57 Ibid.

58 Olivova, *Sports and Games in the Ancient World*, 109.

59 Hughson, 'A Tale of Two Tribes'.

60 Finley and Pleket, *The Olympic Games*, 57–8.

61 Philostratus, *Imagines*, 151.
62 Tertullian, 'De Spectaculis'.
63 Ibid., 267.
64 Ibid., 277.
65 Ibid., 289.
66 Ibid., 291.
67 Auguet, *Cruelty and Civilization*, 23.
68 Ibid., 19.
69 Ibid., 21.
70 Ibid., 23.
71 Ibid., 24.
72 Ibid., 25.
73 Juvenal, 'Satire 10', lines 77–81, as cited by Mahoney, *Roman Sports and Spectacles*, 86.
74 Newby, *Greek Athletics in the Roman World*, 22.
75 Cicero quoted in Grant, *Gladiators*, 116.
76 Kyle, *Sport and Spectacle in the Ancient World*, 270.
77 Pliny the Younger, *Letter 9.6*, as cited by Mahoney, *Roman Sports and Spectacles*, 95–6.
78 Seneca, *Letter 7*, section 1–5, as cited by Mahoney, *Roman Sports and Spectacles*, 93–4.
79 Kyle, *Sport and Spectacle in the Ancient World*, 328.
80 Seneca, *Letter 7*, section 1–5, as cited by Mahoney, *Roman Sports and Spectacles*, 94.
81 Kyle, *Sport and Spectacle in the Ancient World*, 328 and 314.
82 Ibid., 314.
83 Connolly, 'Crowd Politics', 77.
84 Ibid., 78.
85 Collini, *Arnold*, 91.
86 Arnold, *Culture and Anarchy*.
87 Rowse, *Matthew Arnold*, 154.
88 Turner, *The Greek Heritage in Victorian Britain*, 15–76.
89 Arnold, *Culture and Anarchy*, 132.
90 Ibid., 134.
91 Collini, *Arnold*, 83.
92 Arnold, *Culture and Anarchy*, 52–3.
93 McIntosh, *Physical Education in England since 1800*, 104.
94 Arnold, *Culture and Anarchy*, 106.
95 Ibid., 52–3.
96 Plato, *The Laws of Plato*.
97 Ibid., 178.
98 Ibid., 179.
99 Young, '*Mens Sana in Corpore Sano?*'
100 Plato, *The Laws of Plato*, 191–2.
101 Ibid., 192.
102 Ibid., 219.
103 Ibid., 192.
104 DeLaura, *Hebrew and Hellene in Victorian England*, 171–81.
105 Pater, *Plato and Platonism*, 145–6.
106 Pater, 'The Age of Athletic Prizemen'.
107 Ibid., 278–9.
108 Ibid., 282.

[109] The transition from rest to motion in the *Discobulus* figure is superbly captured in Leni Riefenstahl's *Olympia: The Film of the X1 Olympic Games Berlin 1936, Part I: Festival of the People* (1938).

[110] Shuter, *Rereading Walter Pater*, 37.

[111] Pater, 'The Age of Athletic Prizeman', 287.

[112] Ibid., 293. For images and discussion of different copies of *Diadumenus* (*Diadoumenos*) and *Discobulus* (*Diskobolos*) see, Hyde, *Olympic Victor Monuments*, 150–5 and 183–8.

[113] Pater, 'The Age of Athletic Prizeman', 284.

[114] Ibid., 287.

[115] Ibid., 293.

[116] Ibid., 294.

[117] Jenkyns, *The Victorians and Ancient Greece*, 171.

[118] This term which became the catch-cry of the Aesthetic Movement and subsequently the Bloomsbury group was used by Pater in his review of William Morris's poetry published anonymously in 1868 in the *Westminster Review*. A revised version of the review and the famous words reappeared in the conclusion to Pater, *The Renaissance*, 252.

[119] Levey, *The Case of Walter Pater*, 23.

[120] Willey, *Nineteenth Century Studies*, 254.

[121] Tillotson, *Criticism and the Nineteenth Century*, 111, 280.

[122] Hough, *The Last Romantics*, 137.

[123] Grote, *A History of Greece*, vol.I, 37–8.

[124] Turner, *The Greek Heritage in Victorian Britain*, 99.

[125] Pater, 'Demeter and Persephone', 151.

[126] Bush, *Mythology and the Romantic Tradition in English Poetry*, 51–70.

[127] Pater, *Appreciations*, 62–3.

[128] Finley and Pleket, *The Olympic Games*, 132.

References

Arnold, M. *Culture and Anarchy*, edited by J. Dover Wilson. Cambridge: Cambridge University Press, 1932.

Auguet, R. *Cruelty and Civilization: The Roman Games*. London: Routledge, 1972.

Baker, W.J. *Sports in the Western World*, rev. ed. Urbana, IL: University of Illinois Press, 1988.

Balme, M. 'Attitudes to Work and Leisure in Ancient Greece'. *Greece and Rome*, second series 31, no. 2 (1984): 140–52.

Barker, E. *The Political Thought of Plato and Aristotle*. New York: Dover, 1959.

Bowra, C.M. *Pindar*. Oxford: Clarendon Press, 1964.

Brantlinger, P. *Bread and Circuses: Theories of Mass Culture and Decay*. Ithaca, NY: Cornell University Press, 1983.

Bush, D. *Mythology and the Romantic Tradition in English*. Cambridge, MA: Harvard University Press, 1969.

Collini, S. *Arnold*. Oxford: Oxford University Press, 1988.

Connolly, J. 'Crowd Politics: The Myth of the "Populus Romanus"'. In *Crowds*, edited by J.T. Schnapp and M. Tiews, 77–96. Stanford, CA: Stanford University Press.

de Grazia, S. *Of Time, Work and Leisure*. New York: The Twentieth Century Fund, 1962.

DeLaura, D.J. *Hebrew and Hellene in Victorian England*. Austin, TX: University of Texas Press, 1969.

Diogenes Laertius. *Lives of Eminent Philosophers*, rev. ed., trans. R.D. Hicks in two volumes. London: William Heinemann, 1938.

Ehrenberg, V. *Society and Civilisation in Greece and Rome*. Cambridge, MA: Harvard University Press, 1964.

Finley, M.I., and H.W. Pleket. *The Olympic Games: The First Thousand Years*. London: Chatto and Windus, 1976.

Freeman, K. *The Work and Life of Solon*. London: University of Wales Press Board, 1926.

Gardiner, E.N. *Athletics of the Ancient World*. Oxford: Clarendon Press, 1930.

Grant, M. *Gladiators*. London: Weidenfeld and Nicholson, 1967.

Grote, G. *A History of Greece: From the Earliest Period to the Close of the Generation Contemporary with Alexander the Great*, a new edition in eight volumes. London: John Murray, 1862.

Guttmann, A. *Sports: The First Five Millennia*. Amherst and Boston, MA: University of Massachusetts, 2004.

Hamilton, J. *Johnson's Dictionary of the English Language in Miniature*. 8th ed. London: Lee and Hurst, 1797.

Harris, H.A. *Sport in Greece and Rome*. London: Thames and Hudson, 1972.

Homer. *The Odyssey*, translated by E.V. Rieu. Harmondsworth: Penguin, 1946.

Homer. *The Iliad*, translated by E.V. Rieu. London: Guild Publishing, 1987.

Hough, G. *The Last Romantics*. London: Gerald Duckworth, 1949.

Hughson, J. 'A Tale of Two Tribes: Expressive Fandom in Australian Soccer's A-League'. In *Football Cultures: Local Contests, Global Visions*, edited by G.P.T. Finn and R. Giulianotti, 10–30. London: Frank Cass, 2000.

Hyde, W.W. *Olympic Victor Monuments and Greek Athletic Art*. Washington, DC: Carnegie Institution of Washington, 1921.

Jenkyns, R. *The Victorians and Ancient Greece*. Cambridge, MA: Harvard University Press, 1980.

Kyle, D.G. 'E. Norman Gardiner and the Decline of Greek Sport'. In *Essays on Sport History and Sport Mythology*, edited by D.G. Kyle and G.D. Stark, 7–44. College Station, TX: Texas A&M University Press, 1990.

Kyle, D.G. *Sport and Spectacle in the Ancient World*. Malden, MA: Wiley-Blackwell, 2007.

Levey, M. *The Case of Walter Pater*. London: Thames and Hudson, 1978.

Lewis, J. *Solon the Thinker: Political Thoughts in Archaic Athens*. London: Duckworth, 2006.

Livingstone, R.W. *The Greek Genius and Its Meaning to Us*. Oxford: Clarendon Press, 1915.

Mahoney, A. *Roman Sports and Spectacles: A Sourcebook: A Sourcebook*. Newburyport, MD: Focus Publishing, 2001.

McIntosh, P.C. *Physical Education in England since 1800*, rev. ed. London: G. Bell and Sons, 1968.

Miller, S.G. *Arête: Greek Sports from Ancient Sources*. 2nd ed. Berkeley, CA: University of California Press, 1991.

Miller, S.G. *Arête: Greek Sports from Ancient Sources*, 3rd and expanded ed. Berkeley and Los Angeles, CA: University of California Press, 2004.

Mumford, L. *The City in History: Its Origins, Its Transformations and Its Prospects*. London: Penguin (Peregrine), 1987.

Newby, Z. *Greek Athletics in the Roman World: Victory and Virtue*. Oxford: Oxford University Press, 2005.

Olivova, V. *Sports and Games in the Ancient World*. London: Orbis, 1984.

Pater, W. *The Renaissance: Studies in Art and Poetry*. 3rd ed. London: Macmillan, 1888.

Pater, W. *Plato and Platonism: A Series of Lectures*. 3rd ed. London: Macmillan, 1910.

Pater, W. 'The Age of Athletic Prizemen: A Chapter in Greek Art'. In *Greek Studies: A Series of Essays*, 2nd ed., 269–99. London: Macmillan, 1910.

Pater, W. 'Demeter and Persephone'. In *Greek Studies: A Series of Essays*, 2nd ed., 81–151. London: Macmillan, 1910.

Pater, W. *Appreciations with an Essay on Style*. 3rd ed. London: Macmillan, 1920.

Perrottet, T. *The Naked Olympics: The True Story of the Athens Games*. New York: Random House, 2004.

Philostratus. *Imagines*. Trans. A. Fairbanks. London: Heinemann, 1931.

Pindar. 'Olympian Ode V, For Psaumis of Kamarina (Winner, Mule Race, 448 B.C.)'. In *Olympian Odes/Pythian Odes*, ed. and trans. W.H. Race. Cambridge, MA: Harvard University Press, 1997.

Pindar. 'Olympian Ode XI, For Hagesidamos of Western Lokroi'. In *Olympian Odes/Pythian Odes*, ed. and trans. W.H. Race. Cambridge, MA: Harvard University Press, 1997.

Plato. *The Laws of Plato*. Trans. A.E. Taylor. London: J.M Dent and Sons, 1934.

Poliakoff, M.B. *Combat Sports in the Ancient World: Competition, Violence and Culture*. New Haven, CT: Yale University Press, 1987.

Rowse, A.L. *Matthew Arnold: Poet and Prophet*. London: Thames and Hudson, 1976.

Shuter, W.F. *Rereading Walter Pater*. Cambridge: Cambridge University Press, 1997.

Tertullian. 'De Spectaculis'. In Tertullian, *Apology* and *De Spectaculis*. Trans. T.R. Glover and M. Felix, 231–301. London: Heinemann, 1931.

Thompson, J.G. 'Solon on Athletics'. *Journal of Sport History* 5, no. 1 (1978): 23–9.

Turner, F.M. *The Greek Heritage in Victorian Britain*. New Haven, CT: Yale University Press, 1981.

Tillotson, G. *Criticism and the Nineteenth Century*. London: University of London, the Athlone Press, 1951.

Willey, B. *Nineteenth Century Studies*. London: Chatto and Windus, 1961.

Young, D.C. *The Olympic Myth of Greek Amateur Athletics*. Chicago, IL: Ares Publishers, 1984.

Young, D.C. *A Brief History of the Olympic Games*. Malden, MA: Blackwell, 2004.

Young, D.C. 'Mens Sana in Corpore Sano? Body and Mind in Ancient Greece'. *The International Journal of the History of Sport* 22, no. 1 (2005): 22–44.

Science, culture and the sporting body

The previous essay referred to Plato's negative view of the body, which found practical expression in his position on physical education set out in his dialogue *The Laws of Plato*. Previously this theme had been discussed in his famous dialogue *The Republic*. Plato's philosophical position on the body is set out in another earlier dialogue, *Phaedo*.[1] The supremacy of the soul (equated to mind) is clearly established throughout *Phaedo* on the basis of the soul being eternal, the body being impermanent. Accordingly, Socrates lectures: 'the soul is pure at departing and draws after her no bodily taint, having never voluntarily during life had connection with the body'.[2] Once departed from the body the soul is 'secure of bliss and is released from the error and folly of men'. A somewhat different understanding of the mind/body relationship can possibly be deduced from the actually administered educational programme of Solon. Solon's famous 'enactment that every boy should be taught to swim and to read' is commonly cited as a foundation stone of western humanistic education.[3] We can at best speculate on Solon's underpinning philosophy and as to the reasonableness of declaring him an early advocate of the 'well-rounded individual'. Such speculation might take interest in why Plato, subsequent to Solon, believed it necessary to set out an ideal education programme stipulating what he believed to be the correct hierarchy of mind over body.

The Platonic distrust of the body has impacted significantly on how the body has been regarded within western scholarship over the generations. The cultural significance of the body has thus remained somewhat obscured within the academy. Only over the past few decades has the body emerged as a topic of dedicated discussion within such fields as cultural studies. This essay seeks to partially retrace a cultural history of the body and physicality from the Renaissance to the present. This involves considering the philosophical trajectory of the mind/body dualism and the articulation of philosophy with related areas of culture, especially poetry. Of particular interest is how the sporting body has come to occupy a contested intellectual terrain between science and culture. It is argued that should the sporting body be irretrievably drawn into a future of 'scientism', where measurable performance, results and outcomes are paramount, then it surrenders its humanness and is lost from the domain of culture.

The essay commences with a discussion of 'physical culture', a term which if used today in popular conversation would tend to sound arcane and/or eccentric. Within intellectual discussion the term physical culture has also, by and large, become redundant. Certainly this is the case in the institutional context of the academy, where programmes concerned with human physicality are described variously as physical education, human movement and kinesiology.[4] The terminological background is European, especially in Germany where 'physical culture' (*Leibesubungen*) was used in medical enquiry to describe the healthy development of the human body through physical exercise. The sports medical approach to physical culture was, not surprisingly, fundamentally biological, 'human potential and performance' through 'exercise (*Ubung*) [believed to be] rooted in the organic life process...applicable to organisms ranging in size and complexity from cells to human beings'.[5] An institutionalized commitment to physical culture was exhibited by the founding of the German College for Physical Culture in Berlin in 1920 and, in 1924, the first sports medical journal was published by the German Association of Physicians for the Promotion of Physical Culture.[6] The techno-scientific emphasis of the medical approach to physical culture was not unproblematic in Germany as it offended the anti-modernist temperament of the gymnastics movement, which was traditionally associated with physical culture. Furthermore, conservative German intellectuals, such as Oswald Spengler, believed the pursuit of high performance sport sullied physical culture and followed an undesirable Anglo trend. However, as Chancellor, Adolf Hitler favoured the modernizing of physical culture as a means of displaying Germanic superiority in both technology and race.[7] Hitler provided the stage for this display with his sponsoring of the 1936 Olympic Games in Berlin, but – even though the story of Hitler's response has been somewhat embellished – his hubris was punctured by the success of American athlete Jessie Owens.[8]

In English-speaking countries the term 'physical culture' gained currency in the popular context as a descriptor for what would be regarded today as bodybuilding. American editor Bernarr Macfadden used the term specifically with the publication of *Physical Culture* magazine in 1898.[9] The main image of physical culture to appear in the magazine was that of, for the time, the extremely well-developed muscular male body. Viewed today, the images have something of an old circus sideshow look about them, but Macfadden's endeavour was undoubtedly more serious than such recognition would imply. Macfadden was not interested in freakish voyeurism; the bodily development on show in *Physical Culture* evinced, for him, revival of aspiration to 'the Greek ideal'. However, *Physical Culture* was not entirely focussed on representation of the male form. The magazine took up the issue of female 'physical beauty' and expressed Macfadden's view that beauty must be cultivated through physical activity and the development of 'fine muscles'. Macfadden thus questioned traditional notions of female beauty and the dichotomous ideals for male and female bodies. His promotion of a unisex physical culture is thus regarded by Jan Todd as historically important to the pursuit of gender equality within the field of physical exercise and bodily development.[10] In his time, Macfadden was regarded as a controversialist. He was arrested in 1905 under the charge of 'the spreading of pornography', for displaying posters of women in body hugging costumes at the 'Mammoth Physical Culture Exhibition' in New York.[11] 'Vivid pictures' displayed in his later publication the *Graphic* (1924) resulted in this magazine being nicknamed the *Pornographic*, and detracted duly from Macfadden's reputation as a genuine advocate of bodily development under the name 'physical culture'.[12]

Leonardo and Descartes

The different views on 'physical culture' developed respectively in Germany and the United States in the first part of the twentieth century were based on a common belief in the perfect form of the human body. The bodily enhancement advocated by Macfadden and the excellence in athletic performance pursued by German sports medicos bears testimony to this. The perfect proportioning of the human body was discussed in the early years of the first millennium by the Roman architect Vitruvius, who believed that buildings should be modelled with the human anatomy in mind.[13] According to Vitruvius, 'If a man lies on his back with outstretched arms and legs, his fingers and toes will touch the circumference of a circle whose centre is his navel. In the same fashion, a square can be constructed about this human figure.'[14] Leonardo da Vinci's well-known drawing of the 'Vitruvian Man' (*Proportions of the Figure*, c.1485–90) has become the 'definitive visual realisation' of Vitrvius's image of the human body,[15] 'divine proportion' working to a 'golden ratio'.[16] Kenneth Clark, although accepting Leonardo's drawing to be the most accurate of those depicting the Vitruvian man, did not regard it as one of Leonardo's 'most attractive'. This was not criticism of Leonardo as artist, but indication that 'the Vitruvian formula does not provide any guarantee of a pleasant-looking body'.[17]

Leonardo, like Vitruvius, conceptualized architecture in relation to the body. This was part of his holistic approach to intellectual and cultural life, which also incorporated music and art.[18] Leonardo believed that proportion could be found in all things related to nature and that understanding the workings of the human body was fundamental to understanding the dynamism of nature.[19] Leonardo thus developed a *scientific* interest in the body and may be regarded as a pioneer of anatomical study, even though 'science' did not exist as a word in his Renaissance Europe.[20] Importantly, though, Leonardo's interest in the body was not limited to its scientific explication. Leonardo's scientific interest blended with his artistry; indeed he regarded the visual portrayal of the human body as the 'highest form of artistic expression'.[21] Furthermore, Leonardo's representation of the human body was meant to provoke thought about human movement. He believed the original Vitruvian formula to be stationary, whereas his interest was in visual perception of the body in various stages and states of movement and posture, 'harmonic balance' in motion.[22] Leonardo also wrote about human movement to complement his diagrammatic and pictorial representations; however a book dedicated to this topic was reputedly lost.[23] Leonardo's view of the human body in movement – describable as 'intellectualised geometricalization' – influenced subsequent conceptualizations during the Renaissance of 'games, sports, and physical exercises'. For example, Leonardo's influence can be seen in Michelangelo's sketches of the complex movement involved in fencing, an activity described by the latter as, 'this fine art of killing'.[24]

While maintaining a 'holistic' view of human intellectual inquiry – science and art in the service of nature – Leonardo's position on the body exhibited a tension between the mechanic and the organic. In this way he pre-empted the mind/body dualism that appeared in the philosophical writing of René Descartes in the 1600s. Descartes did not share Leonardo's insistence that the human body is the '*ultimate* machine', but accepted that human bodies are machine-like and are to be explained mathematically as mechanical systems.[25] He has been described as an iatro-mechanist in that he believed blood, after coming into contact with thinking substances in the brain, flowed out through the nervous system to activate body parts and produce movement.[26] So, while the body might be an extremely impressive mechanism, it is a decidedly inferior organism to the brain. Descartes thus breaks from Solon-like humanistic holism and, as discussed below, this has impact on the significance given to sport and physical education in what became known as the Age of Science.

The seventeenth century was also known as the Age of Reason, and this name further reflects Descartes' intellectual bearing on the time. Descartes' fiercely scientific outlook held that absolute knowledge was the preserve of the intellect, and that sensory experience should have no place in knowledge claims made about the world and human affairs. Descartes' scienticism did not preclude moral judgement, but he believed morality to be a purely intellectual concern and moral standards to be ascertainable from 'mathematical physics'.[27] Acquisition of knowledge 'is not the work of a disembodied intellect', but the making of judgements by *reason* is, according to Grene's interpretation of Descartes, 'what marks off man from the brutes [animals]'.[28] Descartes was adamant that human will, which he associates with the senses, should not be allowed to overshadow human understanding, achievable only through the mind. From this view, following the directives of the mind, not the body, is the 'proper condition' for humans – the way it is and the way it should be.

Descartes' *cogito*, 'I think therefore I am', is one of the most famous statements in the history of philosophy, the basis for adjudging the intellect as the primary and only reliable source of self-knowledge. However, Grene believes the *cogito* to be 'one of the great falsehoods of philosophy' because 'other selves ... are known to me before and better than I myself am known'.[29] Of course, we only live inside ourselves, but this very 'insideness', according to Grene, is 'mere subjectivity, not knowledge'. Grene suggests that we do not really *know* ourselves at all, at least not by the certainty of reason averred by Descartes. Grene's criticism of Descartes suggests that we speak more appropriately of self-awareness than self-knowledge and that the senses are a much more significant source of subjective human knowledge than Descartes' hard rationalism could allow. This criticism also challenges Descartes' mind/body dualism in a way insightful to historical consideration of the sportive body.

Educators and philosophers

Descartes believed the mind to exist in direct spiritual relationship with the soul, whereas the body does not transcend the secular realm it physically inhabits. Descartes' position, as indicated above, broke with the humanism of the Renaissance period, which denied a mind/body dualism. A form of holistic humanism was particularly evident in the ideas and work of educationalists, who rejected the Scholasticism of the early Renaissance. Scholastic teaching was steeped in the doctrine of original sin and preached against the carnal vice of the body, the body regarded as a human manifestation of evil. Contrarily, humanist educators valued corporeal existence and recommended instruction on physical exercise and games in their programmes for the development of the well-rounded individual. This is not to suggest that humanist educators were not religious, but that they believed in original goodness rather than original sin, a return to the Greek ideal of soul and body in harmony.[30]

Vittorino da Feltre (1378–1446) is widely regarded as the earliest prominent humanist educator of the Renaissance period. Vittorino, himself a well-rounded scholar, was appointed as principal teacher to the children of the Gonzaga court in Mantua (*Mantova*). Vittorino's programme involved teaching Christian principles along with classical studies and 'the Greek passion for bodily culture and for dignity of the outer life'.[31] Vittorino instructed in bodily exercise and deportment not purely for the purpose of preparing the Gonzaga children for military service – although this was part of his expected role as educator – but to instil appreciation of the inherent value of physical culture into his pupils. According to Woodward, 'Vittorino . . . [taught] . . . gymnastics as an art, deserving of perseverance for its own sake'.[32] However, a number of writers have noted, Vittorino's chief concern was that education – including tuition in physical training and sportive activity – be used for the creation of good citizenship, an aim that has continued through to humanist teaching in modern times.[33]

Vittorino's influence became apparent in Anglo society by the 1500s with the emergence of humanist teachers such as Thomas Elyot (1490–1546) and Roger Ascham (1515–68). Elyot was responsible for teaching the sons of the nobility and his programme involved preparing well-rounded gentlemen versed in the arts, science and philosophy. A *prepared* intellect was to be complemented by a prepared physique and, accordingly, Elyot trained young gentlemen in athletic and sportive activities. Elyot was, however, suitably elitist in the sports he recommended. The folk football of his time he recognized as especially anathema to gentlemanly conduct, stating in 1537, 'Foot ball wherin is nothynge but beastlye furie and exstreme violence, whereof proceedeth hurte; and consequently malice and rancour do remain with them that be wounded, where of it is to be putt in perpetuall silence.'[34] Elyot thus rejected football on the grounds that it is both physically and morally injurious, a view shared by Henry VIII who, like previous monarchs, placed a ban on the playing of football-like games.[35] Apart from athletic contests including wrestling and running, sports encouraged within early humanist educational programmes were mainly those associated with hunting. Roger Ascham's book on archery (*Toxophilus*), published in the 1570s soon after the author's death, appeared as an early form of the sport instruction manual.[36] Beyond moral and health benefits, Ascham maintained that sport was needed by students for respite from mental learning. Sport was thus seen as beneficial to the body, soul and mind.

The link between physical activity and the intellect was reiterated by the philosopher John Locke in his *Some Thoughts Concerning Education* published in1693. However, it seems unlikely that Locke's commitment to the well-rounded individual was as balanced as that of the humanist educators of the 1500s. Locke, at certain points in his writing, appears most interested in physical activity as play, a means of relieving students from the rigours of mental work.[37] Locke insisted upon 'useful exercises of the body and mind, taking their turns' within the daily educational regimen.[38] His well-known dictum, 'a sound mind in a sound body is a short but full description of a happy state in this world', appears to support an educational philosophy of holistic humanism.[39] However, Locke held to a dualistic mind/body hierarchy, much in the manner of Descartes. According to Lowe, 'Locke's "person" sounds rather like Descartes' *res cognitans* (literally, a "thing which thinks")'.[40]

Locke's views on education thus reflect his philosophical position on the individual, the position set out in the lengthy *Essay Concerning Human Understanding*, first published in 1690. Like Descartes, he emphasized the paramountcy of reason in the formation of ideas and thus that the education of the mind must take precedence over that of the body. However, Locke differed from Descartes in that he discussed the importance of sensation as a stimulus to the mind's formulation of ideas.[41] Ideas actually result from reflection upon sensation caused by contact with objects external to the individual. Therefore, despite reiterating a dualism reminiscent of Descartes, Locke's discussion of sensation necessitates serious consideration of the body, given that it is through the body that sensation is experienced. According to Gerber, this would have been apparent enough to Locke himself: 'It would be totally inconsistent for a man who believed that the senses were a primary source of knowing, to be unconcerned with the condition of the body.'[42] Locke's position on the senses and human understanding provided a philosophical underpinning to the empiricist tradition of enquiry that dominated Britain during the Enlightenment period following his death. However, for the body to be valued holistically, the philosophical stronghold of reason had to be challenged further than it was in Locke's recasting of Descartes. The challenge to reason was taken up in the 1700s by another famous name within the history of philosophy, David Hume.

A Treatise of Human Nature, arguably his best-known work, was published in 1739–40 when Hume was just 29 years old. It was in this work that Hume set out his staunch and, for the time, radical opposition to a general (a priori) law of reason: 'any hypothesis, that pretends to discover the ultimate original qualities of human nature, ought at first to be rejected as presumptuous and chimerical'.[43] Hume rejected the notion of infallible reason promoted by Descartes, and thus the latter's view on absolute knowledge, because he did not accept the mind as a perfect instrument of judgement. In retreat from what he saw as the arrogance of logical certainty, Hume introduced the term 'impressions' to describe how human awareness and subsequent action is derived from perceptions acquired from experience and observation of the external world: 'those *impressions*, which arise from the *senses*, their ultimate cause is, in my opinion, perfectly inexplicable by human reason'; 'Since it is not from knowledge or any scientific reasoning, that we derive the opinion of the necessity of a cause to every new production, that opinion must necessarily arise from observation and experience.'[44]

Hume's rejection of absolute knowledge evinces a counter philosophy of scepticism whereby explanations of causation based in pure reason are illusory. He wrote of the need for a 'science of man', clearly implying that scientific knowledge should be sought in the physical rather than metaphysical realm, his emphasis on sensation over intellect provocatively suggesting the importance of body over mind. However, the limitations of the mind also make it impossible to intellectually understand the sensory properties of the body, 'we can never pretend to know the body otherwise than by those external properties, which discover themselves to the senses'.[45] What is more important for Hume is recognizing the link between *passions* and morality, and this becomes the theme in the second 'book' of *A Treatise*. Here Hume again breaks significantly with Descartes. Where the latter saw the mind and soul in direct relationship, Hume reinstates the relationship between body and soul. Indeed, he conflates the two, 'Bodily pains and pleasures . . . the source of many passions . . . arise originally in the soul, or in the body, whichever you please to call it, without any preceding thought or perception'.[46] The originality of Hume's body and soul nexus is that it is given material status, rather than ideal status as in Greek philosophy. The 'moral sense' of humans is aroused as they differentiate between earthly feelings of pleasure and pain. Subsequent questions of right and wrong action are thus derived through feeling not intellect, and are experiential rather than transcendental in basis. It thus seems rather odd that Hume goes on to declare an explicit connection between passions and the *imagination*.[47] But, as Basil Willey has noted, by imagination Hume means not the stuff of fairytale but 'that mental screen whereon, *in men of correct judgement*, the customary connexions of "just" ideas are projected'.[48] Such understanding of imagination in connection with passion was developed interestingly in the nineteenth century in what Bertrand Russell saw as a 'natural sequel to Hume's destruction' of reason and philosophical empiricism – the Romantic Movement.[49]

The 'Romantic' body

The Romantic Movement was primarily associated with the arts, rather than philosophy, but the critical writing of its key figures, particularly poets, came to have considerable bearing on intellectual life by the end of the seventeenth century.[50] The Romantics shared Hume's scepticism about reason, but some also called into question the significance of sensory experience. Prominent in this regard was William Blake, who believed reliance on the senses meant falling into another philosophical trap. For Blake, humans do better to surrender to instinct and intuition.[51] This view is based in deeply religious belief via which Blake effectively reconnects the mind to the soul. His related disregard for the human body is more pronounced than in the dualist philosophies of thinkers such as Descartes. According to Blake, 'this world of Imagination is the world of Eternity; it is the divine bosom into which we shall all go after the death of the Vegetated body'.[52] His interest in the body is confined to that of the 'divine body of the Saviour'. Blake's denial of the importance of human bodily sensation was arrived at independently, he was not greatly interested in contemporaneous metaphysical writing, although his poetry did contain dismissive lines about the materialism of science.[53] Shelley, in *A Defence of Poetry*, definitively enunciated the view that poetry is paramount to science: 'Poetry is indeed something divine. It is at once the centre and circumference of knowledge; it is that which comprehends all science, and to that which all science must be referred.'[54]

The celebration of the imagination continued in the work of two of the most famous Romantic poets, Wordsworth and Coleridge, notably in their collaborative collection *Lyrical Ballads*, first published in 1798. Wordsworth and Coleridge were sympathetic to the critique of rationalism and, at a practical level, were critical of the technological applications of science and the attendant environmental damage wrought by the industrial revolution in Britain. Their fascination with nature in its earthly presence involved a focus on the imagination with less direct religious implication than was the case for Blake. This was certainly so for Wordsworth, whose worldview was more secular than that of Coleridge, a difference that eventually led to a rift between the two.[55] Wordsworth's materialist conception of imagination (as opposed to Blake's idealist conception) was influenced by his reading of a philosophical contemporary of Hume, David Hartley. According to Hartley, the imagination is one of the 'sensations of the soul', and spirituality must be viewed as 'the necessary consequence of passing through life'.[56] His privileging of sensory experience over reason was similar to Hume's position, but whereas the latter was often assumed an atheist, Hartley was a non-dogmatic believer in Christian theology, and this is likely to have made him more acceptable than Hume to Wordsworth, and especially to Coleridge who was an initial admirer.[57]

From Hartley's perspective, the powers of the imagination cannot be disconnected from the human body, and he explained the sensory experience from which imagination stems in distinctly physiological terms. According to Porter, 'Hartley's conjectural physiology of the nervous system also offered prototypes for the sensory motor theories later influential in neurophysiology, comprising distant ancestors of Pavlovian notions of conditioned reflexes'.[58] The influence of Hartley's corresponding philosophical position on the senses is evident in a number of the *Lyrical Ballads*, including Wordsworth's 'Tintern Abbey'. Brett and Jones recognize in the poem, 'Hartley's account of how the mind moves from sensation through perception to thought, [being] turned into an analogy of how the individual passes from childhood through youth to maturity'.[59] Wordsworth, furthermore, shared Hartley's view of the senses providing the basis of 'moral principles'. 'Morality, on such a view, was the product of experience, built from the effects of environment upon one's personal development. This is the central importance in much of Wordsworth's poetry.'[60] A clear example of Wordsworth associating morality with a sensuous experience of nature appears in 'The Tables Turned':

> Books! 'tis a dull and endless strife,
> Come, hear the woodland linnet,
> How sweet his music; on my life
> There's more of wisdom in it.
>   And hark! How blithe the throstle sings!
> And he is no mean preacher;
> Come forth into the light of things,
> Let nature be your teacher...
>   One impulse from a vernal wood
> May teach you more of man;
> Of moral evil and of good,
> Than all the sages can.[61]

According to F.R. Leavis, the philosophical dimension of Wordsworth's poetry 'is an expression of his intense moral seriousness and a mode of that essential discipline of contemplation which gave consistency and stability to his experience'.[62] Moral seriousness most certainly, but for Wordsworth, morality is more an outcome of sensory experience than contemplation. We find in Wordsworth's poetry, and in his writing about poetry,[63] what I will refer to as an *embodied morality*; a morality derived from imaginative engagement with the senses. Accordingly, morality is felt rather than thought. This understanding underpins the subsequent discussion of morality in this essay. Interestingly, Wordsworth himself gives glimpse to the moral possibility of sportive activity. In the long poem 'Ruth' he tells the story of the 'Youth from Georgia's shore' who, as time passes, falls from grace after becoming 'the slave of low desires'. In younger days sport had provided a dimension to his 'moral frame':

> And when he chose to sport and play,
> No dolphin ever was so gay
> Upon the tropic sea.[64]

Wordsworth's poetry also suggests a union between the human spirit and a healthy and active body. This state of union is most perfect in childhood, as recognized by the adult narrator in 'Intimations of Immortality':

> And see the Children sport upon the shore,
> And hear the mighty waters rolling ever more.[65]

Wordsworth's 'ode' to the 'child of nature' is a recurring theme, and is matched by corresponding lament to physical demise with age in such poems as 'Simon Lee, the Old Huntsman', another of the *Lyrical Ballads*.[66] Remembrance of Simon's past highlights his athletic ability in youth:

> He all the country could outrun,
> Could leave both man and horse behind;

Victorian lessons

As indicated in the previous essay in the discussion of Mathew Arnold, the need to maintain a healthy body, for the young in particular, became a theme of importance to prominent public figures in the Victorian period. In the Preface of *Unto This Last*, John Ruskin contended, 'the child should . . . be taught, with the best skill of teaching that the country could produce . . . the laws of health, and the exercises enjoined by them'.[67] Herbert Spencer, the social philosopher, also assumed a quasi-legalistic tone in his essay on physical education, initially published in 1859. According to Spencer, 'the sportive activities to which the instincts impel, are essential to bodily welfare. Whoever forbids them, forbids the divinely-appointed means to physical development.'[68] Spencer, here, is criticizing the imposition within school curricula of 'gymnastics' programmes that are 'artificial' and at best result in disproportionate development of the young male body.[69] Preferable is the 'spontaneous exercise' in which children will undertake, 'prompted by Nature'. Children simply need the freedom of time for natural and spontaneous, rather than imposed, physical exercise. Sportive activity, according to Spencer, is as instinctive to girls as boys and they too should be allowed to 'run wild' despite Victorian fears that such abandon fosters 'unlady-like habits'.[70]

George Bernard Shaw was a particularly interesting critic of the role of physical education within the grammar school curricula: 'In our times [a] cynical claim has been made for the right to drive boys through compulsory games in the playing fields until they are too much exhausted physically to do anything but drop off to sleep'.[71] Shaw believed such games had little to do with intended development of a healthy body, but were aimed at tiring the young as a means of keeping them out of mischief. However, the resultant exhaustion, according to Shaw, meant that the child was also too tired for 'poetry, literature, music, meditation and prayer'.[72] Shaw's criticism of athleticism characteristically lapsed into satire. At one point he called for the introduction of 'the shooting of children as a sport' to rival foxhunting. He saw this as a logical (if farcical) extension of a situation where children were treated in schools in the manner of sporting game. Interestingly, Shaw was no supporter of the competitive sport that had emerged by the late 1800s: 'As a humane person I detested violence and slaughter, whether in war, sport, or the butcher's yard.'[73]

A more serious approach to physical exercise and sportive activity prevailed within the public school system of Victorian Britain. Often discussed as a pioneering figure in this regard is Thomas Arnold, Matthew's father, who was headmaster of Rugby School from 1828–42. Thomas Arnold is often regarded as the founder of the educational philosophy of 'muscular Christianity'; however, this ascription arises more from Thomas Hughes's characterization of Arnold in *Tom Brown's Schooldays* than from a non-fictional account of Arnold's historical legacy.[74] Arnold was undoubtedly concerned with developing religious conviction and moral uprightness in young men, but he did not believe these qualities were nurtured through sport and physical games. Arnold did believe in the importance of physical activity but saw such activity as recreation divorced from the work of mental labour. Recreation, for Arnold, involved a release from intellectual and spiritual concerns and, therefore, is intrinsically amoral, although fundamental to a healthy state of well-being for boys.[75] Arnold insisted on young men having 'pure play', not organized team sports such as football and cricket. In regard to the developmental benefit of the team sports, he was somewhat ambivalent. Again, Arnold's popularly assumed interest in these 'consciously value-laden' team sports is derived from Hughes's fictional account of their prominence within the school culture during Arnold's tenure as principal.[76]

As Haley notes, in Victorian England, 'the cricket match had become the symbol of gentlemanly life outside the school'.[77] It extended from Hughes's characterization in *Tom Brown*, to Henry Newbolt's anthemic poem of the 1890s, 'Vitai Lampada'. Paxman claims that the poem – calling on young men to 'Play up! Play up! And play the game!' – 'remains the encapsulation of the belief that all life's problems can be solved by playing a straight bat'.[78] The public school ethos of virtue and respectable conduct was thus carried on and continued by sporting analogy. Yet, ironically, Thomas Arnold, the great moral reformer of the Victorian school and promoter of gentlemanliness – as seen above – was not a sporting moralist. For Arnold a gentleman is created via the training of the mind and soul rather than the body. He did not favour an embodied morality of the type I have associated with Wordsworth. Arnold actually admitted that he lacked an 'imaginative faculty' and was grateful to Wordsworth for enhancing his appreciation of nature in later life when they became neighbours in the Lake District.[79] However, Arnold was neither a Romantic nor a humanistic educator in the manner of Thomas Elyot. The development of sporting culture at Arnold's Rugby occurred through circumstance rather than design. As a result of Arnold's prefect system, sportive activity gained prominence at Rugby, and subsequently throughout the public school system, largely via student initiative.[80]

Although heralded as an educational reformer Arnold advocated a conventional curriculum 'devoted to the teaching of Greek and Latin Grammar'.[81] This curriculum, which took on the misnomer of 'liberal education', was challenged in the later nineteenth century by those who believed it increasingly irrelevant to an industrialized society. For example, T.H. Huxley believed that a continuing concentration on classical languages ignored the need for a 'scientific education', the latter being 'an absolutely essential condition of industrial progress'.[82] This opinion put him at odds with his friend Matthew Arnold. The younger Arnold believed that science should be brought onto the curriculum but not at the expense of literature. The classification of literature should be broad enough to include not only great novels, plays and poems, but also great books of science. Arnold specifically named Euclid's *Elements* and Newton's *Principia* as essential books.[83] Yet, Arnold remained wary of science going beyond its station in the educational system. He was particularly concerned that science would promote specialization to the detriment of humanistic education.[84] However, in the final analysis, Huxley and Arnold may have been not so much hostile combatants as collegial interlocutors in an ultimately harmonious dialogue, 'its traditions located in the accumulated wisdom of both humanism and science'.[85]

The future in their bones or the metal in their limbs

A more heated antagonism between science and the humanities came to a head in the twentieth century in the so-called 'two cultures' controversy surrounding the novelist and scientist C.P. Snow and the literary critic F.R. Leavis. Snow, speaking in 1959, claimed that a gulf had emerged between the sciences and the humanities and that public decision-making was driven by the latter. He maintained that the 'traditional culture' (meaning literary intellectuals) needed to give way to scientists, those with the 'future in their bones'.[86] Leavis's objection, best known for its alleged vituperation, was that Snow's pro-science position was ultimately utilitarian and if instituted into the educational curriculum would sink Britain into a cultural 'vacuum of disinheritance'.[87] Leavis had long been cautious of 'applied science' and its accompanying advents in technology. He believed in the maintenance of an 'older order', an 'organic community' lived within a 'natural environment' according to the 'rhythm of the year'.[88] For Snow 'applied science' would be ignored at mankind's peril because it alone holds the key to the removal of material suffering. Snow's championing of science, whether or not of utilitarian consequence, was driven by genuine concern for the future of humanity and the 'two cultures' might therefore be regarded as two sides of a humanist coin; the scientific humanism of Snow in converse relation to the cultural humanism of Leavis.

A decidedly non humanistic championing of science had occurred early in the twentieth century with the release of *The Futurist Manifesto* in 1909 by the Italian writer Filippo Marinetti. Marinetti was awestruck by the possibilities of machine technology. Point 4 of the Manifesto declared:

> We affirm that the world's magnificence has been enriched by a new beauty: the beauty of speed. A racing car whose hood is adorned with great pipes, like serpents of explosive breath – a roaring car that seems to ride of grapeshot is more beautiful than the *Victory of Samothrace*.[89]

To Marinetti the past was the enemy, 'he attacked history and memory with operatic zeal, and a wide range of objects and customs fell under his disapproval'.[90] In Britain he befriended the painter C.R.W. Nevinson and together in 1912 they presented *The Futurist Manifesto Against English Art*, which denounced, inter alia, the Pre-Raphaelites, Morris dances, fairy stories, Oscar Wilde 'and other kinds of traditionalist rubbish'.[91] Most interestingly, in the affirmative, Marinetti and Nevinson declared, 'that sport be considered as an essential element in art'. Marinetti was an advocate of extremely strenuous physical exercise and clearly favoured a programme for the development of the body in preference to the intellect. He thus advanced, 'a cult of progress and speed, of sport, of physical strength, of fearless courage, of heroism, and of danger, against any obsession with culture, classical education, the museum, the library, and archaeological remains'.[92] Marinetti heralded the fusion of human body and machine, which he called 'geometrical and mechanical splendour': 'an aggressive optimism stemming from a passion for sport and the toning of muscles . . . a passion for success, a pioneering instinct for breaking records . . . the sweet precision of machinery and of well-oiled thought; the harmony of energies converging in one victorious path'.[93] The futurist fusion of body and machine in sport received striking visual representation in Umberto Boccioni's 'Dynamism Studies', in particular the 1913 paintings *Dynamism of a Cyclist* and *The Dynamism of a Soccer Player*.[94]

Marinetti's reputation eventually suffered because of collaboration with Mussolini in the early years of Italian fascism, but he is a problematic figure not only because of this actual association.[95] As Hewitt notes, it is not possible to assess Marinetti's futurism apart from this episode as there is contiguity between the so-called progressive aesthetics promulgated in his manifestos and a reactionary political ideology.[96] Even before the human calamity of European fascism had been revealed, enthusiasm for the machine had been dented by cultural pessimism especially within literature. For example, Aldous Huxley's futuristic novel *Brave New World* (1932) satirized the very idea of scientific progress in a manner consistent with his non-fiction writing. In the essay 'One and Many' Huxley decried the deception of technology, in particular the mechanization of leisure, arguing that machines not only relieve humans of drudgery but deprive us of the 'possibility of performing any creative or spontaneous act whatsoever'.[97]

The dystopian view of machinery expunged the *fin de siècle* optimism of Oscar Wilde who envisioned a socialistic civilization in which machinery will forever shatter human relations of slavery. While human slavery is an abomination, 'on the slavery of the machine, the future of the world depends', so Wilde believed.[98]

In contemporary scholarship postmodernist theorists have returned to the human/machine fusion, but via an inversion of Marinetti's aesthetics > politics formula. In this spirit Haraway delivered her influential 'Cyborg Manifesto': 'by the late twentieth century...we are all...fabricated hybrids of machine and organism; in short, we are cyborgs'.[99] Haraway is confident about a cybernetic future because she sees the cyborg as a disruption to traditional power arrangements, especially gender. Haraway's cyborg manifesto has obvious implications for sport, as recognized in the work of Cole.[100] Cole welcomes the indecipherability of the cyborg and its attendant 'destabilising' of the humanistic binary between the sporting body and machine.[101] The cyborg renders notions of the 'organic body' obsolete.[102] From this recognition, Cole dismisses 'moral valuations' of the sportsperson relying on technologically enhanced performance – particularly in regard to drug use – as irrelevant. Accordingly, she regards drug-testing in sport as little more than intrusive policing, a misguided attempt to reinstate a humanistic distinction between body and machine.

'Mortal Engines'

In opposition to pro-technology positions on sport, John Hoberman warns against the retreat from humanism.[103] Hoberman contends that the 'fusion of sport and science has transformed the generally accepted meaning of sportsmanship' away from traditional notions of 'fair play' to an obsession with 'performance and productivity'.[104] He disputes as historical myth the view that sport enhancement techniques practised in East Germany from the 1950s were an extension of Hitler's ambitions for the creation of super athletes.[105] According to Hoberman, there is little evidence that Hitler promoted biomedical physical enhancement in relation to sport. Rather, the strength of rumour is towards a steroid programme being targeted at various branches of the German army including the SS. The thrust of Hoberman's book *Mortal Engines* is that an untrammelled 'scientism' – transcending political regimes – has drawn sport out of the cultural realm, with moral bearing, into a technological realm where peak performance is paramount. Hoberman's concern that performance-mad coaches unwittingly encourage athletes to overlook their mortality, compares interestingly to Hayles warning that over zealous endorsement of the cyborg creates 'fantasies of...disembodied immortality'.[106] Although positive about 'post-human cybernetics' Hayles 'celebrates finitude as a condition of being' and calls for renewed 'understand[ing of] human life [as] embedded in a material world of great complexity'.

More conventionally Hoberman argues that no matter how successful science has been in enhancing sport performance through the nineteenth century, the human body is, after all, constituted of human matter and, therefore, mortal. Science merely offers an illusion of immortality. The forgetting of mortality simultaneously involves a release from moral judgement, as the necessity for standards of living conduct become philosophically redundant. Dehumanization occurs when moral questions about sporting activity are suspended. Of topical pertinence to such questioning is the issue of drug usage in the pursuit of peak sporting performance. Reported usage of drugs for sporting contest dates back to the 1860s.[107] Cyclists were believed to use 'speed balls' of heroin and cocaine as well as mild stimulants such as caffeine to maintain endurance. Steroid usage proliferated in power sports such as weightlifting following availability in chemical form in the late 1920s.[108] Successful Soviet weightlifters had been suspected of steroid use since the 1950s, and by the 1970s usage was so widespread in the sport that the American heavyweight champion, Ken Patera, boasted that the gold medal at the 1972 Olympics would be won by the 'better' steroids.[109]

However, effective tests to identify steroid 'cheats' were devised in the mid-1970s and widely administered by the 1980s.[110] Perhaps the best-known case of steroid detection remains that involving Canadian athlete Ben Johnson, who was stripped of the gold medal he had been awarded for victory in the 100 metres sprint at the 1988 Olympic Games.

The general protest against steroid usage is made largely on medical grounds, i.e. on the basis that while steroid usage may be beneficial to sporting performance it is ultimately injurious to the consumer's health. As Simon notes, such criticism is paternalistic and if logically extended could be applied to any activity in life that could be agreed upon as having harmful health effects.[111] The protest against drug usage in high performance sport – such as in the Johnson case – is more clearly waged on moral grounds. Simon regards this entirely appropriate because, he believes, by its very nature sporting competition is an agreement between participants involved 'in a mutual quest for excellence through challenge'.[112] Thus viewed, competitors are 'under moral obligations to their opponents' and should accept the sporting challenge 'for its own sake'.[113] *Sport for sport's sake* requires sportspersons to fairly engage with opponents and not seek undue advantage, and to respect the intrinsic human value of the sporting contest. From this perspective, the pursuit of excellence in sport is desirable when undertaken according to basic moral principles to which the sportsperson tacitly agrees by entering the contest. Contrarily, scientism relieves moral and, therefore, 'human' responsibility. Arguments for the relaxation of steroid usage in sport tend to operate on this philosophical basis, in some cases contending that moral imposition should not be placed on the sportsperson. The difficulty with such a position is that in relieving the sportsperson of moral responsibility it at once extracts the humanness from the sporting contest.

As Moran notes, we are all cyborgs in mundane and routine ways: in sportive activity we 'wear trainers designed to improve our athletic performance'.[114] But need this point to the blurring of the distinction between body and machine in a so-called post-human age? After all Roger Bannister was as reliant on footwear to break the four minute mile in 1954 as Hicham El Guerrouj was in breaking the world record for the mile in 1999. Despite increasing mechanical intrusion, sport continues to offer a reminder that the post-human age is yet to arrive. The technological enhancement of sports performance may anticipate 'dehumanisation', but the flow and spillage of blood, sweat and tears ensures that sport is an essentially human activity. Nevertheless, science maintains a position of historical challenge. Should sports competitors come to evince 'disembodied immortality' rather than 'embodied morality', we may well have entered an epoch of post-humanism.

Notes

1. Plato, *The Republic*; Plato, *Phaedo*.

2. Plato, *Phaedo*, 465.

3. Boyd, *The History of Western Education*, 16.

4. For a discussion of the academic history of physical culture see Kirk, 'Physical Culture, Physical Education and Relational Analysis'.

5. Hoberman, 'The Early Development of Sports Medicine in Germany', 260.

6. Ibid., 240.

7. Ibid., 245.

8. Guttmann, *The Olympics*, 67–8.

9. Mrozek, 'The Scientific Quest for Physical Culture', 288. Images from *Physical Culture* magazine can be seen at: http://www.riverflow.com/macfadden/pcmagreview/index.html.

10. Todd, 'Bernarr Macfadden: Reformer of Feminine Form'.

11. Ibid., 213.

[12] Mrozek, 'The Scientific Quest for Physical Culture', 288.

[13] Kemp, *Leonardo*, 66.

[14] Kuhnst, *Sports*, 18 and 20.

[15] Kemp, *Leonardo*, 67. For an image of the drawing see, Monti, *Leonardo*, Plate 75.

[16] Bulent, *The Art and Science of Leonardo da Vinci*, 105.

[17] Clark, *The Nude*, 15.

[18] White, *Leonardo: The First Scientist*, 164.

[19] Ibid., 168.

[20] Ibid., 267.

[21] Ibid., 321.

[22] Kemp, *Leonardo*, 67.

[23] Clark, *Leonardo da Vinci*, 69.

[24] Kuhnst, *Sports*, 21–2.

[25] Russell, *History of Western Philosophy*, 546.

[26] Schofield, *Mechanism and Materialism*, 49.

[27] Grene, *The Knower and the Known*, 65.

[28] Ibid., 82.

[29] Ibid., 86.

[30] Mechikoff and Estes, *A History and Philosophy of Sport and Physical Education*, 80.

[31] Woodward, *Vittorino da Feltre and Other Humanist Educators*, 27.

[32] Ibid., 246.

[33] For example, Gerber, *Innovators and Institutions in Physical Education*, 50.

[34] Rice, *A Brief History of Physical Education*, 126.

[35] Rice, *Start of Play*, 13–14.

[36] Gerber, *Innovators and Institutions in Physical Education*, 64.

[37] Locke, *Some Thoughts Concerning Education*, 166.

[38] Ibid., 138.

[39] Ibid., 25.

[40] Lowe, *Locke on Human Understanding*, 103.

[41] Locke, *Essay Concerning Human Understanding*, 151.

[42] Gerber, *Innovators and Institutions in Physical Education*, 64.

[43] Hume, *A Treatise of Human Nature*, xvii.

[44] Ibid., 84 and 82.

[45] Ibid., 64.

[46] Ibid., 276.

[47] Ibid., 340.

[48] Willey, *The Eighteenth Century Background*, 115.

[49] Russell, *History of Western Philosophy*, 647.

[50] Hume is regarded as having influence on the Romantic Movement; ibid., 651.

[51] Harper, *The Neoplatonism of William Blake*, 235.

[52] Blake from 'A Vision of the Last Judgement', cited in Bowra, *The Romantic Imagination*, 3.

[53] Ibid., 8–9.

[54] Shelley, *A Defence of Poetry*, 38; William Wordsworth was also interested in the 'close relationship between poetry and science'. He regarded the scientist as a 'lonely specialist', the poet as one who 'speaks to all men'. For this reason the latter is more able to illuminate a thoroughgoing understanding of life. See Durant, *Wordsworth and the Great System*, 4–5.

[55] Brett and Jones (eds), 'Introduction' to *Lyrical Ballads*, xxxvii.

[56] Porter, *Enlightenment*, 181. Hartley's major philosophical work, known to Wordsworth and Coleridge, was *Observations on Man: his Frame, his Duty and his expectations*, first published in 1749.

57 Porter, *Enlightenment*, 179.

58 Ibid., 182.

59 Brett and Jones (eds), 'Introduction' to *Lyrical Ballads*, xxxv–xxxvi.

60 Ibid., xxxiv.

61 Wordsworth, 'The Tables Turned; An Evening Scene, on the Same Subject', in Brett and Jones (eds), *Lyrical Ballads*, 104–5.

62 Leavis, *Revaluation*, 164.

63 'Wordsworth's Prefaces of 1800 and 1802', in Brett and Jones (eds), *Lyrical Ballads*, 248–55.

64 Wordsworth, 'Ruth', in Brett and Jones (eds), *Lyrical Ballads*, 174–84.

65 Wordsworth, 'Ode: Intimations of Immortality', 357–61.

66 Knoepflmacher, 'Mutations of the Wordsworthian Child of Nature'; Wordsworth, 'Simon Lee, the Old Huntsman, with an incident in which he was concerned', in Brett and Jones (eds), *Lyrical Ballads*, 60–3.

67 Ruskin, *Unto This Last*, xvii.

68 Spencer, *Education*, 172.

69 Ibid., 171.

70 Ibid., 170.

71 Shaw, 'Treatise on Parents and Children', xliv.

72 Ibid., lxxx.

73 Shaw, 'Mainly about Myself', vi.

74 Hughes, *Tom Brown's School Days*. Muscular Christianity has also been associated with the novelist Charles Kingsley but, although a staunch advocate of the link between Christianity and healthy outdoor living, it was a term he clearly rejected as indicated in his correspondence. For example, see Kingsley, *Charles Kingsley*, 213. Perhaps more willingly associated with the term muscular Christianity was the author and mountaineer Leslie Stephen, well-known as the father of Virginia Woolf and Vanessa Bell. Stephen has been said to have phrased the 'true creed of a muscular Christian' when he declared, 'to fear God and walk a thousand miles in a thousand hours'. Courtney, *Free Thinkers of the Nineteenth Century*, 177.

75 Haley, *The Healthy Body and Victorian Culture*, 143–4.

76 Ibid., 153.

77 Ibid., 260.

78 Paxman, *The English*, 143–4.

79 Campbell, *Thomas Arnold*, 110–11.

80 McIntosh, *Physical Education in England since 1800*, 41.

81 Strachey, *Eminent Victorians*, 187.

82 Huxley, 'Science and Culture', 137–8.

83 Arnold, 'Literature and Science'.

84 Collini, 'Introduction', xv.

85 Paradis and Postlewait, 'Introduction', xiii.

86 Snow, 'Two Cultures and the Scientific Revolution'.

87 Leavis, 'Two Cultures: The Significance of C.P Snow' and 'Luddites? *Or* There is Only One Culture'. For a discussion of the 'two cultures' debate in relation to physical education see Hughson and Tapsell, 'Physical Education and the "Two Cultures" Debate'.

88 Leavis and Thompson, *Culture and Environment*.

89 Apollonio (ed.), *Futurist Manifestos*, 21.

90 Hughes, *The Shock of the New*, 42.

91 Marinetti, *Critical Writings*, 94–5.

92 Ibid., 76.

93 Ibid., 135.

94 Schafer, *The Turn of the Century*, 114. For images and further discussion of these paintings see Coen, *Umberto Boccioni*, 167 and 173.

[95] Hewitt, *Fascist Modernism*, 54.

[96] Ibid., 1.

[97] Huxley, 'One and Many', 49.

[98] Wilde, *The Soul of Man Under Socialism*, 42.

[99] Haraway, *Simians, Cyborgs and Women*, 150.

[100] Cole, 'Addiction, Exercise, and Cyborgs'.

[101] Ibid., 272.

[102] Ibid., 273.

[103] Hoberman, *Mortal Engines*.

[104] Ibid., 21.

[105] Ibid., 214.

[106] Hayles, *How We Became Posthuman*, 5.

[107] Todd, 'A History of the Use of Anabolic Steroids in Sport', 323.

[108] Ibid., 324.

[109] Ibid., 328.

[110] Ibid., 330 and 334.

[111] Simon, *Fair Play*, 75–7.

[112] Ibid., 71.

[113] Ibid., 72.

[114] Moran, *Interdisciplinarity*, 163.

References

Apollonio, U., ed. *Futurist Manifestos*. Boston: artworks, 1970.

Arnold, M. 'Literature and Science'. In *Philistinism in England and America: The Complete Prose Works of Matthew Arnold*, vol. X, edited by R.H. Super, 53–73. Ann Arbor, MI: University of Michigan Press, 1974.

Bowra, C.M. *The Romantic Imagination*. Cambridge, MA: Harvard University Press, 1949.

Boyd, W. *The History of Western Education*. 6th ed. London: Adam & Charles Black, 1952.

Brett, R.L., and A.R. Jones, eds. *Lyrical Ballads* by Wordsworth and Coleridge. London: Methuen, 1963.

Bulent, A. *The Art and Science of Leonardo da Vinci*. Washington, DC: Smithsonian Books, 2004.

Campbell, R.J. *Thomas Arnold*. London: Macmillan, 1927.

Clark, K. *Leonardo da Vinci: An Account of his Development as an Artist*. 2nd ed. Cambridge: Cambridge University Press, 1952.

Clark, K. *The Nude*. Harmondsworth: Penguin, 1960.

Coen, E. *Umberto Boccioni*. New York: The Metropolitan Museum of Art, 1988.

Cole, C.L. 'Addiction, Exercise, and Cyborgs: Technologies of Deviant Bodies'. In *Sport and Postmodern Times*, edited by G. Rail, 261–75. Albany, NY: State University of New York Press, 1998.

Collini, S. 'Introduction'. In *The Two Cultures*, edited by C.P. Snow, vii–lxxi. London: Cambridge University Press/Canto, 1993.

Courtney, J.E. *Free Thinkers of the Nineteenth Century*. London: Chapman Hall, 1920.

Durant, G. *Wordsworth and the Great System: A Study of Wordsworth's Poetic Universe*. Cambridge: Cambridge University Press, 1970.

Gerber, E.W. *Innovators and Institutions in Physical Education*. Philadelphia, PA: Lea and Febiger, 1971.

Grene, M. *The Knower and the Known*. London: Faber and Faber, 1966.

Guttmann, A. *The Olympics: A History of the Modern Games*. Urbana, IL: University of Illinois Press, 1992.

Haley, B. *The Healthy Body and Victorian Culture*. Cambridge, MA: Harvard University Press, 1978.

Haraway, D.J. *Simians, Cyborgs and Women: The Reinvention of Nature*. London: Free Association Books, 1991.

Harper, G.M. *The Neoplatonism of William Blake*. Chapel Hill, NC: University of North Carolina Press, 1961.

Hayles, N.K. *How We Became Posthuman: Virtual Bodies in Cybernetics, Literature and Informatics*. Chicago, IL: University of Chicago Press, 1999.

Hewitt, A. *Fascist Modernism: Aesthetics, Politics and the Avant-Garde*. Stanford, CA: Stanford University Press, 1993.

Hoberman, J. *Mortal Engines: The Science of Performance and the Dehumanization of Sport*. New York: Free Press/Macmillan, 1992.

Hoberman, J. 'The Early Development of Sports Medicine in Germany'. In *Sport and Exercise Science: Essays in the History of Sports Medicine*, edited by J.W. Berryman and R.J. Park, 233–82. Urbana, IL: University of Illinois Press, 1992.

Hughes, R. *The Shock of the New: Art and the Century of Change*. London: Thames and Hudson, 1991.

Hughes, T. *Tom Brown's School Days*. London: J.M. Dent and Sons, 1949.

Hughson, J., and C. Tapsell. 'Physical Education and the "Two Cultures" Debate: Lessons from Dr Leavis'. *Quest* 58, no. 4 (2006): 410–23.

Hume, D. *A Treatise of Human Nature*, edited by L.A. Selby-Bigge (1888), text revised and variant readings by P.H. Nidditch. Oxford: Oxford University Press, 1978.

Huxley, A. 'One and Many'. In *Do What You Will*, 1–51. London: Chatto and Windus, 1929.

Huxley, T.H. 'Science and Culture'. In *Science and Education*, 134–59. London: Macmillan, 1885.

Kemp, M. *Leonardo*. Oxford: Oxford University Press, 2004.

Kingsley, C. *Charles Kingsley: His Letters and Memories of his Life*, edited by his wife [Fanny Kingsley]. London: Kegan Paul, Trench and Company, 1885.

Kirk, D. 'Physical Culture, Physical Education and Relational Analysis'. *Sport, Education and Society* 4, no. 1 (1999): 63–73.

Knoepflmacher, U.C. 'Mutations of the Wordsworthian Child of Nature'. In *Nature and the Victorian Imagination*, edited by U.C. Knoepflmacher and G.B. Tennyson, 391–425. Berkeley, CA: University of California Press, 1977.

Kuhnst, P. *Sport: A Cultural History in the Mirror of Art*. Dresden: Verlag Der Kunst, 1996.

Leavis, F.R. *Revaluation: Tradition and Development in English Poetry*. London: Chatto and Windus, 1959.

Leavis, F.R. 'Two Cultures: The Significance of C.P Snow'. In *Nor Shall My Sword: Discourses on Pluralism, Compassion and Social Hope*, 39–74. London: Chatto and Windus, 1972.

Leavis, F.R. 'Luddites? *Or* There is Only One Culture'. In *Nor Shall My Sword: Discourses on Pluralism, Compassion and Social Hope*, 77–99. London: Chatto and Windus, 1972.

Leavis, F.R., and D. Thompson. *Culture and Environment: The Training of Critical Awareness*. London: Chatto and Windus, 1964.

Locke, J. *Some Thoughts Concerning Education*, edited by F.W. Garforth. London: Heinemann, 1964.

Locke, J. *Essay Concerning Human Understanding*, edited by Peter H. Nidditch. London: Oxford University Press, 1975.

Lowe, E.J. *Locke on Human Understanding*. London: Routledge, 1995.

Marinetti, F.T. *Critical Writings*, edited by Gunther Berghaus, trans. Doug Thompson. New York: Farrar, Straus and Giroux, 2006.

McIntosh, P.C. *Physical Education in England since 1800*, rev. ed. London: G. Bell and Sons, 1968.

Mechikoff, R.A., and S.G. Estes. *History and Philosophy of Sport and Physical Education: From the Ancient Greeks to the Present*. Madison, WI: Brown and Benchmark, 1993.

Monti, R. *Leonardo*. London: Thames and Hudson, 1967.

Moran, J. *Interdisciplinarity*. London: Routledge, 2002.

Mrozek, D.J. 'The Scientific Quest for Physical Culture and the Persistent Appeal of Quackery'. In *Sport and Exercise Science: Essays in the History of Sports Medicine*, edited by J.W. Berryman and R.J. Park, 283–96. Urbana, IL: University of Illinois Press, 1992.

Paradis, J., and T. Postlewait. 'Introduction'. In *Victorian Science and Victorian Values*, edited by J. Paradis and T. Postlewait, ix–xiii. New York: The New York Academy of Sciences, 1981.

Paxman, J. *The English: Portrait of a People*. London: Penguin, 1999.

Plato. *Phaedo*. In *The Dialogues of Plato*, edited by B. Jowett, vol. I, 441–501. New York: Random House, 1937.

Plato. *The Republic*. In *The Dialogues of Plato*, edited by B. Jowett, vol. I, 591–879. New York: Random House, 1937.

Porter, R. *Enlightenment: Britain and the Creation of the Modern World*. London: Penguin, 2000.

Rice, E.A. *A Brief History of Physical Education*, rev. ed. New York: A.S. Barnes and Company, 1929.

Rice, J. *Start of Play: The Curious Origins of Our Favourite Sports*. London: Prion, 1998.

Ruskin, J. *Unto This Last: Four Essays on the First Principles of Political Economy*. London: George Allen, 1902.

Russell, B. *History of Western Philosophy: and its Connection with Political and Social Circumstances from the Earliest Times to the Present Day.* 2nd ed. London: Unwin Paperbacks, 1979.

Schafer. *The Turn of the Century: the First Futurists.* New York: Peter Lang, 1995.

Schofield, R.E. *Mechanism and Materialism: British Natural Philosophy in an Age of Reason.* Princeton, NJ: Princeton University Press, 1970.

Shaw, G.B. 'Mainly about Myself'. Preface to *Plays: Pleasant and Unpleasant*, vol. 1. London: Constable and Company, 1910.

Shaw, G.B. 'Treatise on Parents and Children'. In *Misalliance.* London: Constable, 1930.

Shelley, P.B. *A Defence of Poetry*, edited by A.S. Cook. Boston, MA: Ginn and Company, 1890.

Simon, R.L. *Fair Play: Sports, Values and Society.* Boulder, CO: Westview Press, 1991.

Snow, C.P. 'Two Cultures and the Scientific Revolution'. In *Two Cultures: a Second Look*, 1–52. Cambridge: Cambridge University Press, 1963.

Spencer, H. *Education: Intellectual, Moral and Physical.* London: Routledge/Thoemmes Press, 1993.

Strachey, L. *Eminent Victorians.* Harmondsworth: Penguin, 1971.

Todd, J. 'Bernarr Macfadden: Reformer of Feminine Form'. In *Sport and Exercise Science: Essays in the History of Sports Medicine*, edited by J.W. Berryman and R.J. Park, 213–32. Urbana, IL: University of Illinois Press, 1992.

Todd, T. 'A History of the Use of Anabolic Steroids in Sport'. In *Sport and Exercise Science: Essays in the History of Sports Medicine*, edited by J.W. Berryman and R.J. Park, 319–50. Urbana, IL: University of Illinois Press, 1992.

White, M. *Leonardo: The First Scientist.* London: Abacus, 2001.

Wilde, O. *The Soul of Man Under Socialism.* London: Arthur L. Humphreys, 1912.

Willey. *The Eighteenth Century Background: Studies on the Idea of Nature in the Thought of the Period.* Harmondsworth: Penguin, 1962.

Woodward, W.H. *Vittorino da Feltre and Other Humanist Educators.* New York: Teachers College, Columbia University, 1963.

Wordsworth, W. 'Ode: Intimations of Immortality'. In *The Complete Poetical Works of William Wordsworth*, intro. by J. Morley, 357–61. London: Macmillan, 1907.

The working class and the making of sport

An admirer of Oscar Wilde's well-intentioned socialism, George Orwell nevertheless dismissed the idea of machines becoming the slaves of mankind. Orwell argued there will always be 'dull and exhausting work' requiring the flexibility that only 'unwilling human muscles can provide'.[1] Furthermore, in *The Road to Wigan Pier* Orwell mocks H.G. Wells' vision of a futuristic society in which physical labour has been made redundant. In such a 'Utopian' society the 'inhabitants [presumably] ... would create artificial dangers in order to exercise their courage and do dumb-bell exercises to harden muscles which they would never be obliged to use'.[2] Orwell thus dismissed as blind faith Wells' prediction for 'progress and a scientifically perfected future'.[3] Orwell not only disputed the possibilities of technology, but also the inability of humans in positions of leadership to deploy machines in a way beneficent to society in general. Relatedly he rejected political ideologies – totalitarianism of both left and right persuasion – portending the end of man's problems as at best illusory, at worst insidious. For Orwell, the 'universal humanist', the overcoming of human problems via the harnessing of technology or any other means is an impossibility that should not even be contemplated, as it is through facing ongoing 'disaster, pain [and] difficulty' that humans maintain awareness of their humanness.[4]

Orwell did not foresee a future classless society, and viewed with contempt claims that class divisions were disappearing in Britain during the 1930s.[5] Orwell's description of the working class in *The Road to Wigan Pier* at times betrayed his own middle-class background,[6] but his graphic description, from first hand experience, of work in a coal mine gave the clearest possible insight to a middle-class readership of the punishing physical demands of this relentless form of labour.[7] Not from dumb-bells but as the outcome of work, these men had 'arms and belly muscles of steel'.[8] The human body and spirit were forged – and sometimes broken – by a labour system that was very much a matter of class. To Orwell's ethnographically focussed eye the utopian vision of a classless and leisurely future society appeared wildly fanciful and had no place in either his non-fiction or fictional writing.

Orwell's counter vision was of a dystopic society – as seen in *Nineteen Eighty-Four* – where any semblance of classlessness was crushed by self-perpetuating totalitarian rule. As a number of critics have noted, including Raymond Williams, the spectre of Orwell which hung over the new left in Britain in the 1950s and 1960s, nurtured a politics of pessimism that inhibited radical mobilization.[9] E.P. Thompson, writing in 1960, argued that 'Orwell's pessimism has contributed a good deal to the form of generalised pessimism which has outlasted the context in which it arose'.[10] Thompson took particular issue with the fear of communism that had been roused by Orwell's impact on the left in Britain, based, Thompson believed, on the latter's jaundiced interpretation of communism and an ignorance of its democratic possibilities when pursued in non-totalitarian form. Underlying the differing outlooks is the respective view of the working class held by these writers. Orwell's view was at best sympathetic, at worst pitying. His pessimism was underpinned by a lack of faith in the working class to resist the political tyranny of the minority, whether the leadership happens to be of the right or the left. Against this view,

Thompson believed that the working class possessed a collective agency holding out the possibility of a genuinely progressive politics that Orwell could not envisage.

Thompson and culture as 'struggle'

Thompson's position on class was set out in his monumental *The Making of the English Working Class*, published in 1963. Thompson's book was intellectually radical in that it upturned the tradition of official history writing from a standpoint of interest in the deeds of famous historical figures, to a primary interest in the collective life situation, over time, of the working class. *The Making of the English Working Class* is thus often credited as the key text in scholarship favouring a 'history from below'.[11] In its rejection of historically deterministic accounts of class, the book also challenged left intellectualism, the humanistic pessimism of Orwell and the structural theory of New Left Marxists alike. For Thompson, class is neither a 'structure' nor a 'category', but 'something which in fact happens in human relationships'; 'the notion of class entails the notion of historical relationship'.[12] Thompson, at the very beginning of *Making*, emphatically rejects the construction of the working class by historians. 'The working class did not rise like the sun at appointed time. It was present at its own making.' Thompson spends the almost 900 pages of his book accounting for how the English working class participated in its own historical formation as a class; 'class is defined by men as they live their own history, and, in the end, this is its only definition'.[13]

Thompson believed class relations to be conflictual in nature, a view he held in keeping with his Marxist contemporaries. 'Class happens when some men, as a result of common experiences (inherited or shared), feel and articulate the identity of their interests as between themselves, and as against other men whose interests are different from (and usually opposed to) theirs.'[14] The reference to feeling and articulation highlights Thompson's insistence that class identity involves *conscious* expression of class experience, his key difference from the Marxist understanding of class existing primarily in terms of 'so many men who stand in a certain relation to the means of production'.[15] Thompson's emphasis on consciousness connects directly with his view on the importance of culture. 'Class-consciousness is the way in which these experiences are handled in cultural terms: embodied in traditions, value-systems, ideas, and institutional forms.'[16] So for Thompson, culture does not exist in some form of super-structural relationship to class, it is at the core of a meaningful class existence. To an extent, then, he was in agreement with the position of Raymond Williams but, significantly, he believed that Williams, by sticking too closely to the conservative tradition he sought to criticize, had failed to reveal that culture is the arena in which class conflict is lived out. Thompson was particularly critical in this regard of Williams's usage of the 'whole way of life', a term Thompson – and perhaps Williams himself – suspected T.S. Eliot of using disingenuously in his 'definition' of culture. For Thompson, culture is 'a whole way of *conflict*. And a way of conflict is a way of *struggle*.'[17] It is the responsibility of the cultural historian, according to Thompson, to recount the struggle of the working class in the making of its own (cultural) history.[18]

Thompson wrote little about sport in *Making*, yet it must be noted that his book concentrated on the eighteenth century, and thus the best part of 100 years prior to what is generally accepted as the time when sport was formalized in Britain. He does, though, give occasional glimpse of how sporting culture developed under the impetus of inchoate class relations. For example, he notes the complaint of a Lancashire writer in 1823 that: 'The Athletic exercises of Quoits, Wrestling, Foot-ball, Prison-bars and Shooting with the Long-bow are becoming obsolete ... they are now Pigeon-fanciers, Canary-breeders and Tulip-growers.'[19] Thompson accepts that this account indicates a degree to which the working class became disciplined. Under the 'productive tempo of the clock' the worker became more 'reserved' and less disposed to violence and spontaneity in his leisure time, 'traditional sports were displaced by more sedentary hobbies'. Yet, as Thompson maintained in his essay 'Custom and Culture', 'plebeian culture' of the eighteenth century was resilient and remained 'the people's own' to the extent that it resisted intrusion into its customs and practices by the 'gentry and clergy'. Thompson so viewed taverns, fairs and 'rough music'.[20] A little further into the essay we look at how the working class organizational involvement in the establishment of soccer towards the end of the 1800s might be adjudged from this perspective. Before this, greater consideration of Thompson's claim about cultural history *necessarily* involving the study of class struggle within the cultural realm is appropriate.

Thompson's claim for cultural history has been disputed by at least two prominent historians, Arthur Marwick and David Cannadine. Marwick, from a decidedly non-Marxist disposition, believes that Thompson is ready to read class conflict into any cultural situation involving dissent. A problem arises for Thompson within his own historical account of the eighteenth century because he claims that the working class did not actually take form until the early nineteenth century; thus it is problematic to apply Marxist class theory to the earlier period. According to Marwick, Thompson's historical evidence reveals 'working class awareness' rather than 'working class consciousness', in the Marxist sense.[21] Cannadine contends, similarly, that 'while people were sometimes thinking socially in terms of class', in eighteenth-century England, 'they were rarely thinking *politically* in terms of class'. He thus suggests that Thompson's formulation of 'class struggle without class' should be inverted to 'class without class struggle'.[22] Furthermore, Cannadine challenges Thompson's claim that *the* working class was formed in the period between 1790 and 1830. Rather, according to Cannadine, this period saw the emergence of heterogeneous working classes with a degree of commonality in orientation and attitude to cultural life:

> it was not so much the forging of a new, unprecedented, homogeneous working class, along with its correspondingly new, unprecedented, homogeneous consciousness and identity of interests, that was taking place during these undeniably troubled and tumultuous times. Rather it was an intensification of the traditional, populist way of looking at the world, as being irrevocably divided between 'us' and 'them'.[23]

History from 'below' and 'within'

This strong moral sense of a division between 'us' and 'them' has appeared in subsequent writing about the working classes, as Cannadine notes,[24] finding clearest articulation in regard to the cultural attitude of modern urbanized workers in Richard Hoggart's landmark *The Uses of Literacy: Aspects of Woking-Class Life with special Reference to Publications and Entertainments*, first published in 1957. 'Them' refers to 'the bosses', not only the owners of industry, but also those in management and other positions of public authority. These people inhabit a cultural world entirely removed from that of 'us', members of the working classes.[25] Hoggart notes that the working class generally mistrusts 'Them' and shows no desire to join their cultural ranks. Indeed, he observed the reverse tendency, whereby 'self-made men now living in villas ... like to join the crowd at football matches ... on the terraces rather than in the stands', thus suggesting that some members of the working class might rise above their station economically and socially, but retain attachment to their cultural roots.[26]

Hoggart indicates, unremarkably, that the working class uses its leisure activities as a means of escape from the authoritarianism of 'Them' experienced in the workplace and other areas of public life. As such, any perceived intrusion by 'Them' into the cultural domains of the working class is deeply resented. Hoggart provides an interesting example pertaining to sport. Discussing rugby league, a sport with regionalized working-class popularity in the north of England since the 1890s, Hoggart notes that spectators hold the referee in 'common distrust'.[27] Hoggart believes this distrust to be more than one-eyed barracking, rather it is a 'deeply ingrained feeling' that the referee is little better than a headmaster laying down orders. The dislike of this official does not usually result in violence but it is 'pervasive', suggesting the referee is regarded as an unpopular authority figure and an unwelcome interloping presence – a representative of 'Them' – on the rugby league pitch.

As indicated in the opening essay of this volume Hoggart, along with Raymond Williams and E.P. Thompson, is credited as a founding figure of the academic field that became known as cultural studies. Indeed, Hoggart was responsible for institutionalizing this field in the academy when, as the inaugural Director, he opened the Centre for Contemporary Cultural Studies (CCCS) at the University of Birmingham in 1964. The contribution of Hoggart, in common with that of Williams and Thompson, was to put the study of working-class culture onto the academic agenda. Of the three, Hoggart alone did not embrace Marxist intellectualism, although he was openly sympathetic to left reformist politics. While believing English working-class cultural life of the between war years to be marked by solidarity and neighbourliness, Hoggart did not regard it as a site of class struggle.[28] Hoggart's unwillingness to embrace Marxism or to engage in theoretical debate about class, has left his largely anecdotal account of working-class cultural life open to the claim that it is uncritical and nostalgic.[29] Such potential criticism needs to be checked against Hoggart's own admission in *The Uses of Literacy* that all was not rosy in pre-war working-class life in England. For example, he notes that collective acts of 'hooliganism and rowdyism' were not an infrequent occurrence.[30]

Despite differing on the centrality of class struggle, the scholarship of both Hoggart and Thompson is fundamentally humanistic, this temperament underpinning the respective emphases in their writing on the importance of the cultural – rather than the structural – life of the working class. In ebullient praise for Hoggart's 'literary-sociological flair' Thompson declared, 'I am ready to root for Richard Hoggart as King'.[31] In reciprocal if somewhat more sober praise, Hoggart referred to Thompson – along with Williams – as one of the outstanding figures in the 'Condition of England' debate that had continued since the publication of Matthew Arnold's *Culture and Anarchy* in 1869.[32] Hoggart's auto-ethnographic account of working-class culture in the 1930s is as concerned with the working class' *making* of culture as was Thompson's documentary study of life in the eighteenth century. Relatedly, Hoggart makes interesting reference to his 'efforts to describe [working class culture] from within as it were', a point that resonates with Stephen Yeo's recommendation for 'history-from-within'.[33]

Thompson is often cited as a pioneer of 'history from below', and he undoubtedly reversed the focus of historical study from the familiar top-down to a bottom-up approach. However, 'history from below' is used as a methodological descriptor for social history, and although fair claim is made to Thompson as a social historian, his humanistic interest in the sensuousness of the cultural life of the working class can have him just as rightly described as a cultural historian. We may well speak then of both Thompson and Hoggart, in their different ways, as cultural historians providing a 'history from within'.

Williams's claim that 'we have to return the meanings to experience' in anthro-historical study suggests his sympathy to a 'history from within'.[34] This claim relates to his rejection of the abstract and asserted notion, prominent within conservative cultural criticism, of the 'masses' as undiscerning consumers of popular culture. Williams claimed, 'There are in fact no masses; there are only ways of seeing people as masses'. He continued, 'In an urban industrial society there are many opportunities for such ways of seeing'.[35] The work of Williams, Thompson and Hoggart presents mutual reinforcement against such intellectual opportunism. A common thread running through their work is that the urban working class should not be seen as a mass but as a culturally creative social collectivity.

The crowd and 'mob' culture

The representation of the working class as a mass in modern society is a continuation of the 'negative classicism' discussed by Brantlinger – Juvenal's 'bread and circuses' comment sits readily on the lips of those wanting to denounce sport.[36] Sports crowds have been represented in binary negative, polar oppositional terms as either an active or passive mass. On the one hand, in regard to group spectatorship, sport has been associated with the active mass as crowd. On the other, sport has been reported as being historically handed down to the working class as a passive mass. In neither sense is the working class represented as being involved in the making of sport. In the first sense the sport crowd is associated with the mob – Williams declared masses to be little more than 'a new word for mob'[37] – and to be feared as a dangerous element within the sporting domain. Media generated commentary on so-called football hooliganism has been particularly prominent in this regard. Although attributed as active the crowd is seen to be involved in the un-making of sporting culture as hooliganism is widely regarded with moral opprobrium. In the second sense mentioned above the working class is regarded as an amorphous and passive mass that has sport handed down to it. From this view, even sporting cultures regarded as 'the people's game' – baseball in the US; soccer in Britain – may be seen to be given to the people and passively consumed by them.

The best-known modern characterization of the active mass appeared in Gustave Le Bon's book *The Crowd*. Written in the late 1800s, this book partially anticipates the 'mass society theory' that emerged in the US following the Second World War.[38] Brantlinger identifies *The Crowd* as a continuation of 'negative classicism', given Le Bon's evocation of the plebeian Roman audience in direct comparison to the modern crowd.[39] Le Bon connected his gloomy hypothesis to an emergent popular psychology, sketching an uneasy picture of the crowd deliberately aimed to titillate public alarm about mass gatherings. According to McClelland, 'Le Bon sets out to make the crowd as frightening as possible in order to peddle a particular kind of ideology, and it is a complete ideology in something like the modern sense of the term'.[40] McClelland is suggesting that Le Bon's warning about the dangerous crowd was anti-working class and beneficial to the cultural elite within modern society.

According to Le Bon, the crowd is to be especially feared once a consensus in race – by which he meant values common to a nation – begins to dissipate. At this point a mass mentality comes to the fore and threatens civilized society. Even the 'cultivated individual' can become a 'barbarian' in the presence of the crowd, contended Le Bon; 'by the mere fact that he forms part of an organised crowd, a man descends several rungs in the ladder of civilisation'.[41] According to Le Bon, in the crowd the individual becomes 'a creature acting by instinct … possess[ing] the spontaneity, the violence, the ferocity, and also the enthusiasm and heroism of primitive beings … An individual in a crowd is a grain of sand amid other grains of sand, which the wind stirs up at will'.

Le Bon's *The Crowd* was a best seller from the time of its publication.[42] This seems to have much to do with his ability to tap the general fear of atavism: the violent beast within man will be unleashed in the irrational gathering that is the crowd. This type of concern appears not to have calmed in more recent history. Its representation and expression tends to be episodic and in occurrence with periods of alarm about particular social groupings. The largely media-generated alarm about youth gangs – usefully referred to as 'moral panic' by Stanley Cohen in his study of the conflict between mods and rockers on English beaches in the 1960s[43] – reactivates ongoing concern about the atavistic crowd. This concern stems seemingly from an underlying anxiety about the unruliness of human nature and the wont of most individuals to believe that they are civilized beyond this rank state.

The notion of moral panic has been pertinently used to describe the popular discourse on one of the most disparaged sport crowds, or elements thereof, viz. English soccer hooligans.

Soccer hooliganism emerged as an area of historical and sociological study in the 1970s and divergent attempts to explain its causes have resulted in considerable rancour between academic contributors to the discussion.[44] Early contributions – those of Taylor, Clarke and Critcher – favoured a neo-Marxist explanation that saw hooliganism as symptomatic of the estrangement of working-class youth in post-war England. The aggressive masculinity, stylized in the skinhead and associated soccer-supporting subcultures, was referred to by Clarke as an attempt to 'magically recover' the imagined working-class community of the parental generation.[45] Critcher generally agreed with Clarke and warned against the popular interpretation of soccer hooliganism as part of a general 'social malaise'.[46] He believed that soccer hooliganism evinced a particular circumstantial form of 'cultural alienation'; its violence for some participants was about 'restor[ing] adolescent male working-class identity' and the 'football ground [provided] the established venue for the exploration and expression of this identity'.[47] Taylor's position was even more sympathetic to young men branded as football hooligans. Rejecting the popular portrayal of them as social deviants, he referred to their activities as a 'drift into resistance' that was an enactment not of irrationality but of a culturally acquired 'soccer consciousness'.[48]

Perhaps the best-known academic work on soccer hooliganism to date is that led by Eric Dunning, in the 1980s, at the University of Leicester.[49] While Dunning and his associates accepted that the particular types of youth subcultural groupings identified by Clarke and others were a recent manifestation within the soccer crowd, they presented documentary evidence to show that crowd-related violence could be traced throughout the competitive history of the sport in England.[50] This is no mere point of contention, but, rather, a disputation over a significant issue within the cultural history of soccer. Dunning and his associates are adherents to the 'civilizing process' theory of the historical sociologist Norbert Elias, which holds that western societies, since the time of the Middle Ages, have developed '"higher" levels of civilisation' whereby the lower social groups have taken on the mores, customs and associated forms of behaviour of elite social groups.[51] In class terms, it could be said that the middle classes have been the 'principal standard-setting groups' for the working classes.

According to the 'civilizing process' theory, the lower classes have come to accept that coercive power should rest with the state, and this has resulted in violent conduct becoming generally unacceptable over time. However, Elias did not portend a total disappearance of violence from the public domain and he recognized the need to explain ongoing occurrences of violence as more than social aberration. Elias thus referred to the existence of 'counter civilising' developments and 'de-civilising spurts'; 'the movement of society and civilisation certainly does not follow a straight line … fluctuations [and] counter-movements' against the civilizing trend must be expected to occur. Dunning and colleagues develop a related position on 'de-civilising' trends to explain the occurrence of soccer hooliganism.[52] Accordingly, soccer crowd-related violence is indicative of a 'de-civilising spurt' rather than a breakdown of the civilizing process. Its participants, according to Dunning and associates' research, are not fully 'incorporated' into the civilizing process, a result of their structural location in the lowest rungs of the working class. Accustomed to violence from early life, the young men of the 'rough' working class are predisposed to recruitment into the ranks of football hooliganism.[53]

Both the neo-Marxist and the Eliasian interpreters agree that the phenomenon of football hooliganism has been amplified by media reportage, yet both accept the existence of soccer-related crowd disorder perpetrated by young men from the working class and the need for its intellectual analysis. So whereas the 'moral panic' position developed by Cohen is primarily concerned with examining the media amplification process of deviant labelling, the theorists discussed above are concerned with revealing the 'source and contexts' from which those who engage in the activity known as soccer hooliganism come. Both are, therefore, interested in the roots of soccer hooliganism, and in how social factors pertaining to class have significant bearing on why young men are drawn into such activity. Of the two perspectives, that of Dunning and associates appears the more deterministic in suggesting that young men from the 'rough' working class are almost inevitably destined to engage in unruly, if not violent, social behaviour because they are not fully incorporated into the civilizing process. From this account, it is not surprising that football hooliganism has proven irresistible to some of their number.

The neo-Marxist theorists referred to above give less of an impression of soccer hooliganism being an inevitable outcome of social background. Taylor's work is particularly interesting in this regard. While recognizing the significance of the socio-economic background of soccer hooligans he considers their cultural agency in a manner not evident in the work of the Leicester academics, despite discussion in that work of the rough working-class cultural milieu. Soccer hooliganism is regarded by Taylor as a particular expression of 'soccer consciousness' which itself is a particular form of 'lower-class consciousness'.[54] Such consciousness is culturally embedded, generationally handed down and lived out circumstantially. Taylor thus regards soccer hooliganism as an attempt by 'certain sections of the [working] class to assert some inarticulate but keenly experienced control over "the game that was theirs"'.[55] Accordingly, the public reaction to soccer hooligans as a 'motiveless and meaningless' crowd disregards completely the class sub-cultural context from which the activity stems. The extent to which the sport was historically 'owned' by the working class is contentious, but understanding soccer hooliganism as an attempt by young men to reclaim a sense of 'participatory democracy' lends support to Taylor's recognition of the activity as a 'resistance movement' rather than a rabble. Taylor does not condone soccer hooliganism but suggests that it must be regarded historically as occurring within a tradition of legitimate working-class protest through 'riots'.[56] The unruly crowd by this interpretation, whether or not to be feared, does not signify atavism but collective rational militancy.

'Mass culture' and the exceptionality of sport

Pejorative accounts of the mass as passive (rather than active) continue to exhibit a fear of the crowd, not in physical but in intellectual terms. The related concern with the 'mob mentality' is not indicative of a look back to atavism, but a look forward into a pending near future characterized by cultural stupefaction. Again, Le Bon's *The Crowd* was influential to such accounts, particularly so, his use of the term contagion. Le Bon's usage of the term betrays his cultural prejudice against the working classes of the late nineteenth century; 'contagion, after having been at work among the popular classes, has spread to the higher classes of society … every opinion adopted by the populace always ends in implanting itself with great vigour in the highest social strata, however obvious the absurdity of the triumphant opinion'.[57] 'Contagion' appeared in subsequent theorizing on the crowd, notably in Elias Canetti's *Crowds and Power*. Drawing from a background in chemistry, Canetti likened the crowd to a mass of diseased micro-organisms infecting the moral well-being of humankind in modernizing societies.[58] A related notion of contagion resurfaced in post-war cultural criticism in the US. For example, Dwight Macdonald observed, in correspondence with the breakdown of 'compartmentation' between 'Folk Art and High Culture', the emergence of a 'tepid flaccid Middlebrow Culture that threatens to engulf everything in its spreading ooze'.[59] Macdonald reflected the fear of the American new left, that cultural production in capitalist society for purely commercial purposes had undermined both cultural traditions and standards.

Critical commentaries on mass culture in the US focussed mainly on textual forms, thus excluding sport. For example, a key anthology *Mass Culture: The Popular Arts in America*

(1957) included essays in sections titled Mass Literature, Motion Pictures, Television and Radio, and Advertising.[60] However, although not formally included in the contents of this volume, sport was not entirely ignored by the essayists. Particularly interesting is Irving Howe's reference to baseball. Howe, another intellectual of the post-war American new left, argued a familiar line that 'mass culture ... diverts the worker from his disturbing reduction to semi-robot status by arranging "relaxing" amusements for him', inducing 'passivity and boredom' – culturally and politically. Mass culture thus results, according to Howe, in the 'depersonalisation of the individual'. However, where there is sport there is hope. Howe's contrast of the cultural experience of the movie house with the baseball park is telling:

> The movie house is a psychological cloakroom where one checks one's personality. But baseball, one of the few mass urban activities that seems to retain some folk spontaneity, is different. The game is so paced that one usually has enough time to return to oneself, and the entire atmosphere of the ball park allows for some spontaneity: the audience argues, eats, shouts, participates as an independent group that is reacting to the events on the field. As a result, one encounters a kind of rough and pleasing wit in the ball park, as well as an easy-going camaraderie. The ball park, I find, is one of the few public places where one can converse uninhibitedly with total strangers.[61]

An often quoted writer on the cultural significance of baseball is Jacques Barzun. Barzun, a French-American intellectual historian, declared in his book *God's Country and Mine*, 'Whoever wants to know the heart and mind of America had better learn baseball'.[62] Heralding baseball as the heart and soul of American culture – and making explicit connection to Greek heroism – Barzun suggests that it is classless, being delivered from the gods: 'Happy the man in the bleachers. He is enjoying the spectacle that the gods on Olympus contrived only with difficulty when they sent Helen to Troy and picked their teams.'[63] Barzun is unperturbed by the baseball crowd. He even sees the baseball park as an arena where an uncivilized temperament can be purposefully expressed: 'For those whom civilised play doesn't fully satisfy, there will be provided a scapegoat in a blue suit – the umpire, yell-proof and even-handed as justice, which he demonstrates with outstretched arms calling "Safe!"'.[64]

The class based 'deeply ingrained feeling' of antipathy towards the referee of the English working-class crowd in Hoggart's account of rugby league is thus absent from Barzun's reading of baseball in America, where the match official may be abused but is ultimately respected. Barzun's non-antagonistic view of baseball as a national folk culture is reminiscent of Leavis's discussion of the 'living culture' and 'social arts' of the 'organic community'.[65] It is not surprising that Leavis's non-class understanding of culture would be shared by a relatively conservative commentator on American culture such as Barzun, but more surprising is the tendency of leftist critics of the 1950s such as Macdonald and Howe to neglect a concerted discussion of class in their critiques of popular culture. Their preoccupation with condemning mass culture is not so different from Leavis's attacks on 'mass civilisation' in the 1930s.[66] Leavis criticized emergent popular culture such as Hollywood films not only for its 'levelling down' of cultural standards but for its upturning of traditions of public culture. For Leavis – pre-empting the cultural pessimism of Howe – the culture brought by mass communication forms was atomistic, the cinema being a venue where 'individuals came together to escape from their loneliness and the emptiness of their lives and to nourish their sense of herd solidarity'.[67]

However, as indicated by the quote above, Howe the cultural pessimist regards sport – baseball at least – as an arena of popular culture in which genuine solidarity can be had. This indicates something of an acceptance within cultural criticism of the special nature of sport as a form of culture. Howe's essay goes on to suggest that true fantasy was lost as 'mass culture' became 'inseparably related to common experience'. Baseball is different for him, offering real, albeit ephemeral, possibility of release from 'industrial society'.[68] Howe's positive outlook is in contrast to Huizinga's, who claimed to have seen the play element in American sport disappear as major sports became subject to modernization in the 1920s.

> as a result of the modern capacity for very far-reaching organization and the possibilities created by modern transportation, an element of mechanization enters sport. In the immense sport organizations like those of football and baseball, we see free youthful forces and courage reduced to normality and uniformity in the service of the machinery of rules of play and the competitive system.[69]

Contrarily, Riesman, writing in 1951, cautioned against seeing rationalization processes occurring within American football as the ascension of sporting industry over sporting culture. Such conclusions, he believed, are facile in failing to recognize that 'in the American culture as a whole, no sharp line exists between work and play'.[70] His view is thus contrary to the work/play dichotomy that was articulated most tellingly in Huizinga's book *Homo Ludens*. For Huizinga play is separate from work in the adult world because, unlike work, 'play is superfluous', it is needed only 'to the extent that the enjoyment of it makes a need'.[71] Furthermore, 'Play can be deferred or suspended at any time. It is never imposed by physical necessity or moral duty. It is never a task. It is done at leisure, during "free time".' Huizinga, nonetheless, realizes that play and work are not philosophically distinct activities, but rather, the split has occurred historically. As enjoyment has been extracted from work in industrial society, leisure takes on added significance as the realm of enjoyment.

Christopher Lasch, the historian and author of the best-selling *The Culture of Narcissism*, recognized the modern differentiation between work and leisure but notes the symbiotic connection of these realms. He maintained that leisure exists in historically converse and 'organic relation' to work. Relatedly, he rejected Huizinga's claim that 'play is the direct opposite of seriousness'.[72] Lasch believed that play – stemming from childhood – is very serious and that the intrinsic uselessness of games is the reason why adults take them so seriously. Indeed, as people become increasingly disinterested in the routine of work, 'games take on added meaning', for many they are taken more seriously than work.[73] Lasch's chapter 'The Degradation of Sport' attacks commercialization and related attempts to popularize modern sport, contending that popularization in turn trivializes sport and undermines its seriousness. With the loss of genuine seriousness, sport's quality of illusion is lost and its significance as a form of leisure seriously diminished – there is no better example than sport, from Lasch's view, to show the tyranny of work invading the leisure realm.

In more recent work Lasch notes the importance of Williams and Thompson in providing a corrective to the economic determinism of Marxism, i.e. their provision of a 'serious theory of culture' that foregrounds the significance of culture in 'historical experience'.[74] However, his own work on sport registers a cultural pessimism that Williams and Thompson would regard as only partially reflective of 'historical experience'. While Lasch stands as one of the best-known critics on the impact of capitalism and industrialism on sport he does not incorporate consideration of class agency into his cultural analysis of sport. Howe's brief commentary on baseball, noted above, shows the cultural exceptionality of sport and its ability to jolt an otherwise pervasive pessimism towards popular culture. What distinguishes baseball for Howe, although not stated in explicit terms, is the active engagement of average (or working-class) people in its cultural making. Towards the conclusion of this essay, summary comment is made on the class status – in terms of working class agency – of baseball in the United States, and its generally regarded equivalent as the national sport in Britain, soccer.

Class and the 'people's' games

Baseball was portrayed as the national game of the United States not long after its rules were codified in the mid-1800s.[75] Baseball's heralding as the national game was more a question of timing than a true reflection of its general appeal. Baseball, developed as a rival bat and ball game to cricket, fitted perfectly into a strengthening populist desire for a 'Native American Sport', and was thus promoted by the press as symbolic of the emancipation of home-grown games from foreign influence.[76] More a 'New York pastime' than a national sport, baseball was nevertheless rhetorically invested with qualities regarded as all-American.[77] Adelman contends that this ideology was quickly pervasive and successful and baseball became widely accepted 'as the embodiment of the American temperament'.[78] Relatedly, a number of American authors have noted the popular recognition of baseball as the most democratic of sports. For example, in the well-known book *The Joy of Sports*, the theologian Michael Novak notes how baseball, since its early days, has been regarded as a cultural bastion of equality and fairness. As evidence of this view Novak quotes the comment made by a New York reverend (undated) in *Baseball Magazine*: 'At the baseball match, we encounter real democracy of spirit … we rub shoulders with high and low … we forget everything clannish … we are swayed by common impulse; we are all equal'.[79]

Such depiction of unity and related emphasis on baseball as the national game suggests that sectionalism and class are irrelevant to the sport's cultural and historical understanding. To the extent that baseball does have class-based origins, it is not with the working class but the middle class. Historical record indicates that the game was formalized and coded by young professional men in New York in the 1840s, its popularity as a spectator sport spreading as it professionalized, culminating in the formation of the first National League in the 1870s.[80] As baseball gained in general popularity the middle class became less interested or, as Guttmann puts it, 'the leisure class spurned the baseball diamond'.[81] Despite the rhetoric of classlessness, cultural snobbery thus appears to have played its part in the history of baseball as the 'American elite' retreated from the baseball park to their 'country clubs'. The rapid growth of baseball's popularity in the working class is undoubtedly linked, as numerous commentators have noted, to the processes of modernization that occurred following the Civil War, including the expansion of the railroad.[82]

The link between modernizing industry and baseball as an explanation of the sport's popularity has been referred to by Gelber as a 'congruence hypothesis'; the large majority of people (thus the working class) become enculturated into work life to the extent that they seek out mirroring forms of leisure activity. As baseball became more like 'business', in its operations and values, it thus offered a leisure/work congruent attraction. Opposed to the congruence hypothesis is the 'compensatory hypothesis'; people are compensated in leisure for the dissatisfaction of work life. Accordingly, baseball provides a means through which excitement and creativity, lost in the routine and stultification of the workplace, can be reclaimed.[83] So, on the one hand, we have an explanation for the historical development of baseball based on the view that work positively influences the leisure domain, and a contrasting view that baseball reflects the remedial necessity of leisure as a counter to dehumanized work life. To these hypotheses a third must be added; that the oppression and alienation of work life becomes replicated in the leisure domain. Such a view underpins Lasch's account of the historical 'degradation of sport', baseball included.

Although these hypotheses, or explanations, summarily represent scholarship on the historical development of baseball, none gives much of a view to class agency. In each hypothesis cultural outcomes are shaped by forces beyond the powers of people, the working class is thus written into the history of baseball rather than seen to be present during its making. The American cultural study of sport has tended to reflect the wider tendency to regard popular culture as mass culture, with the resultant reduction of the working class to a mass in receipt of the culture given to it. Both optimistic and pessimistic accounts of popular culture, including those on sport, leave the impression of people being fitted into a cultural milieu set for them.

Historians in Britain have been inclined to give fuller consideration to the involvement of the working class in the *making* of association football. For example, neo-Marxist scholars such as Taylor, discussed earlier, attribute the emergence of hooliganism in the 1960s to a severance of the working class from the 'sub-culture of soccer', i.e. from being 'involved in the building and sustaining' of local soccer teams.[84] Such an interpretation gives an impression of the working class having been historically active in the formation and development of the sport. This impression has been criticized by some scholars. Hill notes that the actual involvement of 'the people' in the so-called people's game was quite limited.[85] From the inception of the English Football League in the 1880s, working-class ownership has been minimal. Even in the early days of the competition, local businessmen predominated as shareholders in clubs and as members of their boards of governance.

However, more important in cultural terms than formal ownership is the issue of class character, the way in which the working class has *made* the sport of association football its own through a history of collective emotional investment, irrespective of a lack in economic control.[86] The working class can be said to have gained cultural control over the sport partly through the power of numbers. As crowds at football matches 'became increasingly working class in composition', rugby emerged as the bastion of amateurism and as the football code of the middle class.[87] Middle-class disapproval of soccer extended into a concern held by employers that the working-class obsession with the sport presented a distraction from work and resulted in 'unexpected absenteeism on Monday morning'.[88] A number of factors facilitated the growth in working-class attendance of professional soccer games, including affordable public transportation via tram and railway, and the inexpensive cost of match tickets.[89] Nevertheless, the apparent higher attendance of football matches by skilled rather than unskilled workers indicates that cost may have been prohibitive for some members of the working class.[90]

The interest of British historians in the involvement of the working class in the cultural development of soccer bypasses hypothesizing of the kind applied to baseball by Gelber. While work conditions may have been arduous for many this need not lead to the conclusion that soccer was primarily a compensation for the endurance of such conditions. According to Walvin, the work/leisure link in association football should be read somewhat differently: 'Football emerged as an industrial game, not as a palliative to the grimness of industrial life, but largely because industrial workers, unlike others, had free time.'[91] Walvin is suggesting, quite simply, that working-class people made the most of the leisure time available to them in a manner of their own choosing. He continues, 'Modern football reflected then a deep-rooted social revolution within industrial society, involving the freeing of the lower strata to enjoy the first meagre benefits of a technically advanced and relatively sophisticated society'.[92] The adult fascination with soccer was transferred to the young who were able to adapt the sport to their living environment. Soccer was the ideal football code for the limited space and hard cobble-stone surfaces of working-class neighbourhoods.[93] Its embedding within working-class culture was thus ensured over generations.

The working-class' preoccupation with association football was criticized not only by industrialists in Britain, but also by labour militants who regarded it as a diversion from politics in the workplace. Some labour leaders deemed the high degree of worker interest in professional, commercially run, football as 'bourgeois dominance' through cultural means.[94] However, this view displayed a misunderstanding of the nature of working-class life in fuller context, involving an articulation between the realms of work and leisure. As Jones has remarked, 'there is no reason why a supporter of a premier football team could not also be a militant trade unionist'.[95] According to Russell, football supporting could at once be a central aspect of working life but 'not necessarily translate into any political programme'. In this way, 'football . . . perhaps generated a consciousness of class rather than a class consciousness'.[96]

Sport as working-class *culture*

Thus understood, the history of soccer in Britain can be reconsidered in regard to Cannadine's phrase about 'class without class struggle'. The historical study of this sport evinces the cultural *activity* rather than *passivity* of the working class, but care must be taken not to overestimate the political power of the working class through active engagement in sport and leisure.[97] We thus return to the question of whether or not we can speak of the *making* of sport by the working class in the absence of struggle. From Thompson's Marxist position this is unlikely to be so. However, as much as scholarship is indebted to Thompson for revealing the importance of writing class agency into historical analysis, non-Marxist scholars of leftist persuasion tend to view such agency primarily in terms of identity and expression rather than conflict and struggle.

Typical of this view is Hoggart's account of working-class leisure in *The Uses of Literacy*. Hoggart has been criticized for his apolitical approach to working-class leisure, but such criticism tends to miss the point that Hoggart is not so much unaware of the relationship between culture and politics but is operating with a deliberate view of culture and politics residing in different spheres of human activity. Mulhern notes that Hoggart's 'conceptual binary' is characteristic of a distinction between *culture* and *civilization*, a distinction which was brought into British cultural criticism from the German *Kulturkritik* tradition stemming from the work of von Herder.[98] The distinction, put simply, is one between the naturalness of culture, a deep aesthetic desire innate to human beings, and civilization understood as the artifice of daily affairs including matters of politics and economy.[99]

This distinction between culture and civilization is discussed further in the next essay as it is used to inform the discussion of sport in relation to the middle and upper classes and the cultural significance of sport within colonialist and, subsequently, post-colonialist contexts. We close this essay by suggesting that the distinction between culture and civilization can be used to support the view that the working class does *make* its own sporting life in a way primarily removed from political struggle. This is to view sport – in the sense of deeply felt aesthetic experience – occupying a sphere of culture separate from that of civilization. This should not be read as a lapse into the old conservative chestnut that sport and politics do not mix, but an appreciation that a *Kulturkritik* distinction between aesthetic and practical life can be extended beyond the realms of the high arts to areas of 'popular' culture, including sport. The collective aesthetic appreciation of sports, such as association football and baseball, within class contexts provides the fundamental justification for being able to speak of sport being *made* by the working class. It also provides grounds for speaking of sport as part of a 'whole way of life' prior to the intrusion of political considerations.

Notes

[1] Orwell, 'Wilde's Utopia', 74–6.
[2] Orwell, *The Road to Wigan Pier*, 170.
[3] Stansky and Abrahams, *Orwell: The Transformation*, 172.
[4] Hitchens, *Orwell's Victory*, 98 and 170.
[5] Hoggart, 'The Road to Wigan Pier', 103.
[6] Ibid., 102.
[7] Orwell, *The Road to Wigan Pier*, 23–6.
[8] Ibid., 31.
[9] Williams, 'Orwell'.
[10] Thompson, 'Outside the Whale', 33.
[11] Dworkin, *Cultural Marxism in Postwar Britain*, 38.
[12] Thompson, *The Making of the English Working Class*, 9.

[13] Ibid., 11.

[14] Ibid., 9.

[15] Ibid., 10.

[16] Ibid.

[17] Thompson, 'The Long Revolution', 33.

[18] Ibid., 32.

[19] Thompson, *The Making of the English Working Class*, 410.

[20] Thompson, *Customs in Common*, 12.

[21] Marwick, *The New Nature of History*, 114–15.

[22] Cannadine, *Class in Britain*, 51–2.

[23] Ibid., 69.

[24] Ibid., 134.

[25] Hoggart, *The Uses of Literacy*, 62. Hoggart tends to use the terms working classes and working class interchangeably.

[26] Ibid., 69.

[27] Ibid., 91.

[28] Dworkin, *Cultural Marxism in Postwar Britain*, 83.

[29] McGuigan, *Cultural Populism*, 50.

[30] Hoggart, *The Uses of Literacy*, 73–4.

[31] Thompson, 'The Long Revolution', 32.

[32] Hoggart, *The Way We Live Now*, 316–17.

[33] Hoggart, 'The Uncertain Criteria of Deprivation', 35; Yeo, his contribution to the chapter 'What is the History of Popular Culture', 129.

[34] Williams, *Culture and Society*, 289.

[35] Ibid.

[36] Brantlinger, *Bread and Circuses*.

[37] Williams, *Culture and Society*, 288.

[38] Le Bon, *The Crowd*. Le Bon's populism is discussed by McClelland, *The Crowd and the Mob*, 207.

[39] Brantlinger, *Bread and Circuses*, 168.

[40] McClelland, *The Crowd and the Mob*, 200.

[41] Le Bon, *The Crowd*, 36.

[42] McClelland, *The Crowd and the Mob*, 196.

[43] Cohen, *Folk Devils and Moral Panics*.

[44] Hughson, 'Among the Thugs', 44–5.

[45] Clarke, 'The Skinheads', 99–102.

[46] Critcher, 'Football since the War'.

[47] Ibid., 173.

[48] Taylor, 'Soccer Consciousness and Soccer Hooliganism'.

[49] Dunning, Williams, and Murphy, *Hooligans Abroad*; Dunning, Murphy, and Williams, *The Roots of Football Hooliganism*.

[50] Dunning, Murphy, and Williams, *The Roots of Football Hooliganism*.

[51] Ibid., 222.

[52] Ibid., 243–4.

[53] Ibid., 227.

[54] Taylor, 'Soccer Consciousness and Soccer Hooliganism', 139.

[55] Ibid., 163.

[56] The most impressive historical argument in this regard remains E.P. Thompson's essay on the 'moral economy' of food riots in the 1700s. The essay appears as Chapter IV of *Customs in Common*.

[57] Le Bon, *The Crowd*, 146.

[58] Canetti, *Crowds and Power*, 47.

[59] Macdonald, 'A Theory of Mass Culture', 63–4.

[60] Rosenberg and Manning White, *Mass Culture*.

[61] Howe, 'Notes on Mass Culture', 498.

[62] Cited in Barzun, 'On Baseball', 437.

[63] Ibid. 440.

[64] Ibid.

[65] Hughson, Inglis, and Free, *The Uses of Sport*, 16–20.

[66] Cf. Ross, *No Respect*, 50.

[67] Leavis and Thompson, *Culture and Environment*, 65.

[68] Howe, 'Notes on Mass Culture', 498.

[69] Huizinga, 'Man and the Masses in America', 115–16.

[70] Riesman (with Denney), 'Football in America', 255.

[71] Huizinga, *Homo Ludens*, 8.

[72] Lasch, *The Culture of Narcissism*, 216.

[73] Ibid., 184.

[74] Lasch, *The True and Only Heaven*, 29.

[75] Tygiel, *Past Time*, 4–5.

[76] Adelman, *A Sporting Time*, 136.

[77] Tygiel, *Past Time*, 6.

[78] Adelman, *A Sporting Time*. 136.

[79] Novak, *The Joy of Sports*, 64–5.

[80] Rader, *American Sports*, 108–11.

[81] Guttmann, *Sports Spectators*, 111.

[82] See for example, Betts, 'The Technological Revolution', 144.

[83] Gelber, 'Working at Playing'.

[84] Taylor, 'Soccer Consciousness and Soccer Hooliganism', 142–3.

[85] Hill, *Sport, Leisure and Culture in Twentieth Century Britain*, 62.

[86] Hargreaves, *Sport, Power and Culture*, 67. Hargreaves refers to the working class stamping 'their own character' on sports like association football and rugby league in opposition to values of the 'bourgeois athleticist tradition'.

[87] Mason, *Associational Football*, 153 and 242.

[88] Walvin, *The People's Game*, 68.

[89] Mason, *Associational Football*, 146 and 150.

[90] Holt, *Sport and the British*, 159.

[91] Walvin, *The People's Game*, 53.

[92] Ibid., 66.

[93] Ibid., 67.

[94] Jones, *Sport, Politics and the Working Class*, 89–90.

[95] Ibid., 90.

[96] Russell, *Football and the English*, 72.

[97] Maguire, 'Conceptual and Methodological Confusion', 41.

[98] Mulhern, *Culture/Metaculture*, 59.

[99] Hughson, Inglis, and Free, *The Uses of Sport*, 8.

References

Adelman, M.L. *A Sporting Time: New York City and the Rise of Modern Athletics, 1820–70*. Urbana, IL: University of Illinois Press, 1986.

Barzun, J. 'On Baseball'. In *A Jacques Barzun Reader: Selections from His Works*, 437–42. New York: Perennial Classics (HarperCollins), 2003.

Betts, J.R. 'The Technological Revolution and the Rise of Sport, 1850–1900'. In *The American Sporting Experience: A Historical Anthology of Sport in America*, edited by S.A. Riess, 141–63. Champaign, IL: Leisure Press, 1984.

Brantlinger, P. *Bread and Circuses: Theories of Mass Culture and Decay*. Ithaca, NY: Cornell University Press, 1983.

Canetti, E. *Crowds and Power*. London: Victor Gollancz, 1962.

Cannadine, D. *Class in Britain*. London: Penguin, 2000.

Clarke, J. 'The Skinheads and the Magical Recovery of Community'. In *Resistance through Rituals: Youth Subcultures in Postwar Britain*, edited by S. Hall and T. Jefferson, 99–102. London: Hutchinson, 1976.

Cohen, S. *Folk Devils and Moral Panics: The Creation of the Mods and Rockers*. St Albans: Paladin, 1973.

Critcher, C. 'Football since the War'. In *Working Class Culture: Studies in History and Theory*, edited by J. Clarke, C. Critcher, and R. Johnson, 161–84. London: Hutchinson, 1979.

Dunning, E., P. Murphy, and J. Williams. *The Roots of Football Hooliganism*. London: Routledge, 1988.

Dunning, E., J. Williams, and P. Murphy. *Hooligans Abroad: The Behaviour and Control of English Fans in Continental Europe*. London: Routledge, 1984.

Dworkin, D. *Cultural Marxism in Postwar Britain: History, the New Left, and the Origins of Cultural Studies*. Durham, NC: Duke University Press, 1997.

Gelber, S.M. 'Working at Playing: The Culture of the Workplace and the Rise of Baseball'. *Journal of Social History* 2 (Summer 1983): 3–22.

Guttmann, A. *Sports Spectators*. New York: Columbia University Press, 1986.

Hargreaves, J. *Sport, Power and Culture: A Social and Historical Analysis of Popular Sports in Britain*. Cambridge: Polity, 1986.

Hill, J. *Sport, Leisure and Culture in Twentieth Century Britain*. Basingstoke, Hampshire: Palgrave, 2002.

Hitchens, C. *Orwell's Victory*. London: Allen Lane, 2002.

Hoggart, R. *The Uses of Literacy: Aspects of Working-class Life with Special Reference to Publications and Entertainments*. London: Chatto and Windus, 1957.

Hoggart, R. 'The Uncertain Criteria of Deprivation'. In *An English Temper: Essays on Education, Culture and Communications*, 31–43. London: Chatto and Windus, 1982.

Hoggart, R. *The Way We Live Now*. London: Pimlico, 1996.

Hoggart, R. 'The Road to Wigan Pier'. In *Between Two Worlds*, 101–9. London: Aurum, 2001.

Holt, R. *Sport and the British: A Modern History*. Oxford: Clarendon Press, 1992.

Howe, I. 'Notes on Mass Culture'. In *Mass Culture: The Popular Arts in America*, edited by B. Rosenberg and D. Manning White, 496–503. New York: Free Press, 1957.

Hughson, J. 'Among the Thugs: The "New Ethnographies" of Football Supporting Subcultures'. *International Review for the Sociology of Sport* 33, no. 1 (1998): 43–57.

Hughson, J., D. Inglis, and M. Free. *The Uses of Sport: A Critical Study*. London: Routledge, 2005.

Huizinga, J. *Homo Ludens: A Study of the Play Element in Culture*. Boston, MA: Beacon Press, 1955.

Huizinga, J. 'Man and the Masses in America'. In *America: A Dutch Historian's Vision from Afar and Near*, trans. and intro. by H.H. Rowen, 1–171. New York: Harper and Rowe, 1972.

Jones, S.G. *Politics and the Working Class: Organised Labour and Sport in Interwar Britain*. Manchester: Manchester University Press, 1988.

Lasch, C. *The Culture of Narcissism: American Life in an Age of Diminishing Expectations*. New York: Warner, 1977.

Lasch, C. *The True and Only Heaven: Progress and Its Critics*. New York: W.W. Norton, 1991.

Le Bon, G. *The Crowd: A Study of the Popular Mind*. London: T. Fisher Unwin, 1917.

Leavis, F.R., and D. Thompson. *Culture and Environment: The Training of Critical Awareness*. London: Chatto and Windus, 1964.

Macdonald, D. 'A Theory of Mass Culture'. In *Mass Culture: The Popular Arts in America*, edited by B. Rosenberg and D. Manning White, 59–73. New York: Free Press, 1957.

Maguire, J.A. 'Conceptual and Methodological Confusion in Analyses of Nineteenth Century Leisure – The Case for Historical Sociology'. In *Sport, Culture, Society: International, Historical and Sociological Perspectives*, edited by J.A. Mangan and R.B. Small, 39–51. London: E & F.N. Spon, 1986.

Marwick, A. *The New Nature of History: Knowledge, Evidence, Language*. Basingstoke: Palgrave, 2001.

Mason, T. *Associational Football and English Society 1863–1915*. Brighton: Harvester Press, 1980.

McClelland, J.S. *The Crowd and the Mob: From Plato to Canetti*. London: Unwin Hyman, 1989.

McGuigan, J. *Cultural Populism*. London: Routledge, 1992.

Mulhern, F. *Culture/Metaculture*. London: Routledge, 2000.

Novak, M. *The Joy of Sports: End Zones, Bases, Baskets, Balls, and the Consecration of the American Spirit*. New York: Basic Books, 1976.

Orwell, G. *The Road to Wigan Pier*. London: Penguin, 1962.

Orwell, G. 'Wilde's Utopia' (from *The Observer*, 9 May 1948). In *Orwell: The Observer Years*, 74–6. London: Atlantic Books, 2003.

Rader, B.G. *American Sports: From the Age of Folk Games to the Age of Spectators*. Englewood Cliffs, NJ: Prentice-Hall, 1983.

Riesman, D. (with R. Denney), 'Football in America: A Study in Culture Diffusion'. In *Individualism Reconsidered: and Other Essays*, 242–57. Glencoe, IL: Free Press, 1954.

Rosenberg, B., and D. Manning White, eds. *Mass Culture: The Popular Arts in America*. New York: Free Press, 1957.

Ross, A. *No Respect: Intellectuals and Popular Culture*. London: Routledge, 1989.

Russell, D. *Football and the English: A Social History of Association Football in England, 1863–1995*. Preston: Carnegie, 1997.

Stansky, P., and W. Abrahams. *Orwell: The Transformation*. London: Granada, 1979.

Taylor, I. 'Soccer Consciousness and Soccer Hooliganism'. In *Images of Deviance*, edited by S. Cohen, 134–64. Harmondsworth: Penguin, 1971.

Thompson, E.P. 'The Long Revolution'. *New Left Review* 9 (1961): 24–33.

Thompson, E.P. *The Making of the English Working Class*. London: Victor Gollancz, 1963.

Thompson, E.P. 'Outside the Whale'. In *The Poverty of Theory and Other Essays*, 24–33. London: Merlin Press, 1978.

Thompson, E.P. *Customs in Common*. London: Merlin, 1991.

Tygiel, J. *Past Time: Baseball as History*. New York: Oxford University Press, 2000.

Walvin, J. *The People's Game: A Social History of British Football*. London: Allen Lane, 1975.

Williams, R. *Culture and Society 1780–1950*. Harmondsworth: Penguin, 1961.

Williams, R. 'Orwell'. In *Politics and Letters: Interviews with the New Left*, 384–92. London: Verso, 1979.

Yeo, S. 'What is the History of Popular Culture'. In *What is History Today?*, edited by J. Gardiner, 128–30. Basingstoke: Macmillan, 1988.

The middle class, colonialism and the making of sport

This essay continues with the theme of the making of sporting culture, initially considering how sport might be *made* by the middle class. Discussion of middle-class sporting culture *in* Britain broadens to an examination of the development of sport in the colonial contexts of Empire. While sport was undoubtedly used within colonies as a means of cementing a collective cultural bond to Empire, the historical development of sports such as cricket clearly show the people of colonized races and ethnic groups as actively involved in the *making* of their own sporting cultures.

The middle class and the making of sport

If it can be contended that certain forms of sporting culture have been made by the working class, can a similar claim hold for the middle class? As discussed in the previous essay, the idea of culture being 'made' is taken from E.P. Thompson's cultural Marxist account of historical agency in *The Making of the English Working Class*. From this perspective, the making of culture occurs within the context of class 'struggle' and has relevance only to the working class. However, furthering the step beyond Thompson initiated in the previous essay, it will be argued here that an understanding of the cultural history of sport benefits from affording agency to the middle class; i.e. in certain regards it is pertinent to say that the middle class has been responsible for the 'making' of sporting culture. A number of sports, including golf and tennis, bear the historical imprint of middle-class agency. As with the case of the working class, this is not to say that these sports were invented by the middle class but that particular sporting cultures of golf and tennis have been 'made' by the middle class, or segments of that class.[1]

To deny that the middle class 'makes' sporting culture not only risks limiting the historical account, but also obscures the critical insight that can be gained from viewing middle-class involvement with sport in this way. The assumption is often put that the middle classes were drawn to particular sporting activities because these activities provided opportunity to commune with nature. Advocacy in the late Victorian and Edwardian periods for certain sports promoted this association. A 1906 edition of the *Yachting Monthly* appealed to middle-class romanticism by declaring that sailing offers 'the solitude of Nature and the presence of the immeasurable'.[2] Even in golf, where the natural landscape is significantly denuded to accommodate the field of play, the appeal to nature was incorporated into the design of courses for the English middle class.[3] The appeal to nature appeared most disingenuous when voiced in connection with hunting. Having initially benefited from the population shift from countryside to town, hunters began to 'feel the pinch' through the 1800s as town sizes expanded to the point of impacting on land used for hunting.[4] The resultant romanticizing by hunters of the rural tradition of their sport and the attachment to land appears more an expression of self-interest than a commitment to preserving the natural order through sport.

A case for the historical connection between foxhunting and nature has been restated in recent times by the well-known philosopher Roger Scruton. According to Scruton, foxhunting has, from the time of its emergence in the latter half of the 1700s, provided humans with the possibility of a return to 'the fold of nature'.[5] A prominent voice in the contemporary debate about foxhunting, Scruton is dismissive of critics who seek to have the sport banned on the basis of accusations of cruelty to animals. Firstly, he argues that foxhunting is not actually cruel because, *inter alia*, it gives the fox a fair chance of escape, only ailing foxes usually fall prey to the pursuing hounds, and the kill is made very quickly. Secondly, and more importantly, he contends critics fail to appreciate that the naturalness of foxhunting, in terms of the union it provides between man, animal and the outdoors, has been a source of moral virtue over generations; 'in those the centaur hours ... real life returns [as] the blood of another species flows through your veins, stirring the old deposits of collective life, releasing pockets of energy that a million generations laboriously harvested from the crop of human suffering'.[6]

Scruton acknowledges that foxhunting commenced as an upper-class sport and ascribes its origins to the need of the aristocracy to escape the travails of 'civilization' – understood in *Kulturkritik* terms as affairs of governance and politics – via a totemic reconnection with natural life. Scruton claims that 'today we are all civilised ... and live from the funds of human artifice'. Accordingly, we could all do with a little foxhunting, but, 'unlike the old aristocracy, we lack culture and ... ready awareness of our condition'.[7] Despite this elitist depiction of the ordinary person, Scruton does not regard foxhunting as an exclusive leisure domain for the socially and economically privileged. Although highly ceremonial it can be, and has been over time, enjoyed on a communal rather than class basis. Anthony Trollope remarked as far back as 1867, that to view foxhunting as 'confined to country gentlemen, farmers and rich strangers' is a misjudgement. Recognizing a broad mix of professions and vocations in attendance on any given hunting day, he referred to the 'democratisation' of 'an average hunting field'.[8] However, according to G.M. Trevelyan, while the colourful image of 'the hunt' enjoyed cross-class appeal, the activity of fox-hunting remained largely exclusive.[9] Trollope would thus appear to extend the popular perception of the hunt, held by non-participants, into an account of its lived character. The social reality of the hunt was quite removed from the liberalist optimism projected by Trollope. During the 1800s, hunting did become 'open to all' in the sense that anyone was welcome to participate, 'the dustman was welcome to ride beside the duke', and on occasion did so.[10] However, while this contact certainly involved 'fraternization', democracy is another matter. The fleeting conservations that took place between those at either ends of the class scale during the hunt and periods of rest did nothing to unsettle ingrained social hierarchies. Indeed, the social inclusiveness of the hunt was made possible 'only because the ideals of deference on which the openness of the hunting field depended were accepted by all'.[11]

The hunting for all argument was more conducive to conservative than liberal ends, hunting being seen as a practical means of keeping classes in place rather than disassembling barriers. Accordingly, it was used by the upper middle class as a 'counterweight to the forces of radicalism' that were strengthening in the nineteenth century.[12] Scruton's claims for the social inclusiveness of foxhunting today are in keeping with the conservative ideal. He indicates that there is no place for 'egalitarians' within the cultural domain of hunting. Such minded people will be put off by the ceremony of hunting and the related necessity of costume as a reminder of 'courtliness'. Foxhunting is thus not about 'the modern idea of equality', but an appreciation for the natural order of life that the hunt symbolizes.[13] This is not to suggest that Scruton's claims for the *cultural* significance of hunting are insincere. His account in *On Hunting* is passionate and makes a convincing case for a *Kulturkritik* demarcation, where hunting exists as culture standing above 'civilization'.

From this perspective, culture is not *made* because it is natural; making would suggest a human intrusion into nature. For Scruton, to speak of foxhunting being made would be a vulgarization, a failure to appreciate the naturalness of the hunt. This outlook effectively relegates matters of social relations to a secondary consideration. The hunt comes first and people find their place within it, unconcerned with thoughts of equality but in a spirit of natural 'communion'. Based on this understanding Scruton dismisses the feasibility of a class analysis of foxhunting. A key argument of this essay is that historical enquiry needs to adopt the view that the middle and upper classes *made* their own sporting cultures. To insist that only the working class *makes* culture risks leaving the type of argument advanced by Scruton, in regard to foxhunting, go unchallenged. To challenge Scruton need not mean rejection of the *Kulturkritik* distinction between culture and civilization. To suggest that forms of culture are *made* collectively by humans is not to diminish the terminological significance of culture or to conflate culture with civilization, but to suggest that the lived experience of culture can only be understood within social context. Nor is the relationship between culture and nature to be denied. What is to be challenged is the slippage – apparent in Scruton's position – of the notion of naturalness into the realm of the social. This slippage risks obliterating the very distinction between culture and civilization on which Scruton's advocacy of foxhunting depends.

Having been made as a cultural expression of the conservatism of the English upper middle class, foxhunting came to serve an important ideological function for that class. Those who uncritically accepted the terms of the hunt, at which ever end of the class scale they may have been located, at once complied with 'the established system'. The contrivance of foxhunting as an activity 'open to all' was logically, if disingenuously, extended to the idea that it benefited all and to be critical of the hunt was to be un-English. Itzkowitz thus suggests that foxhunting has been used to promote patriotism by stealth.[14] The link between foxhunting and patriotism can be interestingly considered in relation to Orwell's definition of patriotism in his 1945 essay 'Notes on Nationalism'. According to Orwell, patriotism is 'a devotion to a particular place and a particular way of life, which one believes to be best in the world but has no wish to force upon other people'. Orwell favoured patriotism over nationalism, because while the latter is aggressive the former is defensive, 'both militarily and *culturally*'.[15] Although Orwell regarded patriotism as a relatively benign expression, his own definition glimpses ideological possibilities. Foxhunting, as discussed here, provides good example. Given its conduciveness to the English environment, foxhunting, by comparison to other sports, did not feature in the cultural extension of the British Empire. Rather, as indicated above, it provided a significant ideological tool for the English upper class to extol *their* way of life to their own countrymen. Such has been the particular patriotic – culturally defensive – end served by the sport of foxhunting.

Sport, nation and empire

Of course, the sentiment of patriotism was not historically confined to British shores. In 1886 Lord Rosebery, future British Prime Minister, suggested that patriotic feeling for home should rightly extend into imperial ambition.[16] In joining the Liberal Party debate on the issue of imperial expansion he argued against 'wild, hot Imperialism' in favour of 'sane Imperialism'. The latter, for Rosebery, involved a 'larger patriotism' – rather than militarism – and the pursuit and maintenance of a British Empire could be morally defended on this basis. While France and Germany tended to directly impose customs and values upon their territories, Britain relied on the velvet glove of 'cultural imperialism'.[17] Towards the end of the Victorian period, sport had come to play an important role in this regard. As Holt notes, 'sports were thought to help create a climate of relations that would bind the Empire together'.[18] Initially, sport served to sustain a cultural loyalty to the homeland amongst emigrants, beyond this to provide a cultural bond between colonizing and colonized peoples. According to J.A. Mangan, it was cricket that emerged, not only as the most prominent sport within the British Empire, but also, as 'the symbol *par excellence* of imperial solidarity and superiority epitomizing a set of consolidatory moral imperatives that both exemplified and explained imperial ambition and achievement'.[19]

An understanding of cricket is, therefore, integral to an understanding of the relations of colonialism within the British Empire. Furthermore, while there are points of commonality to be considered, the cultural experience of cricket differed from one national context within the Empire to the next. The chief interest in this essay is to understand how sporting cultures were *made* in colonial contexts; i.e. not only how these cultures were made by the agents of imperialism but how they were received and re-made by colonized peoples. Cricket is an especially interesting example in the latter regard. While cricket was no doubt a key aspect of British cultural imperialism, in the way identified by Mangan, its most interesting stories are those of reclamation associated with the emergent cultures of that sport in the non-white reaches of Empire such as India and the West Indies. Ashis Nandy's fascinating book, *The Tao of Cricket*, opens with the sentence, 'cricket is an Indian game accidentally discovered by the English'.[20] Nandy's challenge to the view of cricket as quintessentially English can be logically extended to debunk the idea that cricket was merely handed down by the British and compliantly absorbed by the local inhabitants of Empire.

Indeed, this was not the story of cricket from the time of its inception in India. The title of the opening chapter – 'The Homesick Colonial and the Imitative Native' – to Ramachandra Guha's history of Indian cricket is instructive.[21] Cricket was brought to India by the British during the colonial expansion of the 1700s; in 1792 the Calcutta Cricket Club became the first cricket club to be established in at outpost of the Empire.[22] According to Guha, cricket provided 'a source of much comfort to the expatriate Englishman', a means to 're-create memories of life in England'.[23] This idea of 'consolation' suggests to Guha that cricket was initially kept by the British for themselves, there being no apparent 'intention of teaching the natives to play'.[24] The initiative to take up the game was borne of the 'native' people rather than the proselytizing influence of the British. Guha recounts how the Parsis of Bombay, a people given to mercantile affairs, emulated their overlords in both business and pleasure. While Parsi traders were hard at work, their sons used idle time to play the bat and ball game they had learnt from diligent observation of English soldiers playing cricket in an area close to the Army parade ground.[25]

Cricket had some similarity to games already played by Parsi youth but, according to Guha, 'in artistry, technique and dramatic interest [it was] far superior to anything previously played on the sub-continent'.[26] The boys initially played with makeshift bats and on rough and uneven surfaces, hardly conducive to an even bounce of the ball. Reaching manhood, the Parsi boys founded their first cricket club in 1848, the Oriental Cricket Club, which soon became known, and still exists, as The Young Zoroastrians. Over the following 20 years, several Parsi cricket clubs were formed, and in 1890 a select team, the Parsi Gymkhana, struck a blow to imperial pride by defeating an amateur English touring side that included the Yorkshire County Cricket Club captain, Lord Hawke.[27] English pride had previously been dented when the national team lost to Australia in Melbourne in 1877, in what has become known as the first international test match. However, a defeat by 'native' colonials, even though of a reputedly weak English team and in a match of inferior status, was a bitter pill to swallow, as indicated by press reports of the day.[28]

Success against the English by an Indian national team in test cricket was long awaited. India played its first test match against England in 1932 but did not win against that country until the final test in the drawn series of 1951–52, played in India. India's first series win came on home soil in the 1961–62 series. Of the 'coloured' cricket-playing nations of Empire, the West Indies has tweaked the imperial nose most often. An all-West Indies team first played an England team in Trinidad in February 1897, winning the game by three wickets.[29] The first test series to be played in the West Indies against England in 1929–30 was drawn. While losing the subsequent 1933 series in England, the West Indies was victorious in the next series played between the countries at home in 1934–35.[30] The success of the West Indies in these early years of test cricket against England does not, of course, undermine the argument that cricket was used as a means of *cultural imperialism*. But it does, as in the case of that sport's history in India, unsettle the view that cricket was simply handed down to a compliant colonized people.

The *making* of West Indian cricket

Cricket emerged in the late 1800s colonial West Indies, following Emancipation. In a potentially unruly social climate, it was used by 'colonial administrators' as a means of promoting the 'values, norms and prejudices' conducive to their rule.[31] Local elites were supportive of this ideological usage of cricket as it helped firm their position within the British colonial system. Relatedly, 'cricket and its associated moral code' was placed at the heart of the elite schooling system in the Caribbean.[32] Stoddart thus identifies cricket as 'being central in the creation of hegemonic cultural values' that assist the 'social reproduction of class hierarchies'.[33] In this statement Stoddart looks to the work of Antonio Gramsci, in particular his notion of hegemony, to explain how cricket became diffused into the cultural lifeblood of the English-speaking West Indies as a form of power that becalmed potential resistance to colonial authority. Gramsci – writing while imprisoned by the Italian fascists in the 1930s – predicted that governing states in the West would increasingly rely upon consensual rather than coercive means to maintain rule, and this would occur via the dissemination of a dominant value system in 'civil society', schools taking on a particularly significant ideological function.[34] From the 1970s, neo-Marxist scholars have adapted Gramsci's notion of hegemony to account for the role of the mass media in capitalist society.[35] While Gramsci intended his notion of hegemony as an extension of Marx's position on the false consciousness of the industrial working class, scholars have more recently applied it to power relations concerning gender and race.[36]

Gramsci's idea of hegemony involved explaining not only how power works to keep subaltern classes in place, but how these classes may mobilize against such power. Gramsci was a binary thinker, believing power from above fertilizes resistance below. Active resistance, he argued, can result in a 'crisis in hegemony' and destabilize existing authority relations.[37] In regard to the present discussion, if hegemony is considered to be a concept relevant to an historical explanation of cricket in the West Indies, it must be looked at in terms of resistance from below as well as power over, or from, above. British imperialism may have been held in place in the West Indies *culturally* by cricket, but, if this is the case, then conversely, the role of cricket must be regarding as significant to the demise of British rule in the Caribbean. A Gramscian understanding of this kind can be found in the writing on cricket by the late West Indian social critic Tim Hector. Hector writes of the development within West Indian cricket of 'a black style', a style which is oppositional to that of the 'oppressor's style' and is ultimately anti-hegemonic. Relatedly, upheavals in cricket coincided with industrial and political militancy in the 1930s, synergizing into what Hector refers to as a 'revolution from below'.[38]

Michael Manley notes that grassroots political protest in the British West Indies became systematic by the late 1930s, in a way that it had not been before.[39] The widespread experience of hunger and poverty demanded that 'the old order had to change'. The mobilization against the imperial overlord came more readily and apparently through the agency of political parties and trade unions. Cricket largely stood apart from this grassroots radicalism. The conservative organizational structure of the West Indies Cricket Board and its associated clubs and district bodies ensured that cricket, despite its broad-based appeal, remained under the formal domination of 'the upper echelons of Caribbean society'.[40] The impetus for challenging this domination came, not surprisingly, from figures close to the game, and no figure loomed larger in this regard than that of the great West Indian all-rounder Learie Constantine. Constantine, who debuted for the West Indies against England in 1928, openly contended that West Indian cricket reflected the racial inequality that characterized British rule in the Caribbean. He became a prominent advocate from the 1920s for the appointment of a black cricketer as captain of the West Indian team.[41] Constantine and his contemporary, George Headley, were obvious candidates to take on such a role, but the connection between cricket and colonial authority was resilient enough to keep inferior white players in the West Indian captaincy until 1960.

Historical coincidence between politics and cricket can be seen with the appointment of Frank Worrell as the first black player to the captaincy of the West Indies in 1960 and, a decade earlier, the first test victory and series win against England in England (1950) by a touring West Indian team. Occurring subsequent to the Montego Bay Conference of 1947, the 1950 tour to England was the first made by a West Indian team united in the spirit of federation. Agreement had been reached at the conference, by a predominance of the Island colonies, to form a Federation 'at the appropriate time' and to operate according to the principles of 'loose' association in the meantime.[42] Resultantly, according to Manley, 'the 1950 side was the product of a far more confident and sophisticated society than its predecessors in the 1930s'.[43] The Federation of the West Indies, including the main cricket-playing Islands, was formed in January 1958, putting the final process towards independence of governance from Britain in place. Against this political backdrop, the drive for a black West Indian to become national cricket captain gained momentum. Following a disappointing, albeit close, series loss to England in the 1959–60 test series at home, rumblings loudened within the press for the replacement by Worrell of the white West Indian captain Gerry Alexander.[44]

Frank Worrell's first test series as captain of the West Indies was to Australia in 1960–61. The series was narrowly lost to the Australians but Worrell was widely praised for rejuvenating the spirit of the West Indian team and 'restoring adventure to the game'.[45] According to Manley, the West Indies regained 'respect as a cricketing power', earning it by 'playing the cricket that comes most naturally to them, fluent, attacking, attractive'.[46] Coming to the captaincy late in an illustrious career, Worrell's period of on-field leadership was fairly brief (Garfield Sobers became captain of the West Indies in 1965 upon Worrell's retirement from international cricket). However, the attacking spirit developed in the series against Australia continued and reward came with a clean sweep series victory against India in the West Indies in 1961–62, and a commanding series win over England in England in 1963.

Although coming from a middle-class background, Worrell is remembered as a man of the people. Having grown up within 'the unyielding racial hierarchy' of Barbados, Worrell relocated to the less rigidly race-divided Jamaica in 1947, and, following a lengthy period with the Kensington Cricket Club, switched to the decidedly working-class club known as Boy's Town in 1960.[47] Worrell's most eloquent eulogist, C.L.R. James, attributes the move to Boy's Town – unlikely for a middle-class black – to Worrell's 'unbridled passion for social equality'. James continued, 'It was the men on his side who had no social status whatever for whose interest and welfare he was primarily concerned. They repaid him with an equally fanatical devotion.' Worrell's wrangles with cricket authorities for higher pay and involvement in the campaign that eventuated in his elevation to captaincy can, accordingly, be regarded as acts of benevolence rather than self-aggrandizement. Lending further to this interpretation, Worrell was regarded by those who controlled the sport in the West Indies as a 'cricket Bolshevik'.[48]

In retrospect Worrell's appointment to the captaincy of the West Indies might be seen more as indication of the gradual relinquishment of cricket from the grip of colonialism, than a radical break from the racial division within the sport. Worrell was, after all, an atypical black West Indian, middle-class, well-educated and closely associated with England from his experience as a professional playing in the Central Lancashire League. In short, awarding the captaincy to him may have been a compromise solution acceded to by the cricketing elite in grudging response to the groundswell for change.[49] Accordingly, ground was given on race, yet not on class. Nevertheless, whatever the particular interpretation of events, the history of cricket within the West Indies reflects the history of British colonialism and the politics of race embedded within that history.

The 'maple man': C.L.R. James, cricket and colonialism

The superlative account of this historical relationship is given in C.L.R. James's much cited book *Beyond a Boundary* (1963).[50] Written in autobiographical form the book not only identifies the centrality of cricket to James's life, but the centrality of cricket to the cultural life of the West Indies, and the cultural significance of cricket more generally. The most frequently cited phrase from *Beyond a Boundary*, 'What do they know of cricket who only cricket know', makes clear enough James's wont to provide an understanding of cricket as something more than a ludic activity.[51] Indeed, although admitting to blissful incomprehension of the social gravity of cricket during his youth in Trinidad, James acknowledges the formative role of cricket in his preparation as an activist: 'Cricket had plunged me into politics long before I was aware of it. When I did turn to politics I did not have too much to learn.'[52]

Raised within the educated black middle-class community of Port of Spain, James, as a young man, chose to play cricket for Maple, the club that was regarded as appropriate for an individual from his background. In making this choice he declined the opportunity to play for Shannon, a club associated with the black lower middle class. In doing so, he was denied an early life opportunity to become acquainted with his friend and idol of later years, Learie Constantine. James regretted the decision even more so for delaying his personal 'political development' and restricting his contact with people further down the racial hierarchy of the West Indies than himself. James notes how, as a boy, he accepted the 'Puritan' ethic of cricket, which was imparted through the local version of the English public school system: 'I knew what was done and what was not done ... I never cheated, I never appealed for a decision unless I thought the batsman was out, I never argued with the umpire, I never jeered at an opponent ... My defeats and disappointments I took as stoically as I could.'[53]

Significantly, although recognizing the ideological use of cricket by the British, James never rejected its moral code. Resultantly, James has been accused of being so 'seduced' by the sport that he cannot reflexively adjudge the 'values of cricket'.[54] From this critical reading, James's heralding of achievements by outstanding black West Indian players, such as Constantine and Worrell, is not made through indigenous Caribbean eyes per se, but from a perspective jaundiced by the desire to 'prove [oneself] to the "master"'.[55] Amongst his various other activities, James wrote articles on cricket over the years for British newspapers, including the *Manchester Guardian* and the *Glasgow Herald*. He also wrote pieces for specialist organs such as *The Cricketer*. James's prodigious writings on cricket varied from match reports to eulogy and social observation, therefore from more matter-of-fact reporting to critical commentary. Although of the latter category, *Beyond a Boundary* might be seen to sit incongruously within James's scholarly œuvre, which consisted of such highly regarded works as *The Black Jacobins*, a political history of the revolution in Haiti in the late 1700s, and the unfinished *American Civilisation*.[56] Alternatively, *Beyond a Boundary* might be regarded as a work of 'cultural politics' coherently situated further along a publishing trajectory from his works on 'real politics'.[57] In the context of the present volume, mention of this latter reading prompts comparison between James and Raymond Williams.

James's most direct intellectual engagement with Williams was his 1961 review of *Culture and Society* and *The Long Revolution*, in which he acknowledged Williams as 'the most remarkable writer that the socialist movement in England has produced for ten years or perhaps twenty'.[58] His use of the word socialist is decisive as he goes on criticize what he reads as Williams's non-Marxist and, therefore, inadequate account of post-war British society. In particular, James suggests that Williams's analysis is not based in Marx's historical materialism and, as such, explains moments of class upheaval as little more than random events disconnected from the historical inevitability of international revolution. Williams's eventual way forward into Marxist theory and politics came via his turn to Gramsci in the 1970s. While sympathetic to Marxist theory, Williams rejected the economic determinism of classical Marxism. He believed that material social relations are best explained ultimately in cultural rather than economic terms, and hence came to refer to his theoretical position as 'cultural materialism'.[59] James's intellectual maturity and curiosity had peaked by the time Gramsci became available to the English readership in the 1970s. His dialogues on Marx were made via more traditional interpreters such as Trotsky and Lenin, so it is difficult to know what he would have made of Williams' retrieval of Marx through Gramsci. However, the shift to a 'cultural politics' in *Beyond a Boundary* inevitably raises the question of the relevance of the notions of hegemony and counter-hegemony to James's account of the lived politics of cricket in the West Indian context.

James's simultaneous recognition of cricket being used for the purpose of ideological control by the colonial oppressor and as a means of resistance by the socially oppressed may appear compatible with a Gramscian hegemonic model. However, upon closer inspection, the power from above, resistance from below dichotomy is somewhat at odds with the seamless telling of the historical struggle of West Indian cricket proffered by James. To return to a terminology from the previous essay, James tells a 'history from within'. Given the autobiographical nature of *Beyond a Boundary*, James is himself, as author, located within this history, as are the various characters that fight for and find liberation through cricket. For James it would be too simple to say that the cricketing legends whose stories he recounts were leading characters in counter-hegemonic contestation. Cricket was a part of the cultural landscape known to these cricketers from their childhood. What they achieved politically they achieved within the 'code' of the game, not in contravention of it. The hegemony model does not suit James's account because it tends to suggest a cultural uprooting that he does not make case for in *Beyond a Boundary*. James's history tells of a challenge to social relations in the West Indies mirrored in cricket, but in the very same book he argues for the cultural purity of the sport through an attempt to recognize cricket's aesthetic essence.

According to James, the aesthetic essence of cricket has both performative and imaginative dimensions.[60] Cricket's performative beauty is in its inherent drama. Many sports can be regarded as dramatic, yet in a superficial way in that they work up to a dramatic finale. For James, this is but melodrama whereas cricket contains real drama within every component of its play. He contends that each of cricket's 'isolated episodes' are 'completely self-contained', 'each single one fraught with immense possibilities of expectation and realisation'.[61] These episodes constitute the 'total spectacle' of cricket and are indicative of its 'structural perfection'. According to James, cricket, like life, is a continuous drama and this is why 'the end result [of a match] is not of great importance'. Cricket's imaginative beauty is, for James, in its capturing of 'significant form'. In this regard James is inspired by the famous art critic Bernard Berenson,[62] who praised Renaissance artists such as Masaccio and Raphael, because of their ability to evoke 'the imaginary experience of certain complicated muscular movement'.[63] James likens the greatest of cricketers to these painter's works of art, in a player such as W.G. Grace 'significant form [is] most unadulterated and permanently present'. In terms more familiar to cricket, the player with significant form can be said, according to James, to exhibit 'style'.

James's unwavering belief in the aesthetics of cricket gives it *Kulturkritik* like distinction, whereby cricket as culture stands conceptually apart from cricket as socially inscribed human practice. However, James, obviously enough, did not believe that cricket as artistic engagement is sealed off from society. On the contrary, he argues that the embodied history of social relations brought to the game by cricketers characterizes the 'style' they display. This can be seen lucidly in his account of the great batsman Rohan Kanhai: 'in Kanhai's batting what I have found is a unique pointer of the West Indian quest for identity, for ways of expressing our potential bursting at every seam'.[64] Via this recognition James can proclaim without fear of contradiction, 'Cricket is an art, a means of national expression',[65] Art is art, but its resonance is born of place. James is able to share with other West Indians a particular appreciation of Kanhai's art and that of other Caribbean cricketing greats he has witnessed over the years. With 'coloured' countrymen he can share 'the sensation that here was one of us, performing *in excelsis* in a sphere where competition was open ... a demonstration that atoned for a pervading humiliation, and nourished pride and hope'.[66]

In a review of *Beyond a Boundary*, shortly after its publication, V.S. Naipaul declared the book to be one of the finest 'to come out of the West Indies, important to England, important to the West Indies'.[67] This is to recognize, from *Beyond a Boundary*, that the significance of cricket to the West Indies can never be disconnected from its colonial roots. James's story of cricket is not just of relevance to the place(s) called the West Indies, it is a story of relevance to the place called England as well. In a letter to Naipaul, James declares that while his book 'is West Indian through and through' it is also 'very British'. He continues, 'originating as we are within the British structure, but living under such different social conditions, we have a lot to say about the British civilisation itself which we see more sharply than they themselves'.[68] Furthermore, while James condemns the racial oppression of colonialism he retains conviction of the humanistic temper of his public school background, a quality he very much associates with the spirit of cricket. Thus he concludes *Beyond a Boundary*, 'Thomas Arnold, Thomas Hughes and the Old Master himself [viz. W.G. Grace] would have recognised Frank Worrell as their boy'.[69] It is such portrayal that leads to James being accused of writing from the perspective of an English colonial rather than from that of a West Indian of African descent. However, such criticism misses the point made by Mark Kingwell, that James's commitment to what he regarded as the essential values of cricket represented a successful anti-colonial strategy, because those same humanistic values, which may well exist in a purified sense, were never followed by the colonizers in their attempt to impose cultural imperialism. Accordingly, by accepting and adhering to the values of cricket, James 'beat the masters at their own game'.[70]

Sport, colonialism and *cultural traffic*

James's view that the cultural impact of colonialism was felt by not only the colonized country but also by the colonizing country, is similar to a position advanced by the Australian art historian and anthropologist Bernard Smith. In *European Vision and the South Pacific* Smith makes the not initially surprising claim that Australian art needs to be understood through a related understanding of British art.[71] But, further to this, he claims that to understand British art from the late 1700s requires an appreciation of the cultural impact of the voyages made to Australia and the South Pacific by James Cook. Cook's second voyage carried the artist William Hodges whose representations of the people of the South Pacific created considerable interest upon his return to Britain. His paintings revived debate about the dramatist Dryden's notion of the 'noble savage'.[72] On the one hand satirists mocked the primitive characters in Hodges artwork, on the other, some commentators saw splendidly attired natives assumedly happy with their lifestyle. This latter view connected with the impression taken from Cook's journals of an idyllic social existence located at the bottom end of the world. At a time of considerable social concern coinciding with qualms about rampant industrialization, Hodges' paintings were viewed by some as a moral riposte to what had gone wrong with Britain.

According to Smith, 'The idea of an antipodal inversion of natural laws was not an easy one to reconcile with the idea of a carefully ordered hierarchy both physical and moral which was securely held together by the laws of nature'.[73] Following European discovery, the lands of the South became unmoored from their imagined place, in the words of Smith's scholarly interpreter, Peter Beilharz, 'the reflux from below … return[ed] to haunt the metropolitan consciousness'.[74] Beilharz notes that for Smith, the Antipodes is not about place but displacement, the Antipodes suggests a relationship rather than geographical location.[75] The relationship is one of power inequity, but although 'unequal by nature', it involves 'a great deal more fluidity than those formally in control could themselves imagine'. Beilharz uses the term *cultural traffic* to explain the dynamism of the antipodean relationship as discussed by Smith.[76] The term suggests that the relationship involves ongoing reciprocity and mutual impact, and that it features the movement of people and/or cultural practices and items.

In the manner of Smith on the Antipodes, so we might regard the depiction of the Caribbean by James in *Beyond a Boundary*; whereas the West Indies refers to place(s), the Caribbean refers to a relationship. Relatedly, *cultural traffic* can be adapted interestingly as a term to explain the uses of sport within the respective relationships of the Caribbean (cricket) and Antipodes (cricket and rugby) to Britain. In this regard, cultural traffic can refer to the to-and-fro movement of sports people between centre and periphery for such events as test matches and also the residential relocation of players to take up opportunities in, for example, English inter-county cricket and as 'professionals' within county leagues. James discusses how players from the Caribbean such as Learie Constantine – whom James followed to England – were able to attain financial security and develop as cricketers and individuals through their time in England, in remove from the racial hierarchy of cricket in the West Indies. James also notes that Constantine was aware of his atypical experience as a black West Indian living in Britain, both in terms of his sporting profile and his residence in a small northern town. Constantine and James were a rare sight on the streets of Nelson, Lancashire in the 1930s. While Constantine appreciated the adulation he received from local cricket supporters he, and James alike, 'could not get rid of the feeling that whatever [they] did would be judged as representative of the habits and standards of millions of people at home'.[77]

Constantine, and Frank Worrell after him, may well be regarded as unusual representatives of West Indian cricket in Britain. Both were intellectuals, Constantine joined James in a number of public commentary forums. However, as a cricketer Constantine lent to the carnival image that has become popularly associated with Caribbean, or as it has been called, Calypso cricket. A powerful hitting batsman and frenetic fast bowler, the term most often used in England to describe Constantine was 'electric'. Hill argues that such reference gives recognition to Constantine as a 'dazzling virtuoso' who lit up a sport often stereotypically associated with dull English summers.[78] That Constantine's accomplishment in the Lancashire County League occurred in the 1930s prompts Hill to regard him as a 'symbol of this New World modernity'. While this is an interesting consideration, the representation of Constantine as 'electric' also prompts query into the extent to which he fitted with a perception of black physicality and pre-modernity. The image of the highly energetic black athlete can be related back to the idea of the 'noble savage', and, from there, read ambivalently. Constantine's press appears to have been overwhelmingly positive, hence the use of a word associated with brightness and antonymous with darkness. Yet, West Indian cricket has not always been viewed so positively, and although reference to darkness may be avoided, criticism, in relatively recent time, has been couched in terms conjuring savagery from a foreboding and distant place. Thus the successful West Indian fast bowling attack during the era of Clive Lloyd's captaincy in the latter part of the 1970s and early 1980s was accused by the English cricketing press of, inter alia, 'brutalizing the game'.[79]

An interesting early example of ambivalence in response to the appearance of the 'noble savage' within the history of sport and Empire can be traced to what has become known as the Native tour of Britain in 1888–89, by a select rugby team from New Zealand comprising a majority of Maori players. As part of his study of the tour, Greg Ryan examines responses by the English press, at the time, to the exotic sporting visitors. Early reports were cast in the characteristically patronizing terms of the day. *The Daily Telegraph* greeted the tour with a flippant inversion of history;

> We have been invaded, and the Maori is upon us ... Yet the timid may take heart of grace; this invasion of peaceful and pleasant character threatens no new danger to England ... It is but another of those ever-welcome colonial invasions in which our fellow subjects from across the sea come to wage friendly war with us in some of our national sports and pastimes.[80]

Using the tour to profess the virtues of sport as colonizing influence, an article in *The Times* declared:

> The colonising race that can imbue the aboriginal inhabitants of the colonised countries with a love for its national games, would seem to have solved the problem of social amalgamation in those countries ... Wherever the Englishman goes he carries the bat and the goal posts.[81]

While the early press reports continued favourably and the Maori were generally complimented for their behaviour on and off the field, a condescending attitude toward the play of the New Zealand team tended to prevail. Furthermore, a comment in the Sydney *Bulletin* that the team 'appear to combine the best elements of a football team and circus' was a forthright version of similar sentiments expressed in English papers.[82] The performance of the haka prior to matches lent to this misinterpretation. But as Ryan suggests, facile dismissal of the native tour at the time failed to appreciate its cultural significance and has led to its historical neglect.[83] The latter problem is particularly pertinent to New Zealand where, to the current day, the Native tour bears a prefatory historical status. The first official All Blacks tour, by a predominantly Pakeha team, was made to Britain in 1905. The naming of this team as the 'Originals' has done little to acknowledge the rightful place of the Native tour within the history of rugby.

It was on the latter tour that the 'wing-forward' formation was seen for the first time in rugby away from New Zealand. This type of play was invented by Thomas Rangiwahia Ellison and is elaborated in his landmark instructional manual *The Art of Rugby*, published in 1902. Ellison, a prominent player in the Native team, declared the play of his team as innovative in comparison to that of the lacklustre 'Britishers'. On the latter, Ellison remarked, 'Their play generally was of one style and description, from start to finish ... They all seem to have tumbled into a groove, and stuck there.'[84] Ellison's 'wing-game' was deployed by subsequent successful All Blacks touring teams over the next two decades until it was counteracted with the imposition of the eight-man scrum, which was codified into the rules of rugby in 1932. In giving impetus to the changes that would come to international rugby, Ellison, and the Native team of which he was a member, gives an early obvious relevance to Smith's term *cultural traffic* being applied to sport. Interestingly, Ellison was a graduate of Te Aute College, a school for Maori boys founded in 1854 along the lines of the English public school. Like the Queen's Royal College, attended by C.L.R. James in Trinidad, it can be said that Te Aute was concerned with familiarizing its pupils with the gentlemanly 'code' of the Empire. Ellison does not elaborate on his experience at Te Aute but noting that his 'real introduction to the game' occurred at the college, suggests that it was there he learnt to accept defeat in 'good spirit' along with knowledge on the finer points on forward play.[85]

The contemporary Maori scholar Brendan Hokowhitu regards Ellison's claim of originality for the Native team's style of play as, 'an exemplary statement of *tino rangatiratanga*'.

This term, more literally meaning chieftainship, is commonly used as an expression of Maori self-determination.[86] Hokowhitu goes on to suggest that the subsequent historical forgetting of the Native team in New Zealand relinquishes an opportunity for symbolic recognition of an incipient common culture through rugby. The depiction of the 1905 All Blacks team as the 'Originals' and 'trailblazers' in the sport, not only denies the Native team its historical significance but also erased an important cultural connection between Maori and Pakeha.[87] The subsequent history of self-determination for Maori within New Zealand rugby has been one of ongoing struggle, a struggle, as Hokowhitu suggests via Marqusee, involving not only the refusal of oppression but an index of collective and individual creativity.[88] The dominant image of Maori within rugby as hyper-masculine and violent shows little understanding of the cultural impact of Maori on the sport, and the cultural significance of the sport to Maori. Although the Maori elite within rugby may have displayed 'both the strength to lead and the weakness to follow', given the colonial origins of rugby and the related link to such institutions as Te Aute, the involvement of the select school-trained elite, such as Ellison, has been crucial to Maori being able to embrace the game more generally.[89]

Sport and colonialism: the 'long revolution'

In *The Black Jacobins* C.L.R. James examined how the Haitian revolution led by Toussaint L'Ouverture arose from African culture tinged with political radicalism born of Western idea. This mixture of influence encouraged James to regard the slaves engaged in revolt as responsible for the making of their history and legitimating the struggle against colonial oppression.[90] The struggle within sport against colonialism is at best a 'long revolution', but such is the case with culture as the title of Williams's book of that name was meant to illustrate. James's *Beyond a Boundary* gives view to this long revolution in motion, the great black West Indian cricketers playing to the 'code' of the game but at the same time carrying the struggle of their people. This is not to suggest a subversive or conspiratorial struggle against the code. The likes of Constantine and Worrell, as with James himself, loved the sport of cricket too much to use it in such an undertaking. Their belief in the aesthetics of cricket was matched by an admiration for the game's moral virtues. They never regarded cricket as racist, only the social relations imposed on the sport through the circumstances of colonialism could be thus indicted. For these aestheticians much about the goodness of life can be learnt from cricket when played according to the unfettered humanistic spirit of the game.

In an excellent biography on C.L.R. James, Paul Buhle alludes to cricket being double-edged, 'It "proved" to the colonizer ... that "civilizing" had been a successful mission; and to the colonized that civilization was by no means the monopoly of the mother country but a larger game that anyone could play'.[91] Although cricket arrived as the game of the colonizers, unlike other forms of culture and elite institutions, it could not remain the exclusive preserve of white colonists or the local black middle class. As James's famous title indicates, cricket embraced as popular art in the West Indian islands moved beyond social boundaries of privilege and opened up a common culture that bonded the scholarship boy James to the Trinidadian working class. Within this context of lived cultural experience a Caribbean way of cricket emerged, and Manley thus speaks of a natural fluency and attack; James's reference to *style* is reinterpreted by Hector as *black style*. The historical success of the West Indies and New Zealand national teams in cricket and rugby respectively, prompts thoughts of the empire striking back.[92] However, usage of this familiar cinema-speak phrase risks trivializing the cultural significance of cricket and rugby in the places that are the West Indies and New Zealand and, more problematically, failing to observe the *cultural traffic* of sport that moves within the relationships that are the Caribbean and the Antipodes.

Notes

[1] Lowerson, *Sport and the English Middle Classes*, provides an historical account that lends to the idea of golf and tennis being *made* by the middle classes.

[2] Ibid., 51.

[3] Ibid., 135.

[4] Birley, *Land of Sport and Glory*, 118–19.

[5] Scruton, *On Hunting*, 69.

[6] Ibid.

[7] Ibid.

[8] Trollope cited in Lowerson, *Sport and the English Middle Classes*, 4.

[9] Trevelyan, *English Social History*, 406.

[10] Itzkowitz, *Peculiar Privilege*, 25.

[11] Ibid., 177.

[12] Ibid.

[13] Scruton, *On Hunting*, 40–1.

[14] Itzkowitz, *Peculiar Privilege*, 23.

[15] Orwell, 'Notes on Nationalism', 411.

[16] Jacobson, 'Rosebery and Liberal Imperialism', 86.

[17] Holt, *Sport and the British*, 212.

[18] Ibid.

[19] Mangan, 'Britain's Chief Spiritual Export', 2.

[20] Nandy, *The Tao of Cricket*, 1.

[21] Guha, *A Corner of a Foreign Field*.

[22] Ibid., 4.

[23] Ibid., 5.

[24] Ibid.

[25] Ibid., 12–13.

[26] Ibid., 13.

[27] Ibid., 33–4.

[28] Ibid., 35–6.

[29] Manley, *A History of West Indies Cricket*, 22.

[30] Details of these cricket test series are taken from Tyler, *The Illustrated History of Test Cricket*.

[31] Cummings, 'The Ideology of West Indian Cricket', 25.

[32] Stoddart, 'Cricket and Colonialism', 251.

[33] Ibid.

[34] Gramsci, *Selections from the Prison Notebooks*, 10–12.

[35] For example, Connell, *Ruling Class, Ruling Culture*.

[36] For some examples in relation to sport see Hughson, Inglis, and Free, *The Uses of Sport*, 121–32.

[37] Gramsci, *Selections from the Prison Notebooks*, 12.

[38] Hector, 'One Eye On the Ball, One Eye On the World'.

[39] Manley, *A History of West Indies Cricket*, 60.

[40] Ibid., 61.

[41] His position on this issue is emphatically stated in Constantine, *Cricket in the Sun*, 62: 'The West Indies teams, mainly composed as they always are of coloured players, should have a coloured captain … every coloured player who has ever turned out in an international side has been conscious of it, and it rots the heart out of our cricket, and always will until it is changed'.

[42] Anglin, 'The Political Development of the West Indies', 41.

[43] Manley, *A History of West Indies Cricket*, 123.

[44] Ibid., 148–9.

[45] Ibid., 157.

[46] Ibid., 158.

[47] Ibid., 129.

[48] James, 'Sir Frank Worrell', 202.

[49] Stoddart, 'Sport, Colonialism and Struggle', 117.

[50] James, *Beyond a Boundary*.

[51] Ibid., ix.

[52] Ibid., 65.

[53] Ibid., 26.

[54] Tiffin, 'Cricket, Literature and the Politics of De-colonisation', 191.

[55] Ibid.

[56] James, *The Black Jacobins*; James, *American Civilisation*.

[57] Farred, 'The Maple Man', 172–3.

[58] James, 'Marxism and the Intellectuals', 114.

[59] For further discussion of the relevance of Williams's 'cultural materialism' to sport, see Hughson, Inglis, and Free, *The Uses of Sport*, 129–32.

[60] James, 'What is Art?', *Beyond a Boundary*, Chap. 16.

[61] Ibid., 197.

[62] Ibid., 199.

[63] Collingwood, *The Principles of Art*, 147.

[64] James, 'Kanhai: A Study in Confidence', 165.

[65] Ibid., 171.

[66] James, *Beyond a Boundary*, 93. At this point James is discussing the Trinidadian cricketer of the 1920s, Wilton St Hill, but his description could equally apply to Kanhai as a more recent representative of the West Indian people.

[67] Naipaul, 'Cricket', 22.

[68] James, 'Letter to V.S. Naipaul'.

[69] James, *Beyond a Boundary*, 261.

[70] Kingwell, 'Keeping a Straight Bat', 379–80.

[71] Smith, *European Vision and the South Pacific*. The book was originally published in 1960.

[72] Ibid., 82–3.

[73] Ibid., 73.

[74] Beilharz, *Imaging the Antipodes*, 78.

[75] Ibid., 97.

[76] Beilharz, 'Bernard Smith', 433–4.

[77] James, *Beyond a Boundary*, 124.

[78] Hill, 'Cricket and the Imperial Connection', 60.

[79] Williams, *Cricket and Race*, 117.

[80] Ryan, *Forerunners of the All Blacks*, 44.

[81] Ibid., 50.

[82] Ibid., 52.

[83] Ibid., 124–7.

[84] Ellison, *The Art of Rugby*, 66.

[85] Ibid., 61.

[86] Hokowhitu, 'Rugby and *Tino Rangatiratanga*', 76.

[87] Ibid., 87.

[88] Ibid., 90.

[89] Cf. Ibid.

90 James, *The Black Jacobins*. For a comparison of this work with E.P. Thompson's *The Making of the English Working Class*, see Linebaugh, 'What if C.L.R. James had met E.P. Thompson in 1792?'

91 Buhle, *C.L.R. James: The Artist as Revolutionary*, 18.

92 *The Empire Strikes Back* was a title used evocatively by authors at the University of Birmingham, Centre for Contemporary Cultural Studies in a study of the emergence of race issues in British culture in the 1970s. In regard to cricket and colonialism Appadurai uses the somewhat more relevant term 'The Empire Plays Back' as a sub-heading in his article 'Playing with Modernity: The Decolonization of Indian Cricket', 38.

References

Anglin, D.G. 'The Political Development of the West Indies'. In *The West Indies Federation: Perspectives on a New Nation*, edited by D. Lowenthal, 35–62. Westport, CT: Greenwood Press, 1961.

Appadurai, A. 'Playing with Modernity: The Decolonization of Indian Cricket'. In *Consuming Modernity: Public Culture in a South Asian World*, edited by C.A. Breckenridge, 23–48. Minneapolis, MN: University of Minnesota Press, 1995.

Beilharz, P. *Imaging the Antipodes: Culture, Theory and the Visual in the Work of Bernard Smith*. Cambridge: Cambridge University Press, 1997.

Beilharz, P. 'Bernard Smith'. In *Dictionary of Cultural Theorists*, edited by E. Cashmore and C. Rojek, 433–4. London: Arnold, 1999.

Birley, D. *Land of Sport and Glory: Sport and British Society 1887–1910*. Manchester: Manchester University Press, 1995.

Buhle, P. *C.L.R. James: The Artist as Revolutionary*. London: Verso, 1988.

Collingwood, R.G. *The Principles of Art*. London: Oxford University Press, 1963.

Connell, R.W. *Ruling Class, Ruling Culture: Studies of Conflict, Power and Hegemony in Australian Life*. Cambridge: Cambridge University Press, 1977.

Constantine, L.N. *Cricket in the Sun*. London: Stanley Paul and Company, 1946.

Cummings, C. 'The Ideology of West Indian Cricket'. *Arena Review* 14, no. 1 (1990): 25–32.

Ellison, T.R. *The Art of Rugby: With Hints and Instructions on Every Point of the Game*. Wellington: Geddis and Blomfield, 1902.

Farred, G. 'The Maple Man: How Cricket Made a Postcolonial Intellectual'. In *Rethinking C.L.R. James*, edited by G. Farred, 165–86. Cambridge, MA: Blackwell, 1996.

Gramsci, A. *Selections from the Prison Notebooks of Antonio Gramsci*, edited by Q. Hoare and G. Nowell Smith. New York: International Publishers, 1971.

Guha, R. *A Corner of a Foreign Field: The Indian History of a British Game*. London: Picador, 2002.

Hector, T. 'One Eye On the Ball, One Eye On the World: Cricket, West Indian Nationalism and the Spirit of C.L.R. James'. In *Cricket and National Identity in the Postcolonial Age: Following On*, edited by S. Wagg, 159–77. London: Routledge, 2005.

Hill, J. 'Cricket and the Imperial Connection: Overseas Players in Lancashire in the Inter-war Years'. In *The Global Sports Arena: Athletic Migration in an Interdependent World*, edited by J. Bale and J. Maguire, 49–62. London: Frank Cass, 1994.

Hokowhitu, B. 'Rugby and *Tino Rangatiratanga*: Early Maori Rugby and the Formation of "Traditional" Maori Masculinity'. *Sporting Traditions* 21, no. 2 (2005): 75–95.

Holt, R. *Sport and the British: A Modern History*. Oxford: Clarendon Press, 1992.

Hughson, J., D. Inglis, and M. Free. *The Uses of Sport: A Critical Study*. London: Routledge, 2005.

Itzkowitz, D.C. *Peculiar Privilege: A Social History of English Foxhunting 1735–1885*. Hassocks: Harvester Press, 1977.

Jacobson, P.D. 'Rosebery and Liberal Imperialism, 1899–1903'. *The Journal of British Studies* 13, no. 1 (1973): 83–107.

James, C.L.R. *The Black Jacobins: Toussaint L'Ouverture and the San Domingo Revolution*. 2nd ed. New York: Vintage Books, 1963.

James, C.L.R. 'Marxism and the Intellectuals'. In *Spheres of Existence: Selected Writings*, 113–30. London: Allison and Busby, 1980.

James, C.L.R. 'Letter to V.S. Naipaul'. In *Cricket: C.L.R. James*, edited by A. Grimshaw, 116–7. London: Allison and Busby, 1986.

James, C.L.R. 'Kanhai: A Study in Confidence'. In *Cricket: C.L.R. James*, edited by A. Grimshaw, 165–71. London: Allison and Busby, 1986.

James, C.L.R. 'Sir Frank Worrell: The Man Whose Leadership Made History'. In *Cricket: C.L.R. James*, edited by A. Grimshaw, 202–5. London: Allison and Busby, 1986.

James, C.L.R. *American Civilisation*, ed. and intro. by A. Grimshaw and K. Hart. Cambridge, MA: Blackwell, 1993.

James, C.L.R. *Beyond a Boundary*. London: Serpent's Tail, 1994.

Kingwell, M. 'Keeping a Straight Bat: Cricket, Civility, and Postcolonialism'. In *C.L.R. James: His Intellectual Legacies*, edited by S.R. Cudjoe and W.E. Cain, 359–87. Amherst, MA: University of Massachusetts Press, 1995.

Linebaugh, P. 'What if C.L.R. James had met E.P. Thompson in 1792?'. In *C.L.R. James: His Life and Work*, edited by P. Buhle, 212–9. London: Allison and Busby, 1986.

Lowerson, J. *Sport and the English Middle Classes 1870–1914*. Manchester: Manchester University Press, 1993.

Mangan, J.A. 'Britain's Chief Spiritual Export: Imperial Sport as Moral Metaphor, Political Symbol and Cultural Bond'. In *The Cultural Bond: Sport, Empire, Society*, edited by J.A. Mangan, 1–10. London: Frank Cass, 1992.

Manley, M. *A History of West Indies Cricket*. London: Andre Deutsch, 1988.

Naipaul, V.S. 'Cricket'. In *The Overcrowded Barracoon and Other Articles*, 17–22. London: Andre Deutsch, 1972.

Nandy, A. *The Tao of Cricket: On Games of Destiny and the Destiny of Games*. New Delhi: Oxford University Press, 2000.

Orwell, G. 'Notes on Nationalism'. In *The Collected Essays, Journalism and Letters of George Orwell, volume III, As I Please (1943–1945)*, edited by S. Orwell and I. Angus, 410–31. Harmondsworth: Penguin, 1970.

Ryan, G. *Forerunners of the All Blacks: The 1888–89 New Zealand Native Football Team in Britain, Australia and New Zealand*. Christchurch: Canterbury University Press, 1993.

Scruton, R. *On Hunting*. London: Yellow Jersey Press, 1998.

Smith, B. *European Vision and the South Pacific*. 2nd ed. New Haven, CT: Yale University Press, 1985.

Stoddart, B. 'Cricket and Colonialism in the English-Speaking Caribbean to 1914: Towards a Cultural Analysis'. In *Pleasure, Profit, Proselytism: British Culture and Sport at Home and Abroad 1700–1914*, edited by J.A. Mangan, 231–57. London: Frank Cass, 1988.

Stoddart, B. 'Sport, Colonialism and Struggle: C.L.R. James and Cricket'. In *Sport and Modern Social Theorists*, edited by R. Giulianotti, 111–28. Houndsmill, Basingstoke: Palgrave Macmillan, 2004.

Tiffin, H. 'Cricket, Literature and the Politics of De-colonisation – The Case of C.L.R. James'. In *Sport, Money, Morality and the Media*, edited by R. Cashman and M. McKernan, 177–93. Kensington, NSW: University of New South Wales Press, 1981.

Trevelyan, G.M. *English Social History: A Survey of Six Centuries, Chaucer to Queen Victoria*. 2nd ed. London: Longmans, Green and Company, 1946.

Tyler, M., ed. *The Illustrated History of Test Cricket: The First Century*. 2nd ed. London: Marshall Cavendish, 1997.

University of Birmingham, Centre for Contemporary Cultural Studies. *The Empire Strikes Back: Race and Racism in 70s Britain*. London: Hutchinson, 1982.

Williams, J. *Cricket and Race*. New York: Berg, 2001.

On sporting heroes

An essay on the sport hero may appear to sit incongruously in a volume bearing the general proposition that sporting cultures have been made collectively by people, within social milieus, across time. While heroic figures do not exist apart from the societies from which they receive adoration, the very notion of hero suggests leadership, innovation and superiority in a way that places the hero above the common person and his/her quotidian existence. Among the best-known writings on the hero within modern history is Thomas Carlyle's series of lectures collected under the title *On Heroes, Hero-worship, and the Heroic in History*.[1] Carlyle's overriding aim was made clear in the opening of his first lecture: 'Universal History, the history of what man has accomplished in this world, is at bottom the History of the Great Men who have worked here.' His further recognition of these 'Great Men' as the 'creators of whatsoever the general mass of men contrived to do or attain' leaves a reader fairly clear that his was precisely the kind of historical interpretation that Thompson sought to overcome in *The Making of the English Working Class*. Against Carlyle, but not in refutation of a Thompsonian influenced position on cultural history, can we reconcile an acceptance of the heroic sporting figure with the view of sporting cultures being made by the people?

An initial point on which to counter Carlyle is his suggestion that the hero serves as a human approximation of god.[2] As discussed in the second essay of this volume, Solon's heralding of the athletic hero in the sixth century BC already challenged such an antiquarian notion of the hero by emphasizing the significance of human input into the heroic deed. From a modern perspective the elevation of the hero to godlike status is problematic for both the secular humanist and the religious believer. For both, the 'exaggerated veneration' of the hero can lead to the abnegation of human responsibility and, at the very least, profound disappointment for the hero-worshipper once the fallibility of the idol is eventually revealed.[3] Hughes-Hallett contends that acceptance of the 'intoxicating allure' of the hero need not result in idolatry, as long as awareness of the hero's 'feet of clay' is maintained.[4] However, she suggests that most people are aware of the foibles of their heroic subjects, and from here, the interesting question arises as to why people claim as heroes individuals they recognize as imperfect. The answer towards which this essay works is that heroism involves the exhibition of greatness tempered by a display of common humanity. Throughout modern history sport has been one of the key cultural arenas from which heroes have emerged. The popularity of heroes must be understood within historical context and only from such grounding can their lasting significance be appreciated. Coverage of heroes across different sports and national contexts is an immense undertaking, beyond the scope of a single essay. Therefore, I concentrate on a number of sport heroes in relation to key themes. Much of the discussion focuses on baseball in the United States. While baseball is often considered insularly American it has produced heroic figures whose stories have universal appeal.

Writing in the 1840s, as he was, Carlyle declared his heroic subjects, 'Prophets, Poets, Priests', to 'belong to the old ages'.[5] His categories are not easily deployed to examine the modern form of sport hero that has emerged since around the turn of the twentieth century and, even less so, the sport hero of the contemporary mass and electronically mediated age. Hughes-Hallett suggests that we are fortunate to live in a time of peace when our heroes are drawn from popular culture – 'footballers, rock stars and models'[6] – rather than more serious arenas of public affairs such as politics and the military. Accordingly, she appears to support the notion that a happy country is one without heroes.[7] In contemporary western society, Hughes-Hallett claims, hero-worship has become a matter of 'collective frivolity' whereby people give their adoration to sport stars and other prominent figures within popular culture. The point is clear enough and at a superficial level not contentious. However, the reference to frivolity risks underestimating the significance of popular culture within the twentieth century, and, therefore, the role of the sport hero within its history.

Towards a definition of sport heroism

The essay considers the sport hero as a type of cultural hero, who may be understood according to two distinct yet related categories: the *prowess hero* and the *moral hero*. These distinctions bear some relation to two of the meanings given for the word hero in *The Oxford English Dictionary*:[8]

> The man [*sic*] who forms the subject of an epic; the chief male personage in a poem, play or story; he in whom the interest of the story or plot is centred.

> A man [*sic*] who exhibits extraordinary bravery, firmness, fortitude, or greatness of soul, in any course of action, or in connexion with any pursuit, work or enterprise; a man admired and venerated for his achievements and noble qualities.

Let us proceed via discussion of these meanings, prowess and moral heroism, in relation to sport. The term 'prowess hero', taken from Coffin and Cohen, is a doing hero whose feats were relayed to the people by whatever means of communication prevailed at given points in history.[9] With the advent and widespread availability of television, sporting heroes could actually be seen rather than read or heard about. Their prowess – display of expertness – became a matter of visible achievement. Sporting prowess, may be regarded as either scientific or aesthetic, the notion of cultural hero clearly favouring the latter bias, although sometimes artistry might be confused or conflated with a discussion of science as we see further on in the case of baseball great Ty Cobb.

To understand prowess heroism in aesthetic terms it is pertinent to return to James's discussion of artistry in *Beyond a Boundary*. Sporting heroism for James is displayed by those players responsible for the *drama* of cricket. Bradman, Grace, Constantine and Worrell are amongst the heroes responsible for the dramatic moments that make up the 'total spectacle' of cricket. Importantly, though, while this hero emerges within the drama of the cricket match – and thus in analogous relationship to the protagonist of a play or novel – he is at once the artist responsible for the dramatic performance in which he appears. The great player embodies and exemplifies 'style', the 'significant form' that makes cricket visually beautiful. James's example of the cricketer thus shows how the prowess hero in sport is doubly invested with aesthetic quality as artist and artistic subject. These dimensions of heroism are distinct but not unrelated. An appreciation of their potential unity can be gleaned from the literary criticism of the poet and dramatist T.S. Eliot. Eliot also provides unexpected insight into an understanding of the relationship between the sport hero and his/her viewing public.

In his early essay 'Tradition and the Individual Talent' (1919) Eliot argues that the mark of the great poet lies in the awareness of the literary tradition and in the ability to write from a point of articulation with that tradition. Eliot thus speaks of a 'historical sense', which 'involves a perception, not only of the pastness of the past, but of its presence'.[10] Possession of historical sense 'makes a writer... acutely conscious of his place in time, of his contemporaneity'.

Accordingly, Eliot suggests that the heroic mission of the poet lies not in pretension to individual acclaim but in a 'continual surrender' of egoism to the pursuit of 'standards of the past'.[11] Eliot's related notion of 'depersonalization' might appear at odds with the familiar understanding of the sports hero as virtuoso.[12] Even heroics in team sports tend to be attributed to the outstanding performer who rises above those around them. However, this notion of depersonalization has nothing to do with submitting to team-mates. The self-sacrifice of the artistic hero is not to peers but to the heroic tradition to which he/she stands in connection. Sporting heroes possess an 'historical sense' of their achievement and in some cases this extends beyond the realm of sport to the cultural historical significance of sport in their time. Towards the conclusion of the essay the relationship between prowess and moral heroism in sport is discussed in this regard.

While sport may be likened to art, the sportsperson's recognition of his/her artistic achievement remains somewhat different to that of the painter or poet. Unlike the artist, who may have a highly developed knowledge of their connection to an artistic lineage, the sportsperson cannot be expected to have an intellectualized appreciation of tradition. Sport does not have a comparable intellectual history to the fine and literary arts, it does not have particular movements and schools in the manner of art, although outstanding sportspersons can leave a stylistic legacy and some might be said to revolutionize their sport. Sporting history is most commonly recounted in 'facts' stemming from the modern fascination with quantification, as discussed by Allen Guttmann in his well-known book *From Ritual to Record*. Lists of the greatest baseball players of all-time appear more relative when based on one or other statistical method rather than subjective assessment. Sporting records provide a constant reminder of the past as participants and spectators are alerted by the holders of 'expert' knowledge when a new height is within reach. Accordingly, the past is used as an index of achievement to be exceeded, and measurement rather than aesthetics becomes the paramount concern of sporting performance. As noted by Guttmann, even balletic sports such as figure-skating and gymnastics have been quantified to the extent that their star performers are lauded more for their maximum scores rather than the beauty of their movement.[13]

In more recent work Guttmann suggests that the modern sporting obsession with record breaking represents a triumph of 'instrumental rationalization' over aesthetics. He extends Hoberman's argument on technological intrusion into sport to claim, that in the near future, 'mortal engines will be our heroes'.[14] While futurists such as Marinetti might have heralded the arrival of a dynamic heroism in sport via technology, this understanding sits incongruously against the romantic perception of the hero which emerged earlier as a riposte to industrialism. Notable in explanation of the latter is Bernard Smith's essay 'The Death of the Artist as Hero'.[15] Smith notes three historical occasions when the artist emerges as a 'culture-hero'. Relevant to the present discussion is the third occasion in the late eighteenth century when the artist struggles to maintain an aesthetic identity in defiance of the forces of uniformity that accompanied industrialism's prevailing division of labour. Although a comparable 'industrialization' does not occur in sport until modernization gathered pace initially in the US in the early twentieth century, Smith's discussion of art offers an interesting parallel. On the culture-hero's reclamation of artistic practice Smith remarks:

> He now finds himself, as he clings to his own personalized mode of production, increasingly estranged from technological man. His achievements take on an increasingly fictive, ideological form. His activities become a psychological surrogate for mechanized man; he becomes the living persona of that human freedom which lingered in the productive process until the forces of inorganic nature were controlled and substituted for man as the prime mover in production.[16]

There is a 'tragic element' to such heroism because the modern hero tends to look back in hope of reviving an aesthetic sensibility from the past.[17] In some cases the modern hero becomes engulfed by disappointment and cynicism as the struggle to find artistic expression goes unfulfilled. Such is the plight of the 'superfluous' hero of Russian literature exemplified by the character Pechorin in Lermontov's novel *A Hero of Our Time*.[18] Pechorin becomes so disenchanted with modern society and its inhabitants that the idealism of his youth turns to hubris and misanthropy. This type of literary figure from the 1800s can be read as a precursor to the anti-hero that emerges in twentieth-century cultural life. Writing in the 1970s Gary Smith described the sport anti-hero as a person who, while 'admired for their ability', is publicly 'despised because they are too haughty and overbearing'.[19] Smith's examples of sports anti-heroes are two iconic figures from the 1960s–1970s, the American football player Joe Namath and Muhammad Ali. As Smith suggests, these figures came to prominence at a rather distinct historical juncture and their eschewing of conventional heroic qualities earned them kudos within the youth counterculture of the time. Of course, Ali's historical significance is greater than Namath's, extending well beyond the time of his sporting achievement. Possibly the most famous figure in sporting history, his redemptive anti-heroism informs the concluding discussion of this essay.

The Anti-hero and the quest for perfection: John McEnroe

The boastful and controversial sport anti-hero predates modernity. The Athenian Alcibiades won an unheralded three prizes for chariot racing at the Olympic Games of 416 BC, yet despite initially being heralded as a hero, his extravagant displays of wealth and success lost him favour amongst a democratically minded people.[20] Alcibiades may have ultimately fallen victim to his natural gifts. His beautiful looks and superb physique 'made him an object, not only of lust, but also of worship' and Plutarch referred to his irresistible 'personal magnetism'.[21] Yet, description of him cavorting in a long purple robe conjures an image of flamboyant and camp-obnoxious professional wrestlers, the hyper-antiheroes of contemporary sport. Good looks and charisma are traits often associated with the sport anti-hero. One of Joe Namath's biographers claims the footballer had a comparable impact on women to that of Elvis Presley.[22] However, although beauty may be said to exist in the eye of the beholder, mention of good looks does not usually feature in discussion of one the most notorious of modern sport anti-heroes, the tennis champion John McEnroe.

Peter Blackman of the London *Evening Standard* has noted, McEnroe will be remembered primarily for his on-court tantrums rather than his supreme tennis skills and thus by the derogatory sobriquet 'Superbrat'.[23] A more sympathetic account, one that allows for a simultaneous view of McEnroe as anti-hero and prowess hero, is offered by Tim Adams in his excellent book *On Being John McEnroe*.[24] Adams attributes McEnroe's wayward genius to his quest for perfection in tennis. When court officials made rulings that McEnroe believed to be incorrect and thus a hindrance to his quest for perfect tennis, he could not control his outrage. Indeed, not to protest vehemently would have been contrary to his sense of justice. McEnroe's frustration, according to Adams, was exacerbated by the early retirement of Bjorn Borg. To achieve perfection McEnroe required a comparably supreme rival. In his sporting lifetime, the only such rival was Borg. Adams portrays McEnroe as a dejected and dissatisfied figure without Borg as foil for his own virtuosity.

McEnroe's reputation for unruliness became particularly prominent in Britain following his flouting of the gentlemanly etiquettes associated with the Wimbledon championship. Although the rules of tennis allow a player to question umpiring decisions, the convention, certainly in the English game, is not to do so.[25] McEnroe might thus be condemned for failing to honour tradition, or, conversely, lauded for challenging sporting codes steeped in middle-class pleasantry that stifle the improvement of championship tennis. He will undoubtedly be remembered as a prowess hero but his status as a moral hero remains contentious. A purely personal quest for athletic perfection would not be deemed heroic, yet McEnroe's personal quest was accompanied by a vision of the ultimate sporting contest in tennis. His approximation of this vision in realization stands as his heroic legacy.

The showman and the scientist: Babe Ruth and Ty Cobb

The sport of baseball offers up many examples for the discussion of prowess heroes and related debate over names worthy of such acclaim. Disputation over the respective reputations of Babe Ruth and Ty Cobb provides an interesting case in point. Cobb's professional career, spent in the American league, spanned 24 years, from 1905 with the Detroit Tigers and a final two seasons with the Philadelphia Athletics. Cobb remains one of baseball's most prolific record holders for batting (indeed, as of 2007 he holds the record for the most battling titles held during a career). He was also the long-time record holder for stolen bases. Apart from record holding Cobb was proud of his reputation as a superb baseball strategist and outfielder. He was the first player elected to the Baseball Hall of Fame in 1936.[26] Yet despite Cobb's achievements his fame over time barely matches that of his greatest rival in baseball, Babe Ruth. Ruth began his professional career in 1914 with the Boston Red Sox but established his gargantuan reputation with the New York Yankees in 1920. He remained with the Yankees until 1934 and played out a final season in 1935 with the Boston Braves. Among his record achievements are the most season home runs in a career and the most home runs in a season, his record of 60 home runs in 1927 was famously surpassed by Roger Maris of the New York Yankees in 1961. Ruth's fame within baseball is as the sport's most spectacular slugger. His ascendancy coincided with a rule change whereby umpires would replace the ball once it had become dirty, significantly switching the advantage traditionally shared by pitchers to batters, who latterly had much greater chance of following the flight of the ball once it had left the pitcher's hand. Ruth's 1920 debut year with the Yankees coincided with his remarkable record 'slugging average' – total bases divided by times at bat – of 0.847.[27] His career slugging average in the American League of 0.692 remains unbeaten.

Ruth's nicknames, including the 'Sultan of Swat' and the 'Caliph of Clout' give indication of how his big-hitting game was received by the baseball following public.[28] Tales of Ruth's batting exploits have become part of American folklore. The following story about Ruth in the 1932 World Series appeared in the *Southern Folklore Quarterly* in 1943: 'with a 4-4 score, Babe walked up to the plate, accepted the umpire's call of two strikes, and then pointed his finger toward a spot far out in centre field to indicate where he intended to slam the ball, and put it there'.[29]

Ruth's reputation as a slugger was used by his great rival Cobb as a point of criticism. According to Cobb, Ruth was 'the most dedicated to power of all batters'.[30] He suggests that Ruth was largely responsible for revolutionizing the approach to batting, whereby 'baseball teachers continue to tell boys to dig in and plant both feet, to grasp the bat at the very end and swing with all their might'. To Cobb this trend 'cheapened' the game and detracted from traditional tactics such as hit-and-run, base stealing, bunting, and strategically punching hits with the intention of taking singles.[31] Cobb expressed disappointment in his related suggestion that the Ruth style was largely influential upon subsequent leading batters including Ted Williams and Joe DiMaggio.[32] Interestingly, Cobb referred not to a lost art of batting but of a 'lost science'; the 'big swing' detracts from the 'scientific nuances of what once was an act of skill rather than of simple power'.[33] Cobb's reference to science was perhaps inspired by the title of Fred Pfeffer's book *Scientific Baseball* (originally published in 1889), which Cobb had read as a young man.[34] His personal quest for perfection in baseball involved the 'scientific' marshalling of skills and related plays. Miller Huggins, Ruth's Manager at the Yankees during the 1920s, admitted that baseball purists would more likely prefer Cobb's style of play but declared that the non-expert spectator wants to see Ruth: 'the American fan "likes the fellow who carries the wallop"'.[35]

A dichotomy thus apparently emerges between science and showmanship, but the discussion of heroism in relation to these presumed extremities tends to be overshadowed by the personalities of Cobb and Ruth. Cobb is renowned as one of baseball's most ferocious on-field competitors. In *My Life in Baseball* he describes his approach to playing the game as being completely uncompromising to opponents; baseball is nothing less, according to Cobb's crude Darwinism, than a 'survival of the fittest'.[36] Cobb would take any advantage he could over an opponent and was especially uncompromising in his running for bases. It was widely alleged that Cobb sharpened the spikes on his boots as a weapon against baseman who stood in his way.[37] Cobb was also known as a brawler. In 1919 he challenged umpire Billy Evans to a 'no rules' fight under the stands after being incensed by Evans's rulings in a game against the Washington Nationals. Evans, a former semi-professional boxer, accepted the challenge, but his pugilistic background did not prepare him for Cobb's onslaught. Players and ground-staff eventually stopped the bloody confrontation in fear for Evans's life. This story lends understanding to pitcher Rude Bressler's proclamation that Cobb was the 'most feared man in the history of baseball'.[38]

Cobb's attempt to unsettle opponents extended to extreme sledging described by Ruth's biographer Robert Creamer as 'cruel and humourless'.[39] Creamer tells of Cobb embellishing a rumour about Ruth not changing his underwear to humiliate the Babe in front of his Yankee team-mates. Better-known is Cobb's readiness to air his characteristic Southern racism. He seized on rumours regarding Ruth having African-American ancestry, goading Ruth from the dugout with the names 'nigger' and 'nigger lips'.[40] The two came close to blows on a number of occasions and did exchange punches during a riotous game between the Tigers and the Yankees in 1923.[41]

Ruth's heroic status owed significantly to the well-publicized rivalry with Cobb. Cobb played villain to Ruth's hero; Cobb's character was widely regarded as so vile as to disqualify him from discussion as hero despite his outstanding playing achievements. Ruth was no paragon of virtue and tales of his gluttony, sexual promiscuity and general recklessness off the field – as well as often unruly behaviour on the diamond – go unchallenged. Yet Ruth seemed to inspire fondness, his misdeeds tended to be put down to haplessness rather than malice. Indeed, Ruth's juvenile innocence is an important part of his heroic legend. According to Lipsyte and Levine, Ruth's appeal went beyond baseball to an American public 'caught in changing times'; 'Here was a man who not only embraced the greedy new consumerism of the twenties but also evoked nostalgic longings for a less complicated society where traditional values ruled'.[42]

To paraphrase from Ken Burn's documentary *Baseball*, in an age of conspicuous consumption, Ruth was its most conspicuous consumer.[43] Ruth's common touch helped Americans come to terms with the new culture of extravagance that emerged in the 'Roaring Twenties'. Although extraordinarily talented at his sport, Ruth maintained an image – largely erroneous – of being accessible and, therefore, representative of the average person. Furthermore, while the early 1920s were relatively prosperous, as Lipsyte and Levine suggest, the period was nevertheless socially and politically complex. For those wanting to avoid the anxiety of the times, Ruth was a welcome symbol of simplicity and light-heartedness. In contrast Cobb was a lingering darkness reminiscent of the toughness and brutality of past American life. When Cobb was accused of match fixing in the late 1920s – a charge from which he was exonerated – speculation about other players followed. Yet journalist Henry L. Farrell expressed what might have passed for the public sentiment on Ruth, 'Babe has human frailties, but never would you find him involved in anything as messy as this'.[44]

In one particular way Ruth was reminiscent of the classic fictional hero implanted in the comic-novel character Frank Merriwell. The creation of Gilbert Patten (writing as Burl L. Standish) Merriwell first appeared in the *Tip Top Library* in 1896.[45] Merriwell was an all-round adventure hero with sport prominent amongst his activities. Merriwell starred for his school (Fardale) and university (Yale) in a host of sports, including football, baseball, rowing, boxing and in most track and field events. Unlike Ruth, Merriwell was always fair and modest, sportsmanlike at all times, as well as industrious in studies. Little is said about Merriwell's background and there is a sense of detachment from his parents. In this way, significantly, Merriwell is much like Ruth. Ruth was turned over by his parents to an orphanage cum reform school in Baltimore in 1902.[46] Subsequently, the perception of his success is heightened in terms of individual achievement and there is a sense in which he can be regarded as the child of the nation; his success may thus be metaphorically interpreted, and recast collectively, as that of the American people. Cobb symbolically takes on the role of the villains who opposed Merriwell, the win-at-any-cost bullyboy. In interesting diametrical opposition – and a sign of the shift from idealism that occurred by the 1920s – Merriwell's antagonists were at times noble, but never as noble as he, whereas Ruth was at times ignoble, but never as ignoble as Cobb.[47]

A real life superhero: Christy Mathewson

Patten left the *Tip Top Weekly* in 1912 and the demise of Frank Merriwell soon followed. Other writers continued the Merriwell legend post-Patten until 1914, and he was revived in comic-strip form in the 1930s. However, the 'authentic' Merriwell effectively departed with Patten, this to the detriment of the common good it has been argued. According to Gary Smith, Merriwell's 'disappearance is lamented by many for the reason that his stories taught a sense of values that are missing today … there has never been anyone to really take his place'.[48] Nor has there been anyone to take the place of the real life ballplayer most often likened to Merriwell in character, Christy Mathewson.[49] Mathewson, one of baseball's most successful pitchers, played for the New York Giants from 1900–15. He was traded to the Cincinnati Reds in 1916 where, after one game, he became manager before taking up military service in 1918. Mathewson's reputation for fair-play and integrity in sport is second to none and this, in combination with his outstanding pitching ability and blond-haired, blue-eyed good looks, cast his heroic image in the light of Merriwell. Mathewson was different to other baseball players. Of rural middle-class background he was well educated and articulate, and retained the moral principles of a Baptist upbringing, so much so that he was nicknamed 'the Christian gentleman' by sports journalists.[50]

During the first decade of the 1900s, Mathewson became the embodiment of what can be regarded as an American version of muscular Christianity. Mathewson's emergence as a major league player coincided with the Presidency of Theodore Roosevelt. Roosevelt promoted the humanistic ideal of a healthy mind and healthy body, initiating a public agenda for physical education that was followed by some subsequent presidents, notably John F. Kennedy.[51] While Roosevelt may have been genuinely interested in individuals attaining good health through sportive activity, his policy of 'athleticism' was aimed ultimately at the development of moral character.[52] He spoke of the 'strenuous life' as the way toward 'splendid ultimate triumph'.[53] Mathewson's diligence as a student of baseball was the epitome of Roosevelt's doctrine. After a less than impressive start with the Giants, Mathewson, under the tutelage of Manager John McGraw, dedicated himself to honing his pitching technique. He was soon to emerge as baseball's leading pitcher, partly attributable to his detailed knowledge of opposing player's batting styles acquired through keen and painstaking scrutiny. McGraw said of Mathewson, 'In a few years he had in that wonderful brain of his a chart of nearly every ballplayer in the National League'.[54]

Mathewson's biographer, Philip Seib, makes interesting reference to the influential book *The Promise of American Life*, published in 1909 by the liberal nationalist writer Herbert Croly.[55] Croly (via his former mentor George Santayana) claimed that American society needed 'heroes and saints' who could inspire 'the common citizen', not to deeds of 'heroic proportion' but to 'sincere and enthusiastic imitation'.[56] Seib suggests that Mathewson, more than any other public figure, fitted the role model sought by Croly. Although not named by Roosevelt, Mathewson, via the popularity that he undoubtedly attracted, can be seen in historical hindsight as an ideological support for the liberalist notion of athleticism. Relatedly, Mathewson certainly did much, if unwittingly, to improve baseball's rowdy image, making it more acceptable to the middle class. However, this observation should not be construed to suggest that Mathewson was an exclusively middle-class hero. His popularity was widespread, suggesting that the decency in sport that he projected was commonly sought. Furthermore, even if Mathewson did serve as an ideological symbol for Roosevelt's so-called 'progressivism' this need not detract from the genuineness of his moral integrity.

The satirist and sportswriter Ring Lardner – not given to sentimentality – so respected Mathewson that he served as publicity chairman of the Christy Mathewson Memorial Foundation upon Mathewson's passing in 1925 with tuberculosis contracted during war service.[57] Between his retirement as a player and his early death Mathewson maintained involvement in baseball as a manager and as a media commentator, and in both capacities his ethical courageousness came to the fore. In 1918, as manager of the Cincinnati Reds, Mathewson suspended pitcher Hal Chase for 'indifferent play' as a means of removing the well-known, but unproven, cheat and match fixer from his team.[58] The following year Mathewson's expert opinion gave prominent sportswriter Hugh Fullerton confidence to sound a warning that the World Series had been 'fixed' following the bribing of a number of Chicago White Sox players, in what has become known within sports history as the 'Black Sox Scandal'.[59] However, care has to be taken against memorialisation in sport biography, and a critical reader needs to be on guard even with a well-measured biography, such as Seib's on Mathewson.

For example, how might we read the eulogizing statements, '[Mathewson] defined athletic and moral excellence, bridging sport and national culture' and 'Mathewson mirrored and influenced the changing character of America … His story and the story of his country flow together'?[60] Standing alone these statements place Mathewson within a facile evocation of nationalist spirit, yet, as Seib's book shows, Mathewson deserves more than a mere populist portrayal within American cultural history. The intellectual difficulty is that in attempting to avoid popularizing Mathewson we sociologize him in class terms. Mathewson, undoubtedly, offered a respectable face within baseball to the middle class but to reduce him to a particular class identity disconnects Mathewson from the 'structure of feeling' in early twentieth-century United States. His moral heroism cannot be appreciated in analytical detachment from the lived experience of the time and the cultural significance of baseball to that time. Similar consideration can be given to subsequent examples of moral heroism, and, from the sport of baseball, few names deserve such attention as that of Jackie Robinson.

The 'race man' cometh: Jackie Robinson

In his introduction to the reprinted edition of Jackie Robinson's book *Baseball Has Done It*, film director Spike Lee declares Robinson an 'inspiration in his life' and despairs that with the passing of time, Robinson has been forgotten by African-American athletes.[61] Lee claims that African-American athletes not only owe a debt to Robinson's memory for the privilege of their own careers, a debt that involves not just knowing that Robinson was the first African-American to play major league baseball but having some awareness of the cultural setting during

Robinson's time as a pro. Only from such awareness can the enormity of Robinson's achievement and his incredible personal resolve be appreciated. The detail of the Robinson legend is well rehearsed. A successful all-round sportsman Robinson commenced playing professional baseball, following war service, for the Negro American League team the Kansas City Monarchs. He was brought to the attention of Brooklyn Dodgers President and General Manager Branch Rickey, an enthusiast for dismantling the colour barrier within the major leagues. Rickey signed Robinson in 1945 to play for the Dodgers farm club The Montreal Royals with a view to him transferring to the Dodgers upon satisfactory performance. After only one season Robinson graduated to the Dodgers and in April 1947 played first base in the opening game against the Boston Braves.[62]

As a player Robinson turned out to be a star. The importance of this was apparent enough to Rickey; from the outset he recognized that the success of his so-called 'great experiment' depended on a number of 'essential points', including selecting a player at least good enough to hold his own in the majors.[63] Robinson outdid this expectation, winning two rookie of the year awards in his debut season and, over his career, being a key player in six World Series with the Dodgers. Robinson's stardom was a matter of style as much as statistics. He was especially known for bringing deceptive base play back to baseball in a way that had not been seen since the days of Ty Cobb.[64] Another 'essential point' of Rickey's was to choose a player who could attract a strong African-American following. Robinson also succeeded in this regard: from his opening game Robinson drew a large African-American audience to major league baseball.[65] His entrée commenced 'integration' not only on the playing field, but also gave impetus to the demise of the colour segregated baseball crowd. Robinson's break into the majors was soon followed by other African-American players, which, while breaking baseball's 'colour line', depleted the then-named Negro leagues from whence these players came. These leagues have been recognized as 'an important black economic and cultural institution' and their resultant collapse lamented.[66] As discussed below, Robinson's role in this outcome has not gone without criticism.

Robinson's esteem as a moral hero – as indicated by Spike Lee's eulogy – is largely based on his perceived martyrdom as a man who suffered for the betterment of his people. This view pertains directly to Robinson's willingness to comply with Branch Rickey's demand that he not react emotionally to the racist taunting that he would inevitably face once playing with the Dodgers. As recounted by Robinson in a gripping recollection of his meeting with Rickey, Rickey questioned, 'Have you got the guts to play the game no matter what happens?' and then proceeded to subject Robinson to the verbal, and even physical, abuse he would face on the field.[67] Rickey's dry run accurately portended what Robinson would experience. Robinson was racially taunted throughout the season he played with the Royals and the vilification intensified once he turned out for the Dodgers. Robinson's composure was pushed to the limit during an early 1947 three-game series against the Philadelphia Phillies at Brooklyn's Ebbets Field. Robinson was so angered by the abuse he received from the Philadelphia dugout, led by team manager Ben Chapman, that he momentarily considered smashing one of the culprits with his 'despised black fist'.[68] But Robinson did not react and was supported by fellow Dodgers (not all of whom had initially welcomed him onto the team) who complained to the press about Robinson's mistreatment by Philadelphia players. Subsequent news reports condemned the racist abusers, Chapman in particular, and complimented Robinson for his 'admirable restraint' and gentlemanly conduct.[69]

Cornell West hails Robinson as a 'transracial figure beloved by blacks and whites who rails against the absurdities of white racism and the seductive security of black xenophobia'.[70] According to West, Robinson 'is a great American hero who refuses to be a mythical hero'. Robinson's heroism is not mythical because it comes from a genuine projection of his humanity.

Robinson's struggle was to have his 'God-given humanity seen ... by those who questioned it'.[71] By achieving this in baseball he played no small part in exposing both the senselessness and unfairness of racial discrimination in other areas of American life. Robinson's appearance for the Dodgers occurred only three years after the publication of The Carnegie Foundation funded project *The American Dilemma*, led and authored by the Swedish sociologist Gunnar Myrdal.[72] The *dilemma* to which Myrdal's voluminous report refers is the existence of racial prejudice towards, and inequality of, the African-American population within a polity supposedly based on the democratic ideals of 'liberty, equality, justice, and fair opportunity for everybody'.[73] Myrdal thus contended that the 'Negro problem' becomes the 'white man's problem'. The moral guilt of racial disparity necessarily weighs on the conscience of those who subscribe to the *American Creed*. However, Myrdal suggested that segregation helped to ease the white conscience by creating a 'convenience of ignorance' whereby the black persons' plight remains unknown.

Branch Rickey's 'great experiment', within which Robinson was the chief protagonist, was intended as a direct assault upon segregation in baseball. Although Rickey's motives have been questioned over the years, mainly the suggestion that he was driven by the financial gain to be had from bringing black players to the Dodgers, his 'great experiment' put into action the position on racial equality in baseball to which he had long been committed. Robinson has defended him tirelessly in this regard.[74] Rickey was drawn to the writing on race by the sociologist Frank Tannenbaum, and used that theorist's term 'physical proximity' to describe not just what was needed to bring the races together in baseball but in American society at large.[75]

Whatever the intention, the so-called 'integration' that occurred following the success of Robinson has, as indicated above, been criticized for destroying the Negro leagues, the existence of which seemingly relied upon the continuation of segregation. In the most vitriolic of criticisms the writer Amiri Baraka describes Robinson as a 'synthetic coloured guy' and his compliance with Rickey's interventionist agenda as a 'farce' that conned African-Americans.[76] Malcolm X's antagonistic correspondence with Robinson in the early 1960s suggests a similar view, by accusing Robinson of kowtowing to 'white bosses', principally Branch Rickey, and not being a true champion to African-American people. X's barb was directed as much at Robinson's post-sporting career political activities as a civil rights moderate as it was at his role in baseball's integration.[77]

The Negro leagues undoubtedly had their own heroes, 'invisible men' as the title of Don Rogosin's book describes them, who lived in the shadow of Robinson, as the subtitle of a biography on the great pitcher Satchel Paige suggests.[78] Paige is an interesting case in point, a charismatic figure he had a Babe Ruth like popularity within Negro baseball from the 1920s through to the 1940s.[79] Paige played for a number of teams in Negro leagues as well as in Cuba and Mexico. At the time of Robinson's signing by Rickey, Paige was a team-mate of Robinson on the Kansas City Monarchs. Paige, having starred for a number of years in Negro leagues and being highly regarded by leading players in the majors, was shocked and 'hurt' by Robinson's elevation after only one year as a professional in so-called blackball.[80] Paige, in his early 40s, was the oldest rookie in major league baseball when he joined the Cleveland Indians for a very successful season in 1948, the year after Robinson's debut for the Dodgers. However, he was too old by this stage for sustained success in the majors, although he continued playing baseball at one level or another into his final years. Whether Robinson deserved his chance ahead of other leading black players such as Paige is a moot point, but acknowledging the unfairness of denial so long experienced by Paige need not detract from Robinson's heroic achievement.

Nor need the demise of the Negro leagues be a matter of discredit to Robinson. As culturally important as these leagues were to African-Americans, they essentially existed on the basis of the racial discrimination that Robinson endeavoured to overcome. Furthermore, care needs to be taken with sentimentalizing the Negro leagues. According to Daniel A. Nathan, 'For some … African Americans, remembering and reconstructing the Negro leagues is an act of recovery … a way of reconnecting with a simultaneously "heroic and tawdry" historical episode'.[81] Robinson's heroism is necessarily at odds with such remembering as long as he is held accountable for the demise of the Negro leagues. But while these leagues should be historically recounted, as they have been in the work of writers such as Rogosin and Tygiel, their history need not be used to recreate a binary opposition between separatism and integration. As Nathan suggests, via Early, the disappointment of race relations post-integration has resulted in the tendency to romanticize black community life under segregation.[82] However, in the 1940s the need for integration was widely supported by African-Americans as a matter of urgency. Rickey was thus able to draw upon support for his plan to sign Robinson from black intellectuals and community leaders as well as sportswriters such as Wendell Smith.[83] Even the politically radical performer and former athlete Paul Robeson actively supported the desegregation of baseball.[84]

The contradiction of sporting heroines: Althea Gibson and 'Babe' Didrikson

Criticism of Robinson shows, even in the case of this most revered sportsman, that heroism is a contestable status. Such criticism serves a useful function by not allowing the heroic legend to be reduced to populist rhetoric. It is through a critical dialogue that Robinson as hero is able to maintain moral relevance. Robinson remains widely regarded as a historical 'signifier of racial progress and national transformation', a heroic inspiration to other African-Americans who challenged ongoing discrimination in their sports, for example, Arthur Ashe in tennis and Tiger Woods in golf.[85] Prior to Ashe's success in the 1970s, Althea Gibson effectively broke the colour barrier in tennis by becoming the first African-American to play in the US Lawn Tennis Association national championships in 1950.[86] She went on to win the women's singles title at the French championship in 1956 and was women's singles winner at Wimbledon and the US championship in the consecutive years, 1957 and 1958. Gibson's achievement was made against the odds of both class and race. Gibson grew up in the slums of Harlem and was more accustomed to playing basketball and other street games than tennis in early life. Recognition of her talent during a random visit to a neighbourhood tennis court led to Gibson joining the Cosmopolitan Club and being exposed to the etiquettes of Harlem's black middle class.[87] By 1947 Gibson had won the women's singles title in the exclusively black national championship of the American Tennis Association – she subsequently won the next ten ATA women's single titles. Her move into white-dominated tennis brought her fame denied to previously successful African-American women, including the earlier doyen of the ATA, Ora Washington. Under the conditions of segregation Washington was refused the chance to play against the great American champion of the 1920s and 1930s Helen Wills, significantly curtailing the fame that she may have otherwise experienced.[88]

Althea Gibson is also remembered for bringing an early 'era of explosive power' to women's tennis.[89] Such an association is more problematic for a female sport hero than for the male sport hero. Writing in the 1930s, Lewis Mumford observed that for a sport hero to be a woman, 'her qualities must be Amazonian in character'.[90] As Jennifer Hargreaves notes, the female sport hero, or heroine, faces a contradiction by very definition.[91] The idea of the hero has been framed in the image of man – as the definitions stated at the outset of the essay indicate – and the socio-biological construction of the term has compounded the problem. Heroism being achievement-oriented aligns with the functionalist sociological view of the instrumental male and is at odds with the converse view of the female as expressive and naturally given to nurturing rather than family-external goal attainment.[92] Thus for a woman to be heroic places her feminine identity in jeopardy. This contradiction has had particular implications for women who have aspired to the heights of heroism in sport. An interesting case is Mildred 'Babe' Didrikson, an outstanding all-round athlete. Didrikson initially excelled in 'amateur' baseball before a phenomenal one-day performance at the American Athletic Union championships in 1931 led to her inclusion in the track and field team for the 1932 Olympics in Los Angeles. Didrikson won gold in the javelin and 80 metre hurdles, setting new world records, and was denied victory in the high jump because judges frowned on her unconventional technique. In 1935 she took up golf and through the 1940s and into the 1950s was the world's leading player, winning every major women's title.[93]

Didrikson, a sportsperson possibly unrivalled in versatility, is unarguably one of history's foremost prowess heroes. She may also be considered as a moral hero for her refusal to conform to the feminine stereotype, and in so doing overcame the contradiction of heroism discussed above. Didrikson, often referred to as a 'tomboy', forthrightly admitted that she had no interest in being a glamorous woman. She wore her hair unfashionably short and was known for not wearing dresses or makeup during her athletic career.[94] The press struggled with her image, wanting to laud her sporting accomplishments while downplaying her lack of socially acceptable femininity. Subsequently, journalists made the most out of any skerrick of information to portray Didrikson's womanliness, reference being made to her abilities in sewing, cooking and curtain-making. Didrikson's marriage to wrestler and impresario George Zaharias in 1938 prompted reference to her transformation from a 'man-girl' into a 'feminine woman'.[95]

Althea Gibson was also described as a 'tomboy' and Susan K. Cahn believes press references to her personality 'complexes' insinuated, with pejorative intent, that Gibson was a lesbian.[96] Like Didrikson, Gibson was subsequently reported to have undergone transformation from tomboy to 'little lady' and was elevated to role model figure as 'America's Gibson Girl' once a feminine image had been constructed for her.[97] A more readily adoptable role model was offered by women who appeared to combine high sporting achievement with motherhood. An exemplary historical example is the Dutch athlete Fanny Blankers-Koen, the next great female track and field star after Didrikson, who won four gold medals at the London Olympics in 1948. An avowedly family-orientated woman, Blankers-Koen was heralded as much for her devotion to husband and children as she was for her sporting success.[98]

Conclusion: sport and humanised heroism

The essay has proceeded with a discussion of sport heroes according to two categories: prowess heroes and moral heroes. It concludes with fuller consideration of the relationship between these categories. To foreshadow the concluding point: the categories are best seen to exist in symbiotic relationship to sport heroism. Some sportspersons are regarded as prowess heroes but make no obvious claim to moral heroism. In some cases, as seen with Ty Cobb, a prowess hero's image is severely tarnished by questionable moral behaviour. Mike Tyson provides a modern example in this regard. Conversely, moral heroics in, or associated with, sport need not have any association with prowess heroism. While both heroic dimensions are important to sport heroism, prowess heroism enjoys primacy because of the particularity of prowess in given sports. The moral heroism of a ballplayer may be akin to the moral heroism of an athlete or tennis player. Accordingly, Reetsma notes, 'Only because Muhammad Ali was a great boxer was he other things, too'.[99]

According to Gerald Early, Muhammad Ali and Jackie Robinson stand, arguably, as the 'two most influential American athletes of the twentieth century'.[100] Arguments as to who was the greatest boxer of all time are notoriously heated and irresolvable, yet it is fair to say that Ali would feature prominently in most such discussion. Jackie Robinson's reputation as a baseball player – although he is generally considered one of the great second basemen – is not usually seen as comparable to Ali's as a boxer. Nevertheless, both were undoubtedly prowess heroes in their given sports and their recognition as moral heroes is inextricably related to their sporting kudos. Both have a cultural significance within American history that goes beyond sport yet cannot be detached from it. Their respective moral stances on race were made as sportsman with a gravitas that came with only the highest level of performance accomplishment. And as divergent as they may have been on the race issue – Robinson the 'race man' and Ali the 'man of race'[101] – their moral resilience is what has won them enduring popular respect. Both forced America to face its democratic 'dilemma' as recognized by Myrdal: Robinson, the integrationist, by 'insisting that he was an American' and Ali by bemoaning that he was never accepted as an American.[102]

Contrary to Robinson, Ali supported the concept of segregation, declaring that Black Muslims would be better off either living in certain southern states under secession or to take flight from the US altogether.[103] Although rejecting this view and the arrangement Ali advocated as not in the best interests of democracy, Robinson defended Ali's right within a democratic society to hold and articulate such a position.[104] More important to Robinson was Ali's refusal to be a 'tame Negro' who 'stays in place'. As early as 1964 Robinson appeared to detect the note of irony – subsequently recognized by other writers[105] – in the then Cassius Clay's cry, 'I am the greatest'. Robinson read this as a collective message to African-Americans, not that 'they are greater than anyone else ... but ... that they are just as great as other human beings'. Ali's heroism, like Robinson's, involved the humanizing of his sporting life, an 'actual self-determination' that showed the viewing public 'the enormous possibility of true meaning'.[106] The ability to achieve sporting excellence while projecting a common sense of humanity – behind a façade of vanity in Ali's case – is the gift of the sporting hero. Via the reconciliation of prowess and morality the sporting hero stands simultaneously above and with the people.

Notes

[1] Carlyle, *On Heroes*.

[2] Only Carlyle's early lectures in *On Heroes* concentrate on religious heroes, although an appeal to the religious quality of heroes pervades the series.

[3] Hughes-Hallett, *Heroes*, 3.

[4] Ibid., 4.

[5] Carlyle, 'The Hero as Man of Letters: Johnson, Rousseau, Burns', *On Heroes*, fifth lecture, 143.

[6] Hughes-Hallett, *Heroes*, 2.

[7] Ibid., 330. The notion is derived from Bertolt Brecht's line spoken by the character Galileo in *The Life of Galileo*. The common translation from the German is, 'Unhappy the land where heroes are needed'. Brecht, *The Life of Galileo*, Scene 13, 98.

[8] *The Oxford English Dictionary*, vol.vii, 171.

[9] Coffin and Cohen, *The Parade of Heroes*, 52–3.

[10] Eliot, 'Tradition and the Individual Talent', 49.

[11] Ibid., 52 and 50.

[12] Ibid., 53.

[13] Guttmann, *From Ritual to Record*, 52.

[14] Guttmann, *Sports*, 201.

[15] Smith, 'The Death of the Artist as Hero'.

[16] Ibid., 20.

[17] Ibid., 19.

[18] Lermontov, *A Hero of Our Time*.

[19] Smith, 'The Sport Hero', 117.

[20] Hughes-Hallett, *Heroes*, 56–7.

21   Ibid., 47.

22   Borstein, *SuperJoe*, 4.

23   Blackman, 'Tennis', 96. McEnroe was included in the 250 most famous people of the twentieth century for a BBC documentary series in the early 1990s on the basis of his 'bad behaviour' rather than his tennis playing ability. James, *Fame in the Twentieth Century*, 7.

24   Adams, *On Being John McEnroe*.

25   Ibid., 32.

26   Stump, *Cobb*, 24.

27   Ward and Burns, *Baseball*, 156.

28   Ibid., 159.

29   Coffin and Cohen, *The Parade of Heroes*, 156. While Coffin and Cohen maintain this tale is apocryphal, Paul Gallico gives eye witness testament to its veracity. Gallico also tells of Ruth promising a home-run to a bed-ridden boy in hospital and fulfilling the promise that afternoon. See Gallico, *Farewell to Sport*, 42–3 and 37–8.

30   Cobb, *My Life in Baseball*, 146.

31   Ibid., 145.

32   Ibid., 147.

33   Ibid., 145. These comments appear in Chap. 11 of Cobb, *My Life in Baseball*, 'Batting: The Lost Science'.

34   Stump, *Cobb*, 50.

35   Ward and Burns, *Baseball*, 159.

36   Cobb, *My Life in Baseball*, 280.

37   Cobb is defended against this claim by veteran Detroit sportswriter E.A. Alexander in the preface to Cobb, *My Life in Baseball*, 10–11.

38   Ward and Burns, *Baseball*, 86.

39   Creamer, *Babe*, 329.

40   Ward and Burns, *Baseball*, 159.

41   Stump, *Cobb*, 357.

42   Lipsyte and Levine, *Idols of the Game*, 95.

43   This point is supported by the historian Warren Susman who describes Ruth as 'a heroic producer in the mechanized world of play … an ideal hero for the world of consumption'. Susman, *Culture as History*, 146.

44   Stump, *Cobb*, 383. Ruth defended Cobb against the allegations, saying, 'he's as clean as they come'.

45   Cf. Oriard, *Dreaming of Heroes*, 27–9.

46   Creamer, *Babe*, 29.

47   For an alternative position claiming that Cobb's image as a villain is a recent construction based on contemporary values, see Hathaway, 'Cobb as Role Model'.

48   Smith, 'The Sport Hero', 114.

49   Further to the Merriwell likeness, Mathewson is said to have been the 'model for Lester Chadwick's *Baseball Joe* stories'. Riess, *Touching Base*, 23.

50   Ward and Burns, *Baseball*, 70.

51   Dyerson, 'The Emergence of Consumer Culture', 210–11; Kennedy's position on the importance of physical exercise was set out in a contribution to *Sports Illustrated* in 1960. See Kennedy, 'The Soft American'.

52   Dyerson, 'The Emergence of Consumer Culture', 211.

53   Seib, *The Player*, 31.

54   Ibid., 29.

55   Ibid., 36.

56   Croly, *The Promise of American Life*, 454.

57   Yardley, *Ring Lardner*, 40.

58   Seib, *The Player*, 117.

59 Asinof, *Eight Men Out*, 46–7.

60 Seib, *The Player*, ix and 2.

61 Spike Lee introduction to Robinson, *Baseball Has Done It*.

62 Ward and Burns, *Baseball*, 284–93. For an outstanding lengthy account of Robinson's life and career see Rampersad, *Jackie Robinson*.

63 Holland, 'Mr. Rickey and the Game'.

64 Ward and Burns, *Baseball*, 292.

65 Ibid., 291.

66 Early, 'Baseball and African American Life', 413.

67 Robinson, *I Never Had It Made*, 30–4.

68 Ibid., 59.

69 Ibid., 60.

70 Cornel West introduction to Robinson, *I Never Had It Made*, xi.

71 Ibid., xii.

72 Myrdal, *An American Dilemma*; The link between Robinson and Myrdal's report is briefly discussed in Tygiel, *Baseball's Great Experiment*, 7–9.

73 Myrdal, *An American Dilemma*, volume 1, *The Negro in a White Nation*, lxxii.

74 Robinson claimed Rickey both as 'baseball's most farsighted innovator' and a 'sincere and dedicated idealist', who 'happily … has survived the puny darts of his adversaries'. Robinson, *Baseball Has Done It*, 51. For a contrary view based on Rickey's alleged disinterest in Negro leagues see, Rogosin, *Invisible Men*, 206.

75 Holland, 'Mr. Rickey and the Game', 188.

76 Baraka, *The Autobiography of LeRoi Jones*, 45.

77 For the 1963 correspondence between Jackie Robinson and Malcolm X, see 'An Exchange of Letters' in Tygiel, *The Jackie Robinson Reader*, 237–47.

78 Ribowsky, *Don't Look Back: Satchel Paige in the Shadows of Baseball*.

79 Ibid., 12–13.

80 Ibid., 230–1.

81 Nathan, 'Bearing Witness to Blackball', 466.

82 Ibid.

83 See Smith's 1946 piece 'It Was a Great Day in Jersey' in Tygiel, *The Jackie Robinson Reader*, 95–100.

84 Smith, 'The Paul Robeson–Jackie Robinson Saga and a Political Collision', 177–8. As discussed by Smith, Robinson controversially testified before the House Un-American Activities Committee in regard to Robeson's pro-communist and anti-American government pronouncements.

85 Smart, *The Sport Star*, 137.

86 Blue, *Grace Under Pressure*, 26.

87 Gibson, 'I Always Wanted to be Somebody'.

88 Blue, *Grace Under Pressure*, 27–8.

89 Lichtenstein, 'Net Profits', 64.

90 Mumford, *Technics and Civilization*, 306.

91 Hargreaves, *Heroines of Sport*, 2.

92 Parsons and Bales, *Family, Socialization and Interaction Process*, 45–54.

93 Blue, *Grace Under Pressure*, 69–70 and 110–11.

94 Cahn, *Coming on Strong*, 115–16.

95 Ibid., 214–16.

96 Ibid., 181.

97 Ibid., 214.

98 Ibid., 110.

99 Reetsma, *More Than a Champion*, 14.

100 Early, 'Introduction: Tales of the Wonderboy', ix.

[101] The reference to Robinson as a 'race man' in Ward and Burns, *Baseball*, 284–5 compares interestingly to Ali's self-proclamation as a 'man of race' as recalled by Malcolm X. See Plimpton, 'Miami Notebook: Cassius Clay and Malcolm X', 33.

[102] Early, 'Introduction: Tales of the Wonderboy', ix.

[103] Ali, '*Playboy* Interview', 151.

[104] Robinson, 'Clay Explodes the Liston Myth', 43–44 and 'In Defense of Cassius Clay', 72.

[105] For example, Early, 'Introduction: Tales of the Wonderboy' and Lemert, *Muhammad Ali: Trickster in the Culture of Irony*.

[106] Early, 'Introduction: Tales of the Wonderboy', xiv.

References

Adams, T. *On Being John McEnroe*. London: Yellow Jersey Press, 2004.

Ali, M. '*Playboy* Interview'. In *The Muhammad Ali Reader*, edited by G. Early, 135–62. Hopewell, NJ: Ecco Press, 1998.

Asinof, E. *Eight Men Out: The Black Sox and the 1919 World Series*. New York: Henry Holt, 1987.

Baraka, A. *The Autobiography of LeRoi Jones*. Chicago, IL: Lawrence Hill Books, 1997.

Blackman, P. 'Tennis'. In *Sporting Strife: Rebels and Rebellion in World Sport*, edited by M. Herd, 94–106. London: Ward Lock, 1991.

Blue, A. *Grace Under Pressure: The Emergence of Women in Sport*. London: Sidgwick and Jackson, 1987.

Borstein, L. *SuperJoe: The Joe Namath Story*. New York: Tempo/Grosset and Dunlap, 1969.

Brecht, B. *The Life of Galileo*, trans. J. Willett. London: Eyre Methuen, 1980.

Cahn, S.K. *Coming on Strong: Gender and Sexuality in Twentieth Century Women's Sport*. Cambridge, MA: Harvard University Press, 1994.

Carlyle, T. *On Heroes, Hero-worship and the Heroic Ideal in History*. London: Chapman and Hall, 1889.

Cobb. T. (with Al Stump). *My Life in Baseball*. Lincoln, NE: University of Nebraska Press, 1993.

Coffin, T.P., and H. Cohen. *The Parade of Heroes: Legendary Figures in American Lore*. New York: Anchor Press/Double Day, 1978.

Creamer, R.W. *Babe: The Legend Comes to Life*. New York: Fireside, 1992.

Croly, H. *The Promise of American Life*. Cambridge, MA: Belknap Press of Harvard University, 1965.

Dyerson, M. 'The Emergence of Consumer Culture and the Transformation of Physical Culture: American Sport in the 1920s'. In *Sport in America: From Wicked Amusement to National Obsession*, edited by D.K. Wiggins, 207–23. Champaign, IL: Human Kinetics, 1995.

Early, G., 'Baseball and African American Life'. In *Baseball: An Illustrated History*, edited by G.C. Ward and K. Burns, 412–7. New York: Knopf, 1994.

Early, G. 'Introduction: Tales of the Wonderboy'. In *The Muhammad Ali Reader*, G. Early, vii–xx. Hopewell, NJ: Ecco Press, 1998.

Eliot, T.S. 'Tradition and the Individual Talent'. In *The Sacred Wood: Essays on Poetry and Criticism*, 4th ed., 47–59. London: Methuen, 1934.

Gallico, P. *Farewell to Sport*. New York: Knopf, 1945.

Gibson, A. 'I Always Wanted to be Somebody' (an excerpt from her autobiography, 1958). In *Out of the Bleachers: Writings on Women and Sport*, edited by S.L. Twin, 130–42. New York: Feminist Press, 1979.

Guttmann, A. *From Ritual to Record: The Nature of Modern Sports*. New York: Columbia University Press, 1978.

Guttmann, A. *Sports: The First Five Millennia*. Amherst and Boston, MA: University of Massachusetts, 2004.

Hargreaves, J. *Heroines of Sport: The Politics of Difference and Identity*. London: Routledge, 2000.

Hathaway, T. 'Cobb as Role Model: Ty Cobb in Juvenile Periodical Literature: 1907–29'. *Nine: A Journal of Baseball History and Culture* 11, no. 2 (2003): 64–72.

Holland, G. 'Mr. Rickey and the Game'. In *The Baseball Reader: Favourites from the Fireside Books of Baseball*, edited by C. Einstein, 180–94. New York: Lippincott and Crowell, 1980.

Hughes-Hallett, L. *Heroes: Saviours, Traitors and Supermen*. London: Fourth Estate, 2004.

James, Clive. *Fame in the Twentieth Century*. London: BBC Books, 1993.

Kennedy, J.F. 'The Soft American'. In *Sport and Society: an Anthology*, edited by J.T. Talamini and C.H. Page, 367–72. Boston, MA: Little Brown and Company, 1973.

Lemert, C. *Muhammad Ali: Trickster in the Culture of Irony*. Cambridge: Polity Press, 2003.

Lermontov, M. *A Hero of Our Time*, trans. and intro. by P. Foote. Harmondsworth: Penguin, 1966.

Lichtenstein, G. 'Net Profits'. In *Nike is a Goddess: The History of Women in Sport*, edited by L. Smith, 57–77. New York: Atlantic Monthly Press, 1998.

Lipsyte, R., and P. Levine. *Idols of the Game: A Sporting History of the American Century*. Atlanta, GA: Turner Publishing, 1995.

Mumford, L. *Technics and Civilization*. New York: Harcourt, Brace and Company, 1934.

Myrdal, G. *An American Dilemma*. New York: McGraw Hill, 1964.

Nathan, D.A. 'Bearing Witness to Blackball: Buck O'Neil, the Negro Leagues, and the Politics of the Past'. *Journal of American Studies* 35, no. 3 (2001): 453–69.

Oriard, M.V. *Dreaming of Heroes: American Sports Fiction, 1868–1980*. Chicago, IL: Nelson-Hall, 1982.

Parsons, T., and R.F. Bales. *Family, Socialization and Interaction Process*. Glencoe, IL: Free Press, 1955.

Plimpton, G. 'Miami Notebook: Cassius Clay and Malcolm X'. In *The Muhammad Ali Reader*, edited by G. Early, 27–40. Hopewell, NJ: Ecco Press, 1998.

Rampersad, A. *Jackie Robinson: A Biography*. New York: Ballantine Books, 1997.

Reetsma, J.P. *More Than a Champion: The Style of Muhammad Ali*. New York: Knopf, 1998.

Ribowsky, M. *Don't Look Back: Satchel Paige in the Shadows of Baseball*. New York: Simon and Schuster, 1994.

Riess, S.A. *Touching Base: Professional Baseball and American Culture in the Progressive Era*. Westport, CT: Greenwood Press, 1980.

Robinson, J. *I Never Had It Made: an Autobiography*. New York: Ecco/Harper Collins, 1995.

Robinson, J. 'Clay Explodes the Liston Myth'. In *The Muhammad Ali Reader*, edited by G. Early, 43–44. Hopewell, NJ: Ecco Press, 1998.

Robinson, J. 'In Defense of Cassius Clay'. In *The Muhammad Ali Reader*, edited by G. Early, 72. Hopewell, NJ: Ecco Press, 1998.

Robinson, J. *Baseball Has Done It*. Brooklyn, NY: Ig Publishing, 2005.

Rogosin, D. *Invisible Men: Life in Baseball's Negro Leagues*. New York: Atheneum, 1985.

Seib, P. *The Player: Christy Mathewson, Baseball, and the American Century*. New York: Thunders Mouth Press, 2003.

Smart, B. *The Sport Star: Modern Sport and the Cultural Economy of Sporting Celebrity*. London: Sage, 2005.

Smith, B. 'The Death of the Artist as Hero'. In *The Death of the Artist as Hero: Essays in History and Culture*, 8–29. Melbourne: Oxford University Press, 1988.

Smith, G. 'The Sport Hero: An Endangered Species'. In *Play, Games and Sports in Cultural Contexts*, edited by J.C. Harris and R.J. Park, 107–22. Champaign, IL: Human Kinetics, 1983.

Smith, R.A. 'The Paul Robeson–Jackie Robinson Saga and a Political Collision'. In *The Jackie Robinson Reader: Perspectives on an American Hero*, edited by J. Tygiel, 169–88. New York: Dutton, 1997.

Stump, A. *Cobb: A Biography*. Chapel Hill, NC: Algonquin, 1994.

Susman, W.I. *Culture as History: the Transformation of American Society in the Twentieth Century*. Washington, DC and London: Smithsonian Institution Press, 2003.

The Oxford English Dictionary. 2nd ed., prepared by J.A. Simpson and E.S.C. Weiner in 20 volumes. Oxford: Clarendon Press, 1989.

Tygiel, J. *Baseball's Great Experiment: Jackie Robinson and His Legacy*. New York: Vintage Books, 1984.

Tygiel, J., ed. *The Jackie Robinson Reader: Perspectives on an American Hero*. New York: Dutton, 1997.

Ward, G.C., and K. Burns. *Baseball: An Illustrated History*. New York: Knopf, 1994.

Yardley, J. *Ring Lardner: A Biography*. New York: Random House, 1977.

The modern city and the making of sport

The focus of this essay is on the 'modern' city, the origins of which are usually attributed to the urban expansion that followed the growth of industrialization in the eighteenth century. This is not to propose a complete rupture between the ancient city and the modern city. For example, the Athenian city-state has remained influential to those who have looked to antiquity as an ageless guide to urban planning. As such, Athens has served as an ideal referent of lived humanism. According to Blackham, 'Never before nor since has there been such an integration and florescence of human activities and genius carried to the pitch of perfection'.[1] The city of Renaissance Italy is widely regarded as having been invested with the artistic dimension of this spirit. Florence, Turin and, for that matter, Rome are seen as works of art in themselves as much as places of artistic nurture and excellence.[2] The essay proceeds in a way sympathetic to the notion of the city as a work of art. The city understood as a work of art at once suggests the idea of a 'city of culture', an idea which runs counter to the anti-humanistic understanding of the city as a place of utilitarian outcomes. The essay is largely concerned with how sport might be placed historically within modern cities thus considered as cities of culture. It proceeds with a discussion of the writing on cities by the architectural and urban historian Lewis Mumford (1895–1990) and goes on to discuss the cultural significance of sport within cities via historical reflection on baseball in the United States and association football in Britain.

Mumford, the city and sport as 'bitch-goddess'

The idea of the city of culture is traceable within modern historical writing to the work of Lewis Mumford, in particular his 1938 book *The Culture of Cities*. Mumford sees the city as both a 'fact of nature' and as a 'conscious work of art'.[3] However, unlike the discussions within art and architectural history, which view the city as a canvas to be worked upon by individual artistic genius, Mumford recognized the city as a 'collective work of art', an artwork resulting from 'the daily communion of its citizens'. Yet, this view of the city remained one of unfulfilled hope as Mumford's enthusiasm was constantly tempered by his concern with the direction that modern urban life was taking. Mumford's particular bugbear was technology (following Oswald Spengler, he used the term *technics*), which he believed had been historically deployed purely for the economic benefit of private industry and to the detriment of the 'organic' development of cities. Relatedly, Mumford recognized utilitarianism as the prevailing form of 'political regulation' within western societies since the time of industrialization.[4] By Mumford's account utilitarianism promoted a laissez-faire belief that the modern economy was self-regulating and in little or no need of interference from the state. Laissez-faire economics undermined traditional 'municipal authority' and brought about a condition referred to by Mumford as *Abbau* – the 'un-building' of the city.[5]

Abbau coincides with a 'stage' of city development named by Mumford as *Megalopolis*. The Greek word meaning Great city was used contrarily by Mumford and in a similar sense to other organic social theorists, principally Oswald Spengler and Patrick Geddes.[6] Megalopolis marks a stage of decline, beyond the metropolis, whereby the city has become overgrown, bloated and an ecological burden to its surrounding region. A number of cities across history are declared by Mumford to have undergone a megalopolis stage. The first megalopolis he cites is Alexandria of the third century BC and the latest, to his time of writing, New York in the early twentieth century.[7] According to Mumford, the 'megalopolis ushers in an age of cultural aggrandizement' in which 'mechanical reproduction takes the place of original art'.[8] Related features of the megalopolis are 'bigness tak[ing] the place of form' and 'voluminousness tak[ing] the place of significance'. Mumford regarded developments in sport as indicative of this cultural tendency. The 'vulgarization' of culture within the megalopolis promotes the mass spectacle satisfied by such events as 'boxing matches, wrestling bouts … motor races and air races'.[9] The sporting spectacle promotes a pseudo form of communal interaction, referred to by Mumford as '*residual* sociality'. Within the modern city the stadium provides the point of assembly for the staging of this sociality, where the spectators come to view the 'essential drama' of near or potential death experience in the sporting contest.[10] Sports events in the megalopolis thus carry an 'inverted sense of life' and present to an unaware public a metaphor of the city in a state of collapse.

Mumford goes on to speculate that as the megalopolis descends into *tyrannopolis* 'mass-sports' will be increasingly used as a form of 'bread and shows' to pacify and becalm a growing under-class.[11] His claim that 'criminals whose activities do not debar them from respectability' within the tyrannopolis, may be read as a portent of the contemporary day situation whereby premier level sports teams in major world cities are owned by individuals of dubious repute. Mumford's denunciation of sport commenced in his earlier book *Technics and Civilization* in a subsection titled 'Sport and the "Bitch-goddess"'. This title reflects Mumford's view that sport in modern times has been absorbed into the world of business concerned almost entirely with material success. Sport becomes a means to an end rather than an end itself in the form of play.[12] The potential of sport as a 'spontaneous reaction' against the machine has been lost, mass-sport being prone to adjustment in keeping with a technological outlook to make it faster and more spectacular. Yet despite the pessimistic historical account presented in his work, Mumford dismisses an inevitably gloomy forecast for the future of the city. Towards the conclusion of *The Culture of Cities* Mumford considers 'possibilities of renewal' within a 'new urban order'. Important here to Mumford is the reinstatement of the play element within sport. In material terms, he claims stadiums need to be more than modern 'gladiatorial arenas', the humanistic city must create stadiums as 'collective facilities for sport and play'.[13]

Mumford drew upon the Victorian critic John Ruskin's claim for environmentally clean cities to be surrounded by fields in which an 'afternoon's walk or game' could be had.[14] This view later appeared in the 'garden city' vision of Ebenezer Howard.[15] Mumford found significant appeal in Howard's vision, especially the idea of a happy union between town and country to be materialized in the formation of small, decongested cities.[16] The politically reformist rather than radical views of Howard were also of appeal to Mumford. As his biographer Donald L. Miller indicates, Mumford's urban agenda may have demanded radical change but his limited political vision suggested evolution rather than revolution.[17] Although regarding cities as communal projects, Mumford gave little insight into how the general public would actively contribute to the renewal of urban culture. This is largely because of the lack of faith he had in working-class activism. Indeed he believed the American working class had been sucked into an abyss of consumerist complacency.[18]

Sport spectatorship was a particular matter of concern for Mumford. He recognized sport watching as a prominent example of an increasing cultural lethargy in the American city. In yet another modern version of 'negative classicism', Mumford believed the shiny spectacle of sport appealed readily to those whose critical faculties were already numbed by consumerism. By regarding its spectators as a passive mass Mumford denied sport possibility as a source of renewal and the sport stadium as being an urban site where people could have a collective input into a cultural life of their own making. However, Mumford's technological determinist position on the historical development of modern sport is challenged by an even-handed reading of the cultural histories of key urban sports such as baseball in the United States and association football in Britain. The collective human input to the development of these respective sporting cultures has been much more enduring than Mumford's negativism suggests.

Sport and the city at the *fin de siècle*

At the turn of the century the urban American sport crowd was regarded as anything but passive, tending to be associated with a 'mob' mentality. Boxing was particularly prone to crowd violence, but 'rowdyism' also occurred at baseball matches especially when fans believed that their team was on the wrong end of poor umpiring decisions. The catch-cry 'Kill the Umpire' became so well known that it was used as a Hollywood film title in 1950. However, a near fatality in 1907, when an umpire was hit by a soda bottle thrown by a spectator, led to the sanctioning of baseball audiences to the extent that 'fans were socialised to respect the authority and integrity of umpires'.[19] Although barracking of umpires and rival players continued, albeit in a less confrontational manner, Riess claims that 'supporters could sit in the stands together, argue about their heroes … and shake hands once the contest was over'.[20] He notes that this culture differed from the volatility of urban supporter cultures that developed elsewhere, particularly in connection with association football. The lack of 'deep-seated antagonisms' between supporters of rival baseball clubs in American cities, imputed by Riess, did not characterize the relations between fans of soccer clubs in some parts of Britain and Europe.

The intensity of fan rivalries in soccer has much to do with the tradition of 'local derby' matches between clubs representing townships in close proximity and between clubs representing districts within large cities such as London. The term 'local derby' is derived from the English East Midland's city Derby which hosted an annual football game each Shrove Tuesday between residents of the Saint Peter and All Saints parishes.[21] The 'battle' between the respectively aligned participants within the amorphous gathering sprawled across the town for the day or two duration of the game was 'so fierce' that *derby* became the still-used generic name for keenly felt local rivalries between soccer fans and their clubs.[22] Such rivalries proliferated in England given its compressed urban development within conurbation systems. Conurbation, a term devised by Mumford's mentor Patrick Geddes to describe an area made up of adjoining administrative districts that were once discontinuous townships, eventually became official nomenclature in the 1951 British Census when a number of geographical units, including Greater London, the West Midlands and Merseyside, were so named.[23] Each of these conurbations features traditional football rivalries reflective of population density and intra-regional tensions. Enduring rivalries exist between the north London clubs Arsenal and Tottenham Hotspur, on Merseyside between Liverpool and Everton football clubs, and in the 'Black Country', to the west of Birmingham, between Wolverhampton Wanderers and West Bromwich Albion football clubs.

Strong sporting rivalries also exist in the conurbation-like area of central Lancashire. The best-known soccer derby rivalries in this area are those between the supporters of Preston North End and Blackpool, and Blackburn Rovers and Burnley. Derby rivalries are heightened during periods when the respective clubs are located in the same division, especially at the top flight of football competition. The Preston/Blackpool rivalry peaked when both teams were in the First Division of the Football League during the 1950s. The derby rivalry between Blackburn and Burnley commenced early on as both clubs competed in the first league season in 1888–89.

It recommenced in 1913–14 with Burnley's promotion to the First Division and continued through the 1920s following an interregnum caused by the First World War. The early 1960s also featured derby battles between these teams in the First Division of the Football League.[24] While derby rivalry is most apparent during periods of on-field contestation, this has not meant that traditional antagonisms abate when respective teams are located in different divisions. Indeed, location in a higher division is customarily regarded by the supporters of the ascendant club as indication of superiority over the local adversary. On the other hand, during periods when clubs have not enjoyed on-field success 'civic patriotism' has been maintained within the local press via backhanded compliment or outright denigration of the successes of the rival club.[25]

Nevertheless, as Russell notes, 'civic pride was never more intensely and graphically expressed than at celebrations which followed the League and Cup successes'.[26] Dominance in football could belie the adage of 'it's grim up north' in towns such as Preston and Blackburn and bring a swagger to their high streets. Indeed, soccer developed free of the rural romanticism often associated with English sport, especially cricket. From its competitive inception in Britain, association football thrived in urban population belts and the size of a town correlated with the prospect of success for its soccer team. Russell notes that a population of less that 100,000 was insufficient for a town to sustain support for a championship club at the turn of the twentieth century.[27] Preston had a population of 117,000 when it became the first winner of the League and FA Cup 'double' in 1888–89. The club won the subsequent First Division title but since then has not won a top division league trophy (it won the FA Cup on one further occasion in 1938). The demise in football status coincides somewhat with Preston's demise as an industrial town in conjunction with the decline of the British cotton industry through the 1900s. In substantiation of Russell's claim on the linkage between competitive football success and urban growth, the First Division title, following 1890 and into the early years of the twentieth century, was won by teams from thriving industrial heartlands, Aston Villa from Birmingham, Sunderland and Newcastle from the shipbuilding North-East, and Liverpool and Everton from the River Mersey port region.

Preston North End's victory in the first competitive season of the English Football League coincided with the Preston Guilds, which existed between 1842 and 1922.[28] The Guilds were a cooperative arrangement between employers and workers, representatives of the latter becoming closely involved with the organization of the annual town march from 1882. The term 'proud Preston', which emerged around that time and in association with the marches, must have been received by many locals as a welcome riposte to the town's rather dire reputation as an industrial wasteland. Preston's particular notoriety sprang from Charles Dickens using the town as an actual model for the fictional Coketown, which he lambasted in the novel *Hard Times*:[29]

> Coketown ... was a town of red brick, or of brick that would have been red if the smoke and ashes had allowed it; but, as matters stood it was a town of unnatural red and black like the painted face of a savage. It was a town of machinery and tall chimneys, out of which interminable serpents of smoke trailed themselves for ever and ever, and never got uncoiled ... It contained several large streets all very like one another, and many small streets still more like one another, inhabited by people equally like one another, who all went in and out at the same hours, with the same sound upon the same pavements, to do the same work, and to whom every day was the same as yesterday and tomorrow, and every year the counterpart of the last and the next.[30]

Dickens fictional representation of Preston displayed the 'social anguish' that he genuinely felt for working people living within the smokestack-blighted urban environments of industrial England.[31] However, while Dickens's remark about each day and year being no different to the next speaks poignantly to the feeling of drudgery in labour, his concern with the monotony of working lives overlooks the possibility of release through leisure. Interestingly, though, Dickens gives clue to the 'vital human impulse' gained through sportive leisure in his description of a visiting circus to Coketown. As F.R. Leavis has noted, the physical prowess displayed by the circus horsemen is to the workers of Coketown 'not merely amusement, but art, and the spectacle of triumphant activity that, seeming to contain its end within itself, is, in its easy mastery, joyously self-justified'.[32] Leavis believed that Dickens' account of the circus performers gives explicit acknowledgement to the non-utilitarian value of leisure, in stark contrast to the totally utilitarian sphere of work.

Soccer in *Coketown*: the case of Preston North End

Association football had not taken shape in the 1840s when Dickens wrote *Hard Times* so any thoughts of how, or even whether or not, he would have accounted for it as a leisure activity had the book been written towards the end of the 1800s are entirely speculative. Yet it is reasonable, following from Leavis, to contend that the non-utilitarian nature of football underpinned its early appeal to the British urban worker. Importantly, whereas the circus came to town, the football club and its team emerged endogenously if not from the working people then in close relationship to them. The Prestonian journalist James Catton recalled an 'atmosphere which developed an inborn love of men's games'.[33] His earliest memory of Preston North End is a cricket club that played on a 'ground called Deepdale, which was leased from the Corporation'. By 1881 the 'Soccer code' had taken hold and Deepdale became the permanent home of Preston North End FC.[34] Although of local roots the team quickly took on a cosmopolitan look with the importation of a number of players from Scotland by the mid 1880s. The arrival of Nick Ross from Heart of Midlothian FC gave Preston the first star player to emerge within League football.[35] Ross became the 'lynchpin' of the 'Invincibles', the Preston team that went unbeaten throughout the 1888–89 season to win the 'double'.

Player importation and professionalism were two sides of a controversy that quickly manifested once the League had been established. Protest against professionalism came predominantly from middle-class critics who, *inter alia*, believed that paying players would make them mercenaries concerned only about winning the game and not about the spirit in which the game was played.[36] Similarly, it was assumed supporters would become disinterested in football as sport and follow it with the 'partisan frenzy of the mob', as one critic put it in 1906.[37] In such circumstance, it is suggested, an appreciation of the skill and finer points of football will be lost to mean-spiritedness and resentment. Such opinion, as Mason notes, smacks of class prejudice and is ill-founded.[38] Firstly such a view is unable to comprehend the particular investment that working people began to place in football teams from the time of the late 1800s. Although working people had relatively small financial investment in football clubs, it was one area of life in which they were able to experience a feeling of collective ownership. It is hardly surprising that partisanship emerged in the football support of people who lived in a social milieu that denied them so much. Football provided a common means of 'civic pride', as discussed by both Russell and Holt.[39] For some fans pride did turn to parochialism and in its fanatical manifestation to incipient forms of hooliganism.[40] The early critics of professionalism were thus portentous, to an extent, in their pious alarmism about the 'frenzy' of the football 'mob'.[41]

Secondly, recent research indicates that parochial support for the local club may have been less common than customarily assumed. Oral history testimonies gathered by Mellor from football supporters who were youthful in the 1950s, suggest that fandom, if not allegiance, extended beyond the local team.[42] A number of Mellor's interviewees recalled visiting different grounds to watch the best players of the era, Tom Finney (Preston North End), Stanley Matthews (Blackpool) and Nat Lofthouse (Bolton Wanderers) are specified. During the 1950s the 'affluent worker' disputably emerged and, without getting into that thorny sociological debate, it can be said that some working-class people had the means to attend matches other than those involving the home team. This had not been the case for football enthusiasts of previous working-class generations. In the 1930s, as Kelly notes, football supporters from the working class were restricted to attending fortnightly home matches as they lacked the wherewithal to travel.[43] However, records indicate that home attendance increased whenever press celebrated 'star' players – such as the young Stanley Matthews of Stoke City and 'Dixie' Dean of Everton – were members of the visiting team. Such popularity suggests that had working-class people had the means, they too, like those after them, would have travelled to see the big name players of other clubs. This dimension of football support displays a certain connoisseurship that goes against culturally elitist representations of indiscriminate working class fandom. It also suggests that the historical connection between urbanism and football was double-edged in that it simultaneously promoted contradictory tendencies towards both the development and dismantling of partisanship.

The historical emergence of 'star' football players since the 1930s as civic ambassadors is apparent today by way of public statues in dedication, outside the stadiums of their former clubs. Related examples include statues honouring 'Dixie' Dean (Everton) at Goodison Park, Stanley Matthews (Stoke City) at the Britannia Stadium, Jackie Milburn (Newcastle United) at St James's Park, Billy Wright (Wolverhampton Wanderers) at Molineux, and Tom Finney at Preston North End's Deepdale. In at least two of these cases – Milburn and Finney – nearby roadways have been named after the players; giving municipal imprimatur to the iconographic recognition afforded them by their former clubs. Each of these players were locally born, in the towns of their clubs in the cases of Matthews and Finney, and in nearby or adjoining areas as in the cases of Dean, Milburn and Wright. In a contemporary age when few players are 'locals', the memorialization of these past stars becomes increasingly significant.

The demise of localism in player ranks emerged in tandem with professionalism. Although William Sudell, one of the pioneering figures in the professionalization of football, had maintained that professionalism could go ahead without importation,[44] this would appear in hindsight a disingenuous claim. The two trends proceeded hand-in-hand, and Sudell, as secretary of Preston North End, actively brought top players to Preston by lure of financial incentive. Fans seem to have accepted both professionalism and importation over the years in a desire for the competitive success of their clubs. Yet, a history of acceptance and even welcoming of imported players is matched by a converse tradition of reverence for those home-grown. The local talent made good is not just *representative of us* but, in an extended familial sense, *one of us*. Association football as a quintessentially urban sport thus fostered a spirit of cosmopolitanism that has remained tempered by a residual sentiment of insularity.

The best-known of English football clubs, Manchester United, has been accused of loosing its civic attachment, not because of the importation of non local and non-English players, but on the presumption that its fan base is predominantly domiciled outside Manchester and even the United Kingdom.[45] From the standpoint of such criticism, the cosmopolitan football club attracting exogenous players retains civic credibility, but not so the club that enjoys global fan popularity. In this light it is interesting to consider the National Football Museum (NFM), located at Preston North End's home stadium, Deepdale. The rationale for the museum, opened in 2001, being located at Preston North End's home appears twofold. Firstly, Deepdale has been a home-ground to a League club longer than any other and, secondly, Preston North End was the inaugural winner of the League championship title in 1888–89.[46] Preston has not appeared in the top division of English football since the beginning of the 1960s, but the lack of 'global' profile accompanying this absence appears to have strengthened the case for the national museum to be housed at Deepdale rather than at a home-ground of one of the currently better-known Premier League clubs.

The global profile of clubs such as Manchester United and Chelsea elevates them symbolically above nation, hence disqualifying their home-grounds as suitable locations for a national museum of English football. This exemplifies how sport's competitive nature and related organizational arrangements distinguish it from other forms of culture and human endeavour. National museums are familiarly found in large and capital cities – global cities such as London (The British Museum, The Imperial War Museum, The National Gallery, Tate Britain) and Manchester (The National Museum of Labour History, The Imperial War Museum North, The Museum of Industry and Commerce, Urbis – Centre for Urban Culture). But not so the national museum of the *people's game*. Although the rules of association football were sanctioned in London in 1863,[47] and the Football League was formally established in Manchester in 1888,[48] football's historical shrine finds location elsewhere.

Soccer on show: museums, stadiums and the *SuperCity*

The historical background to this occurrence is not so much a matter of the metropolis being shunned by football, but football being shunned by the metropolis. Kevin Moore notes that major museums in Britain have tended to take little interest in housing items of football culture, even the ball that was used at Wembley in England's 1966 World Cup Final victory.[49] Football, and sport in general, has suffered from the traditional bias whereby '"low culture" was outside the remit of museums as temples of high culture'. Yet, at the time he was writing in 1996, Moore observed a 'significant shift in museum attitudes' to football.[50] That year marked the first time England had hosted a major soccer tournament – the European Championship (Euro '96) – since the World Cup Finals 30 years earlier. By then the barrier between high and 'low' culture was diminishing and football's cultural legitimization was underway; football was featured in exhibitions at, *inter alia*, the Museum of Liverpool Life and Glasgow's Peoples' Palace museum.[51] The eventual location of the NFM within a football stadium may itself be seen as indicative of a shift from traditional museum custom. However, in appealing to a non-traditional museum audience the NFM appears to have struggled for attendance numbers. Despite confident expectations when the NFM was first touted for location at Deepdale in 1996 early attendance figures were so poor following the 2001 opening that closure was threatened within the first year.[52] Entrance fees to the NFM – most major museums in England have free entry – did not help attendance and eventually, following Government intervention and via regional funding support, the fee was waived. A positive impact on attendance appears to have subsequently resulted. According to the 2007 NFM Annual Report, attendance figures are 106,338 for the financial year, comfortably exceeding the agreed target with the Department of Culture, Media and Sport of 100,000.[53]

To survive over time the NFM may need further reconfiguration into a regional tourism profile.[54] Anecdotal evidence suggests that Preston does not appeal as an urban tourist destination and the prospect of people making an effort to travel an appreciable distance for a one site tourist stop is not great. The prominent architect Will Alsop has proposed the idea of the 'SuperCity' whereby motorways are more creatively used as humanized corridors linking cities and towns across parts of England into singular entities.[55] In his plan for 'Coast-to-Coast', stretching from Liverpool in the west to Hull in the East, Alsop mentions in passing that sport will be part of the cultural profile of the 'SuperCity'. How this would work given longstanding rivalries within football and other sports popular within the lower-northern expanse, including rugby league, is hard to imagine. Preston misses out altogether in Alsop's 'Coast-to-Coast' plan, but this need not be so if the 'SuperCity' were extended to incorporate satellite locations running off key tributary routes. But would historical sites and related museums find popular acceptance within the 'SuperCity'? Not so, if the past is as irrelevant to the average person as some commentators suggest.[56] Yet care needs to be taken within cultural analysis against privileging youth, and the accompanying tendency to overlook the cultural interests of the middle-aged and above.

As a former colleague at the University of Otago remarked, 'people grow into an appreciation of history',[57] a promising portent for a continuing interest in the past within popular culture.

An example of such interest is the popularity of the BBC television programme *Restoration*. First screened in 2003 the series presented to viewers, over six weeks, 18 buildings, mostly heritage listed, in various states of disrepair. During the course of the series, viewers were asked to vote for funding plans for the restoration of particular buildings. Buildings ranged from leisure sites and former factories to aristocratically owned houses. The eventual first prize winner was the Victoria Baths building located in Manchester. The Victoria Baths received not only the prize money associated with the television programme but a subsequent Heritage Lottery Fund grant that will significantly contribute to the restoration plan and bring the building's Turkish Baths back into public use.[58] The selection of the Victorian Baths for the *Restoration* prize indicated a favouring of public historical buildings over those in private forms of ownership. It is of further interest that the Baths is an historical site given to public recreation and that a significant aspect of the restoration plan is for a return to active recreational usage. While some might regard as undignified the very idea of a popular vote for the restoration of one heritage building, as opposed to another, *Restoration* might contrarily be seen as a mediated means of democratic expression conducted by the BBC in its capacity as a public service agency. In a so-called 'postmodern culture' in which 'pseudo-authenticity' disrupts a genuine historical understanding of the past,[59] giving the people an informed say in architectural preservation is no small offering. The selection of the Victoria Baths for the award indicates the public spiritedness with which the competition was received by BBC viewers.

John Bale uses the term 'repositories of history' to describe buildings which 'mimic the past'.[60] The Victoria Baths might be regarded more in terms of replication of the past, yet any attempt at architectural replication does necessarily involve imitation. But although authenticity remains a contentious term within cultural theory, a project such as the restoration of the Victoria Baths constitutes an attempt at effecting rather than affecting the past. For building projects clearly involving historical affectation Bale applies the term 'new-old fashioned'.[61] He relatedly discusses Oriole Park baseball stadium which replaced Baltimore's former Memorial Stadium in 1992.[62] The new stadium was deliberately designed to evoke fan memories of ballparks of yesteryear. Features include a ground entrance with iron gates and brick arches and seating replicating old style bleachers. Bale regards Oriole Park as a 'Disneyfield sportscape *par excellence*'. MacCannell's term 'staged authenticity', referring to the commercial fabrication of an imagined former reality, would also appear appropriate.[63] 'Staged authenticity' implies that people living an alienated urban existence are lured by tourist and leisure experiences that seemingly offer a nostalgic return to better times.

This is not so apparent with modern soccer stadiums, the design of which evince a stark rationalism rather than a playful, if disingenuous and deceptive, historical romanticism. Contemporary stadium design was marked by the crowd tragedies of the late 1980s at Valley Parade (Bradford), Heysel Stadium (Brussels) and Hillsborough Stadium (Sheffield). Although different in cause and circumstance these tragedies revealed safety inadequacies and exposed soccer stadiums – certainly those in Britain – as dilapidated blots on the urban terrain. A major finding of Lord Taylor's report into the tragedy at Hillsborough in April of 1989 was that football stadiums in upper level professional divisions in Britain needed conversion to an all-seated capacity. Inglis notes that Taylor's findings were delivered as 'the inevitable culmination of years of complacency, neglect, low investment, and in many cases, rank bad management'.[64] Soccer stadiums have since been incorporated into plans for the re-imaging of British cities and their quest for recognition as 'cities of culture'.[65] However, the city of culture is not an unambiguous goal, its very discussion being replete with buzzwords – regeneration, gentrification, economic impact – reflecting tension between community and commercial priorities. Large sport stadiums, by nature of purpose, have a discrepant existence within cities. Unlike most buildings of work and leisure, which close only during evenings (some on weekends), the sport stadium remains 'closed and quiet' for most of the week until match times when it becomes a focal point of public congregation.[66] The Taylor Report exposed a history of slapdash safety provision revealing that those responsible for administering soccer stadiums in Britain had totally failed to comprehend this major imperative associated with the stadium's function. The infrequent use of stadiums had perhaps led to a lackadaisical attitude to public safety developing over time. Whether or not the response was alarmist is arguable, but the Taylor Report certainly led to something of a safety-first 'moral panic', resulting in a preoccupation with steel and concrete bowl stadium development.

Relatedly, soccer stadium (re)design in 1990s Britain did not deviate significantly from functionalist intent. However, inventiveness and idiosyncrasy was not entirely absent. Again, the case of Deepdale is of interest. In contrast to the prevailing drab trend in reconstruction, Preston North End adopted the plan of graphics designer, and club supporter, Ben Casey for a stadium influenced by architect Vittorio Gregotti's Stadio Luigi Ferraris in Genoa.[67] The main feature of Casey's mock-Italianate design, floodlight towers connected to the roof structure by diagonal metal riggings, was first unveiled with the opening of the Tom Finney Stand in March 1996. To make way for this new stand, Deepdale's 'much-loved' West Stand was demolished. This stand, originally named the Grand Stand, had stood at Deepdale since 1906.[68] A supporters-led campaign to preserve a part of the wooden panelling of the West Stand led to a small section being housed in the NFM. As the NFM is located within the Tom Finney Stand, a material memory of the old has been physically encapsulated within the new. Since the opening of the Tom Finney Stand the former terraced ends have been converted to seated stands to match the Genoa design influence. The only remnant of the old Deepdale remaining in use, the 1936-built Pavilion Stand, is about to undergo demolition at the time of writing.[69] Suggestions that retaining in use a pre-war style grandstand would be in keeping with Deepdale's heritage theme fell on the deaf ears of the Preston North End administration. Safety concerns notwithstanding, it would have been interesting to see how a postmodern mix of old and new might have come together in the final stage of Deepdale's renovation.

'It happened in Flatbush': Relocation and the demise of the Brooklyn Dodgers

The reconstruction or renovation of football stadiums has understandably been a matter of controversy. More controversial, even upsetting, has been the relocation of clubs to new grounds, especially when this has involved the club transferring to a new town or city. The move of Wimbledon FC from south-west London to Milton Keynes, accompanied by a name change to the MK Dons, caused such uproar that many fans withdrew their allegiance from the team. Analogy was drawn between the re-invented club and the 'prefabricated' post-war 'new town' to which it had been relocated.[70] Such upheavals, still uncommon in the United Kingdom, have been much more familiar within North American sport. Arguably the most famous sport club relocation occurred when the Brooklyn Dodgers were transferred to Los Angeles by their owner Walter O'Malley at the end of the 1957 season.[71] One of baseball's best-known and successful teams metamorphosed in cross-national transit to become the LA Dodgers. The move did not go unchallenged, a resistance campaign being formalized in the Keep the Dodgers in Brooklyn Committee. The Committee received support from none other than the former Dodgers manager, Branch Rickey. Rickey's words seemingly characterize the feelings of those opposed to the move:

> One could not live for eight years in Brooklyn and not catch its spirit of devotion to its baseball club, such as no other city in America had equalled. Call it loyalty and so it was. It would be a crime

against a community of three million to move the Dodgers … A baseball club in any city in America is a quasi-public institution, and in Brooklyn, the Dodgers were public without the quasi.[72]

An image of the Dodgers closely affiliated with community has been well-rehearsed within American literature and popular culture. Isaac Asimov's autobiography, Betty Smith's novel *A Tree Grows in Brooklyn*, a short story 'Brooklyns Lose' in *Sports Illustrated* and Paul Auster's screenplay and subsequent film with Wayne Wang *Blue in the Face*, variously portray the Dodger's as integral to life in Brooklyn.[73] Related portrayal is found in two 1990s television documentaries, *When it Was a Game* – featuring home-movie camera footage shot on 8 and 16 millimetre film – and Ken Burns's celebrated epic *Baseball*. In the former, the voiceover of writer Donald Honig maintains, 'The team was a very important part of the community and their neighbours who they would see in the supermarket and in the playground, playing with their children, were Brooklyn Dodgers; they lived in the neighbourhood'. The voiceover is accompanied by moving images of players involved in everyday activities, including rookie pitcher Roger Craig unloading groceries from his car boot. This is followed by the voiceover of star pitcher Carl Erskine recalling how Dodgers players were feted by Brooklynites. He tells of a local grocer who would bring bags of goods to his door then refuse to receive any payment in belief that, 'you guys shouldn't pay rent; you shouldn't have to pay anything to be in Brooklyn'.[74] In *Baseball* the comedian Billy Crystal, a Yankees fans, recalls from his boyhood the Dodgers move from Brooklyn being like 'a death in the family'. *Baseball* shows a number of other rival supporters sharing Crystal's sympathetic observation.[75]

While the unfavourable public response to the move from Brooklyn can be assessed as a mixture of opprobrium and consternation, the subsequent closure and demolition of the Dodgers' home ground Ebbets Field in the central Brooklyn district of Flatbush seemed to result in a collective sentiment of melancholy. If the Dodgers were emblematic of Brooklyn neighbourhood, then Ebbets Field was the symbolic home. Evocative newsreel footage of Ebbets Field's demolition in February 1960, including a wrecking ball distastefully camouflaged as an oversized baseball crashing into the dugout and outfield perimeter walls, is shown in both *When it Was a Game* and *Baseball*. In the former, these images are accompanied by the following poem read in voiceover mode:

> Don't tear the treasured ballpark down long has it brought me joy,
> as many a Brooklyn player has that I have watched as a boy.
> Above it rings Red Barber's voice amidst the crowd's deep roar,
> for sounds that would be heard by Brooklyn's fans no more.
> Oh let the mighty field stand as tribute to her past,
> the loyalty of all her fans can never be surpassed.
> Forget the California gold, let loyalty prevail,
> for loyalty of Brooklyn fans can never be for sale.

Ebbets Field had a reputation of intimacy and a related connectedness to its fans since opening in 1913. This seems largely due to the man whose name it bore, Dodgers owner Charles Ebbets. An architect by profession, Ebbets had long envisioned a grand stadium for Brooklyn. He wanted a facility that would well serve spectators in terms of safety and comfort, yet have charm and maintain distinction as a ballpark in contrast to the surfeit of 'stadiums' being erected in other urban centres. Accordingly, Ebbets Field was purposely given a recognizable façade and neo-Italianate features including a Rotunda entrance with marble columns and outer wall, and a marble mosaic tile floor.[76] This mock pretension to classicism was offset by the quirky addition of a ball-and-bat chandelier hanging above the centre of the Rotunda. But it was the closeness of stands to the outfield that fostered a homely regard for Ebbets Field:

> If the Manhattan skyline bristled with the icons of the imperial capital, Brooklyn was its complement, the paradigm of home – the new urban American home, which spoke many languages but found a common focus of identity in the democratic myths and loyalties of baseball. To millions across the country, Ebbets Field seemed the distilled essence of Brooklyn: home as a passionately occupied urban turf. It was home to its baseball club as no other park has ever been; its slightly shabby gentility and cramped angularity offered a semiotic key to the whole sprawled web of its neighbourhoods.[77]

But this popular and pervasive view of the Brooklyn Dodgers as a cultural cement that drew together potentially disparate social elements into a harmonious urban community symbolically centred at Ebbets Field has, not surprisingly, been challenged as an exaggeration. According to Carl Prince, 'the Dodgers formed an ameliorating force for unity in Brooklyn, but the team's local mystique did not miraculously bring all the people to love each other'.[78] As indicated by the quote from Nielson, Brooklyn's communal image has much to do with how the borough has been historically perceived in binary opposition to Manhattan. While Manhattan has been known as 'the City' to residents of other boroughs, a place of hustle, bustle and anomic living, Brooklyn has been regarded as relatively tranquil and neighbourly, despite a demographic history of ethnic diversity. Lewis Mumford chose its northern extremity below Manhattan as home, Miller tells of Mumford's fondness for Brooklyn Heights in its 'near-perfect mix of urbanity and community, gracious green places and spirited street life'.[79] Baseball rivalry came to signify the competing images of Brooklyn and the City throughout the twentieth century, up to and beyond the demise of the Dodgers. Such rivalry can be traced to at least the 1860s and newspaper evidence even suggests that the first baseball game was played between a New York and a Brooklyn 'Club' in 1845.[80] The intra-city rivalry intensified during the 1930s when the Dodgers struggled and their National League competitors the New York Giants excelled, and through the 1940s and the 1950s the New York Yankees emerged as the key rival when the two teams played off in seven World Series, the Dodgers winning only once in 1955.[81]

Brooklyn's rivalry with New York underpins the ongoing popularity that has resulted in the Dodgers being remembered as 'America's other team'. Roberts claims that the Dodgers have provided a metaphoric bridge to a 'more traditional' America, a celebration of rural over urban existence.[82] Peculiarly, the most populous of New York's boroughs has kept a passion for the myth of baseball's rural ancestry smouldering within the nation's imagination. The Dodger's 'urban' legend hinges on a memory of match-day at Ebbets Field as an approximation of idyllic life in the countryside. It is not unreasonable to hypothesize that the 'Dodger's myth' took over the role of the 'Abner Doubleday myth' – Albert Spalding's promotion of the fabrication that baseball had been 'invented' by a Civil War General in his youth at Cooperstown, New York in 1839 – which was exposed by Robert W. Henderson's historical investigation into the origins of ball games, published in 1947.[83] The 'Dodger's myth' is perpetuated by what John Bodnar refers to as 'public memory'. Public memory typically emerges from the intersection of official and vernacular cultural expressions.[84] While official culture is handed down from above by people in positions of authority, vernacular culture is developed at grassroots or ground level often in contradiction of official cultural discourses. The 'public memory' of the Brooklyn Dodgers has been formed and reformed predominately via a vernacular culture passed on initially by word-of-mouth, then disseminated through popular literature and film.

Myth and reality: Sport in the city – a contested terrain

According to Bodnar, 'public memory is a body of beliefs and ideas about the past that help a public or society understand both its past, present, and ... future'.[85] The public memory does not suggest an accurate memory; it exists beyond the conventions and strictures of academic history. Yet as Raphael Samuel remarks in discussion of his related term 'popular memory', 'the *sense* of the past, at any given point in time, is quite as much a matter of history as what happened in it ... the two are indivisible'.[86] From this perspective, historians may well discuss a 'Dodger's myth', but a factual challenging will not necessarily dint the myth's cultural efficacy. Although baseball developed as an urban game its folklore has continually suggested otherwise. Americans have perhaps always wanted to believe that baseball 'would have been invented by a guy named Abner'.[87] Spalding's promulgation of the 'Doubleday myth' was essentially driven by a 'chauvinistic determination' to prove baseball American in origin.[88] The enduringness of the myth was undoubtedly aided by its rural legend. Baseball, via the dusty base area of its infields and the green of its outfields, has maintained an 'unbroken connection to earth', an allegorical link with 'American soil'.[89] Relatedly, the artificial playing surfaces of the like seen in American football have been largely absent from baseball. Similarly, an experimental trend towards artificial grass at some soccer grounds in Britain in the 1980s quickly lost favour, an example being Deepdale where a 'plastic pitch' was in place between 1986 and 1991.[90] The retention of 'natural' playing fields in both baseball and soccer has arguably enhanced supporters' love of place and undoubtedly promoted related reference to 'sacred turf'.[91]

The blurring of the sacred and profane is perhaps the historical hallmark of sport in the city. If urban ballparks and soccer grounds have become modern cathedrals, then baseball and soccer can be spoken of as civic religions.[92] Yet the varying temporal arrangements of these sports makes baseball seem closer to the sacred than soccer. Through governance by clock time soccer is more akin to American football and basketball than it is to baseball. Baseball's lack of attention to the clock has been noted by a number of authors. Unlike American football and basketball, baseball appears to have defied urbanism by running at its own pace; by ignoring the discipline of measured time 'baseball belongs to the kind of world in which people did not say, "I haven't got all day"'.[93] The unhurriedness of baseball enhanced for the working man a feeling of release into a leisure domain, 'going to the ballpark meant surrender to the spell of baseball'.[94] However, while the ballpark no doubt gave workers a sense of rustic freedom, baseball also provided a reminder of the increasingly rule-bound nature of modern city life. The competitiveness of the game and the readiness of players to infract rules as a means of winning also resembled the way of business within the city.[95] The extent to which sports such as baseball were codified and conducted according to middle-class prerogatives for the purpose of inculcating capitalist values is debatable. With regard to Britain, Holt maintains that the development of urban sport, association football in particular, can only be understood within a context of 'rational recreation' planned by the middle class for workers.[96]

However, it is important to clarify that 'rational recreation' applied more to participative sport than spectator sport. Modern spectator sport emerged at the cusp of the nineteenth and twentieth centuries, marked especially by the establishment of the Football League in England in 1888 and the commencement of baseball's World Series in 1903. Along with other forms of popular culture such as vaudeville in the US and music hall and variety in Britain, baseball and soccer came to signify 'the quintessence of urban leisure: watching others do things'.[97] A formerly privileged dimension of life was thus opened to people of the working classes. However, the new spectator domains – those of music and comedy as well as sport – were no more generously given to the working class than they were a working class invention. The cultural history of baseball in the US and soccer in Britain must be told within a historical discussion of those countries' cities. These sports are part and parcel of Mumford's idea of the city as a 'collective work of art' made by 'the daily communion of its citizens'. Joseph Rykwert's words remind us that if the city is viewed as an artwork in this way, then it is an unfinished and contested project: 'Cities and towns are not entirely imposed on us by political or economic direction from above; nor are they quite determined from below by the working of obscure forces we cannot quite identify, never mind control'.[98] As this may be for the city, so too for its sports. Once the contested history of sport in the city is recognized, then sport's contribution to the making of urban cultures can begin to be appreciated.

Notes

[1] Blackham, *Humanism*, 86.

[2] Scott, *The Architecture of Humanism*.

[3] Mumford, *The Culture of Cities*, 5.

[4] Ibid., 152.

[5] Ibid., 155 and 150.

[6] Spengler, *The Decline of the West*; Geddes, *Cities in Evolution*.

[7] Mumford, *The Culture of Cities*, 290.

[8] Ibid., 289.

[9] Ibid., 268.

[10] Ibid., 269.

[11] Ibid., 291.

[12] Mumford, *Technics and Civilization*, 307.

[13] Mumford, *The Culture of Cities*, 429–30.

[14] Ibid., 222; Ruskin, *Munera Pulveris*, 204.

[15] Howard, *Garden Cities of To-morrow*, 85. Howard calls for cricket-fields, lawn-tennis courts and playgrounds to be incorporated into urban parkland and green belt areas.

[16] Mumford, *The Culture of Cities*, 396.

[17] Miller, *Lewis Mumford*, 362.

[18] Ibid., 297.

[19] Riess, *City Games*, 225.

[20] Ibid., 226.

[21] Walvin, *The People's Game*, 14.

[22] Bowden, 'Soccer', 99.

[23] Geddes, *Cities in Evolution*, 34; Waller, *Town, City and Nation*, 74.

[24] For tables on teams' league positions during this period see Nawrat and Hutchings, *The Sunday Times Illustrated History of Football*, 158–9.

[25] Russell, *Football and the English*, 65–6.

[26] Ibid., 65.

[27] Ibid., 53.

[28] Joyce, *Visions of the People*, 183.

[29] David Craig, Introduction to Dickens, *Hard Times*, 16.

[30] Dickens, *Hard Times*, 65.

[31] Snow, *The Realists*, 72.

[32] Leavis, 'Hard Times: The World of Bentham', 257–8. The relevant account of the visiting circus is in chapter six, 'Sleary's Horsemanship', of Dickens, *Hard Times*, 70–83.

[33] Catton, 'Preston North End', 391.

[34] Ibid., 392.

[35] Russell, *Football and the English*, 47.

[36] Mason, *Association Football and English Society*, 230.

[37] Ibid.

[38] Ibid., 231.

[39] Russell, *Football and the English*, 65; Holt, *Sport and the British*, 159–79.

[40] Dunning, Murphy and Williams, *The Roots of Football Hooliganism*.

41   Cf. Mason, *Association Football and English Society*, 230.

42   Mellor, 'The Social and Geographical Make-up', 34.

43   Kelly, *Terrace Heroes*, 2.

44   Catton, 'Preston North End', 395.

45   This criticism has particular currency with fans of Manchester City FC who, in turn, promote their own club as English football's genuine Manchester representative. See Brown, '"Manchester United is Red?"'.

46   Johnes and Mason, 'Soccer, Public History', 123.

47   Melvyn Bragg, introduction to *The Rules of Association Football 1863*, 16.

48   Russell, *Football and the English*, 32.

49   Moore, *Museums and Popular Culture*, 123. A dedicated critical discussion of sports museums can be found in Vamplew, 'Facts and Artefacts'.

50   Moore, *Museums and Popular Culture*, 124.

51   Ibid., 123.

52   Brabazon, *Playing on the Periphery*, 57–8.

53   National Football Museum, Annual Report 2007.

54   Brabazon, *Playing on the Periphery*, 59.

55   Alsop's 'SuperCity' concept and related plans were featured in an exhibition at Manchester's Urbis Gallery, 20 January–15 May 2005. 'Coast to Coast' was one of three 'Supercities' featured in a television series of that name on Channel Four in 2003. See also the book from the Urbis exhibition, *Will Alsop's SuperCity*.

56   Brabazon, *Playing on the Periphery*, 41.

57   Comment made to author by John 'Rowdy' Maxted, June 2005.

58   http://www.bbc.co.uk/history/prgrammes/restoration/2003/#victoriabaths.

59   Andrews, 'Dead and Alive?', 78.

60   Bale, *Landscapes of Sport*, 170.

61   Ibid., 169.

62   Ibid., 170.

63   MacCannell, *The Tourist*.

64   Inglis, *Football Grounds of Britain*, 9.

65   Hughson, 'Sport in the "City of Culture"'.

66   Gumbrecht, *In Praise of Athletic Beauty*, 227.

67   Inglis, *The Football Grounds of Britain*, 302. For a dedicated discussion of the Stadio Luigi Ferraris see Inglis, *The Football Grounds of Europe*, 23–7.

68   Ibid., 301.

69   *Lancashire Evening Post*, 29 May 2007. http://www.lep.co.uk/news?articleid = 2910690

70   Hughson and Free, 'Paul Willis, Cultural Commodities', 82–3.

71   For a summary account see Ward and Burns, *Baseball*, 347–8; For a detailed account that goes against the bulk of anti-move sentiment see Sullivan, *The Dodgers Move West*.

72   Ward and Burns, *Baseball*, 348.

73   For discussion of the former three examples see Roberts, 'A Myth Grows in Brooklyn', 5-6; For discussion of the film *Blue in the Face* see Hughson, '"Smoke and Mirrors"'.

74   *When It Was a Game*. HBO, 1992.

75   *Baseball*. Dir. Ken Burns, 1994.

76   McGee, *The Greatest Ballpark Ever*, 61–2.

77   Neilson, 'Baseball', 47.

78   Prince, *Brooklyn's Dodgers*, 102. For related evidence and discussion of fractious dimensions within Brooklyn's baseball fandom see Roberts, 'A Myth Grows in Brooklyn' and Golenbock, *Bums: An Oral History of the Brooklyn Dodgers*.

79   Miller, *Lewis Mumford*, 218.

80   Riess, *City Games*, 35; Adelman, 'The First Baseball Game'.

[81]   Ward and Burns, *Baseball*, 321 and 339–44.
[82]   Roberts, 'A Myth Grows in Brooklyn', 12.
[83]   Henderson, *Ball, Bat and Bishop*, 170–81.
[84]   Bodnar, *Remaking America*, 13.
[85]   Ibid., 15.
[86]   Samuel, *Theatres of Memory*, 15.
[87]   Kissane, 'Baseball and the Urban Crisis', 96.
[88]   Voigt, *American Baseball*, 5.
[89]   Blount, 'Soil is the Soul of Baseball', 80.
[90]   Inglis, *Football Grounds of Britain*, 302.
[91]   Bale, *Landscapes of Sport*, 134.
[92]   A related term 'civil religion' is used in Evans, 'Baseball as Civil Religion'.
[93]   Mandelbaum, *The Meaning of Sports*, 41.
[94]   Barth, *City People*, 148–9.
[95]   Ibid., 149.
[96]   Holt, *Sport and the British*, 137–8.
[97]   Barth, *City People*, 148.
[98]   Rykwert, *The Seduction of Place*, 5.

References

Adelman, M.L. 'The First Baseball Game, the First Newspaper References to Baseball, and the New York Club: a Note on the Early History of Baseball'. *Journal of Sport History*, Notes, Documents and Queries section 7, no. 3 (Winter 1980): 132–5.

Andrews, D.L. 'Dead and Alive?: Sports History in the Late Capitalist Moment'. *Sporting Traditions* 16, no. 1 (1999): 73–83.

Bale, J. *Landscapes of Sport*. Leicester: Leicester University Press, 1994.

Barth, G. *City People: The Rise of Modern City Culture in Nineteenth-Century America*. New York: Oxford University Press, 1980.

Blackham, H.J. *Humanism*. Harmondsworth: Penguin, 1968.

Blount, Jr., R. 'Soil is the Soul of Baseball'. In *Baseball Diamonds: Tales, Traces, Visions and Voodoo From a Native American Rite*, edited by K. Kerrane and R. Grossinger, 80–2. Garden City, NY: Anchor Press/Doubleday, 1980.

Bodnar, J. *Remaking America: Public Memory, Commemoration, and Patriotism in the Twentieth Century*. Princeton, NJ: Princeton University Press, 1992.

Bowden, M. 'Soccer'. In *The Theatre of Sport*, edited by Karl B. Raitz, 97–140. Baltimore, MD: Johns Hopkins University Press, 1995.

Brabazon, T. *Playing on the Periphery: Sport, Identity and Memory*. London: Routledge, 2006.

Brown, A. '"Manchester United is Red?": Manchester United, Fan Identity, and the "Sport City"'. In *Manchester United: A Thematic Study*, edited by D.L. Andrews, 175–89. London: Routledge, 2004.

Catton, J. 'Preston North End – The Pioneers of Professionalism [1926]'. In *The Footballers Companion*, edited by B. Glanville, 391–401. London: Eyre and Spottiswoode, 1962.

Dickens, C. *Hard Times*, intro. by David Craig. Harmondsworth: Penguin, 1986.

Dunning, E., P. Murphy, and J. Williams. *The Roots of Football Hooliganism*. London: Routledge, 1988.

Evans, C.H. 'Baseball as Civil Religion: The Genesis of an American Creation Story'. In *The Faith of Fifty Million: Baseball, Religion and American Culture*, edited by C.H. Evans and W.R. Herzog II, 13–33. Louisville, KY: John Knox Press, 2002.

Geddes, P. *Cities in Evolution: An Introduction to the Town Planning Movement and to the Study of Civics*. London: Williams and Northgate, 1915.

Golenbock, P. *Bums: An Oral History of the Brooklyn Dodgers*. New York: Pocket Books, 1984.

Gumbrecht, H.U. *In Praise of Athletic Beauty*. Cambridge, MA: The Belknap Press of Harvard University, 2006.

Henderson, R.W. *Ball, Bat and Bishop: The Origin of Ball Games*. Urbana, IL: University of Illinois, 2001.

Holt, R. *Sport and the British: A Modern History*. Oxford: Clarendon Press, 1992.

Howard, E. *Garden Cities of To-morrow*. Cambridge, MA: MIT Press, 1965.

Hughson, J. 'Sport in the "City of Culture"'. *The International Journal of Cultural Policy* 10, no. 3 (2004): 319–30.

Hughson, J. '"Smoke and Mirrors": Evocations of the Brooklyn Dodgers and Ebbets Field in *Blue in the Face*'. *Sport in Society* 11, no. 2/3 (2008): 265–78.

Hughson, J., and M. Free. 'Paul Willis, Cultural Commodities and Collective Sport Fandom'. *Sociology of Sport Journal* 23, no. 1 (2006): 72–85.

Inglis, S. *The Football Grounds of Europe*. London: Willow Books/Collins, 1990.

Inglis, S. *Football Grounds of Britain*. 3rd ed. London: Collins Willow, 1996.

Johnes, M., and R. Mason. 'Soccer, Public History and the National Football Museum'. *Sport in History* 23, no. 1 (2003): 115–31.

Joyce, P. *Visions of the People: Industrial England and the Question of Class 1848–1914*. Cambridge: Cambridge University Press, 1991.

Kelly, G. *Terrace Heroes*. London: Routledge, 2004.

Kissane, J. 'Baseball and the Urban Crisis'. In *Baseball & the Game of Ideas: Essays for the Serious Fan*, edited by P.C. Bjarkman, 93–7. Delhi, NY: Birch Book Press, 1993.

Leavis, F.R. 'Hard Times: The World of Bentham'. In *Dickens the Novelist*, by F.R. and Q.D. Leavis, 251–81. Harmondsworth: Penguin, 1972.

MacCannell, D. *The Tourist*. New York: Schoken, 1976.

Mandelbaum, Michael. *The Meaning of Sports: Why Americans Watch Baseball, Football, and Basketball and What They See When They Do*. New York: Public Affairs, 2004.

Mason, T. *Associational Football and English Society 1863–1915*. Brighton: Harvester Press, 1980.

Mellor, G. 'The Social and Geographical Make-up of Football Crowds in the Northwest of England'. *The Sports Historian* 19, no. 2 (1999): 25–42.

Miller, D.L. *Lewis Mumford: A Life*. Pittsburgh, PA: University of Pittsburgh Press, 1989.

Moore, K. *Museums and Popular Culture*. London: Cassell, 1997.

Mumford, L. *Technics and Civilization*. New York: Harcourt, Brace and Company, 1934.

Mumford, L. *The Culture of Cities*. London: Martin Secker and Warburg, 1938.

Nawrat, C., and S. Hutchings. *The Sunday Times Illustrated History of Football*. London: Hamlyn, 1994.

Neilson, B.J. 'Baseball'. In *The Theatre of Sport*, edited by K.B. Raitz, 30–69. Baltimore, MD: Johns Hopkins University Press, 1995.

Prince, C.E. *Brooklyn's Dodgers: The Bums, the Borough and the Best of Baseball, 1947–1957*. New York: Oxford University Press, 1996.

Riess, S.A. *City Games: The Evolution of American Urban Society and the Rise of Sports*. Urbana, IL: University of Illinois Press, 1991.

Roberts, F. 'A Myth Grows in Brooklyn: Urban Death, Resurrection, and the Brooklyn Dodgers'. *Baseball History* 2, no. 2 (1987): 4–26.

Ruskin, J. *Munera Pulveris: Six Essays on the Elements of Political Economy*. 3rd small ed. London: George Allen, 1898.

Russell, D. *Football and the English: A Social History of Association Football in England, 1863–1995*. Preston: Carnegie, 1997.

Rykwert, J. *The Seduction of Place: The City in the Twenty-First Century*. New York: Pantheon Books, 2000.

Samuel, R. *Theatres of Memory (volume 1): Past and Present in Contemporary Culture*. London: Verso, 1994.

Scott, G. *The Architecture of Humanism*. 2nd ed. London: Constable, 1924.

Snow, C.P. *The Realists: Portraits of Eight Novelists*. London: Macmillan, 1978.

Spengler, O. *The Decline of the West*. London: Allen and Unwin, 1954.

Sullivan, N.J. *The Dodgers Move West*. New York: Oxford University Press, 1987.

The Rules of Association Football 1863, intro. by Melvyn Bragg. Oxford: Bodleian Library, 2006.

Vamplew, W. 'Facts and Artefacts: Sports Historians and Sports Museums'. *Journal of Sport History* 25, no. 2 (1998): 268–82.

Voigt, D.Q. *American Baseball: From Gentleman's Sport to the Commissioner System*. Norman, OK: University of Oklahoma Press, 1966.

Waller, P.J. *Town, City and Nation: England 1850–1914*. Oxford: Oxford University Press, 1983.

Walvin, J. *The People's Game: A Social History of British Football*. London: Allen Lane, 1975.

Ward, G.C., and K. Burns. *Baseball: An Illustrated History*. New York: Knopf, 1994.

Will Alsop's SuperCity. Manchester: Urbis, 2005.

Sport and history on the ground: documentary and the feature film

For the most part this volume has been concerned with the historical development of sport in western society from the latter part of the nineteenth century. It has been particularly interested in how distinctive sporting cultures have been *made* collectively and with how sport has held tremendous significance within people's lives over time. This essay looks at how the history of sport is maintained for posterity on moving film in the form of documentary programmes, series and feature films. This interest is driven by the assumption that moments in history are increasingly learnt about by the majority of people via the medium of film, whether this be in the cinema or in the home watching a television broadcast or a DVD. Documentaries and feature film, obviously enough, have quite a different status, the former generally expected to be news-like and based in fact, the latter, if historically themed, to be afforded some artistic license in the interpretation of events. Yet both occupy a terrain of what is discussed in this essay as 'popular history', and as such are of interest to the scholar of history and popular culture. The essay commences with a discussion on the nature of documentary, laying the ground for a consideration of the sport documentary, focus being placed on Ken Burns's epic series *Baseball*, a programme which has been the topic of considerable debate within sport history circles. Historical episodes addressed in *Baseball* prompt a comparative discussion of the feature films *A League of Their Own*, *Soul of the Game* and *Eight Men Out*. The intention is not to establish one filmic form as superior to the other but to give an appreciation of how documentary and feature film can function complementarily in the provision of historical knowledge.

Documentary: actuality and creativity

The actual term 'documentary', in relation to film, is often traced back to John Grierson, a British filmmaker commonly regarded as one of the founding fathers of the genre. Grierson recognized that although the suspension of aesthetic judgement was assumed for the documentary-making endeavour, documentary makers inevitably rely on such judgement when assembling their work.[1] That is to say, documentary making is necessarily creative. Grierson himself was renowned for the highly realistic nature of his filmmaking in social documentaries of 1930s Britain such as *Drifters*, a study of Scottish herring fleets.[2] Regarding documentary as a source of 'public education', he used film as a medium to show what was actually going on in the world from the perspective of people in their everyday lives.[3] But, as indicated, Grierson also recognized documentary making to be a creative activity, the representation of reality in documentaries always being intruded upon by the creative impulses of the filmmaker. Kilborn and Izod specify the 'two counterpoised tendencies' suggested in Grierson's discussion of documentary making. Firstly, there exists an actuality component, whereby 'the documentarist is claiming our attention on the strength of her or his ability to reproduce or represent events which have occurred in the external world'. Secondly, there is a creative component whereby a 'series of structuring and narrativising ploys [are] brought to bear in order to heighten the impact of the film or programme on an audience'. The 'whole documentary enterprise' exists in a perpetual state of tension between these tendencies.[4]

Of course, documentaries differ in the seriousness of their intent and educative purpose. Documentaries used explicitly for means of education, for example within the context of Open University broadcasts, bear high expectations of factual accuracy. On the other hand, some documentaries aspire to no more than 'infotainment' and as such enliven the old journalistic adage, 'never let the facts get in the way of a good story'. Presentation of, and access to, documentaries of these different kinds has become jumbled within the surfeit of documentary and history channels available on pay television networks. Documentaries on crime solving and UFOs are intermingled with histories of famous battles from the Second World War and biographies of past monarchs. Interestingly, an acknowledged classic documentary made in the early days of colour television in the United Kingdom has featured in recent years on the Australian and New Zealand versions of the global *History Channel*. *Civilisation*, a 13-episode documentary, which first appeared on the British Broadcasting Corporation (BBC) television channel BBC2 in February 1969, showed its writer and presenter Kenneth Clark, former Director of Britain's National Gallery, speaking within famous art galleries and in front of various cultural monuments, which he adjudged within an historical overview of western aesthetic endeavour. Clark had previously made documentaries that were effectively televised lectures, but in partnership with director Michael Gill produced a programme that achieved both general popularity and critical acclaim.[5]

Clark believed in the democratic possibilities of television, to the extent that the medium provided a lively and engaging means of bringing the arts into the homes of average people. In the forward to the book accompanying *Civilisation* Clark maintained, 'I am convinced that a combination of words and music, colour and movement can extend human experience in a way words alone cannot do'.[6] Clark accepted the Arnoldian inspired concept of public service broadcasting; he believed that television held a humanizing 'power', as long as it provided programmes of educative worth and artistic quality to outweigh the descending 'vulgarity' threatened by unregulated commercialism.[7] Although much current television within the UK may have lived up to Clark's worst fears, his influence within documentary making can still be seen, especially within television history documentary. Noteworthy in this regard is the 16-episode *History of Britain*, written and presented by the eminent historian Simon Schama. *History of Britain*, which first screened on BBC2 in 2000, has been praised by Arthur Marwick as providing a 'history on the ground' whereby Schama popularizes scholarship, without intellectual sacrifice, by incorporating quotations from primary sources into visual re-enactments conducted at the locations where history occurred. Marwick refers to Schama as an 'auteur', a master of the 'interpretative synthesis', which we might take to mean the synthesis of the actuality and creative components in documentary making and presentation.[8]

The term 'history on the ground' was used to describe work immediately prior to that of E.P. Thompson's 'history from below'.[9] The outstanding work of the earlier 'movement' was W.G. Hoskins's *The Making of the English Landscape*, published in 1955. Hoskins defined history on the ground, if somewhat unintentionally, in his description of the historian going beyond the work of the geologist:

> He [the geologist] explains to us the bones of the landscape, the fundamental structure that gives form and colour to the scene and produces a certain kind of topography and natural vegetation. But the flesh that covers the bones, and the details of the features, are the concern of the historian, whose task it is to show how man has clothed the geological skeleton during the comparatively recent past.[10]

The Making of the English Landscape inspired another BBC2 documentary programme, *English Landscapes* (1973), which was written and presented by Hoskins.[11] In the book published to accompany this programme Hoskins refers to his prevailing interest in the 'powerful [human] imprint made upon the landscape'.[12] This phrase highlights the fundamental difference between Hoskins and Thompson and their respective understandings of what is meant by the term *the making of*. Despite reference elsewhere to local history being essentially concerned with 'striv[ing] to hear the men and women of the past talking and working, and creating what has come down to us ... for our present enjoyment',[13] Hoskins's emphasis on landscape and topography, while considering the impact of humanity, tends to leave human voices unheard. His 'history on the ground' is thus more a history of the ground and, in this way, quite distinct from Thompson's 'history from below'.

Hoskins's chapter on the Industrial Revolution in *The Making of the English Landscape* is especially telling. Unlike Thompson, he was not concerned with how the working class made a way of life, but with how a 'landscape of Hell' was made in such areas as the Potteries and the Black Country.[14] Hoskins, as a recent critic has pointed out, was above all a rural romantic who craved the 'the gentle unravished landscape' of his imagined England past.[15] Hoskins's paean to romantic sensibility is explicit enough. He commences *The Making of the English Landscape* in genuflection to Wordsworth and by acclaiming, 'poets make the best topographers'.[16] However, the romantic outlook can hinder the possibility of the documentary realism that Hoskins, assumedly, wants to achieve in both his books and filmic work. Furthermore, the romantic vision of a countryside trammelled by various aspects of modernity has been associated with the promotion of a conservative national consciousness fearful of any development posing potential threat to a presumed natural state of affairs.[17]

In what follows, this discussion of Hoskins, history on the ground and the related themes of romance and landscape are drawn upon in a consideration of the television sport documentary. The focus of analysis is placed on Ken Burns's nine-episode (divided into 'innings' mostly relating to decades), over 18-hour long, *Baseball*, completed in 1994 and screened in the US on the Public Broadcasting Service (PBS).

Baseball and the 'vernacular landscape'

A connection between Hoskins and Burns is not particularly obvious and cannot be made directly, as Hoskins's work contained 'no reference to North American or other generalizing traditions'.[18] Nevertheless, Hoskins's humanistic approach to landscape studies has appeal extending beyond Britain, as the naming of a volume *The Making of an American Landscape* surely indicates.[19] Hoskins's work – despite key differences – has been likened to that of the foundational American figure in humanistic geography John Brinkerhoff Jackson. The term 'vernacular landscape' has been used to capture Jackson's insistence on the need to understand how landscapes are culturally inhabited.[20] Ken Burns's *Baseball* helps to make sense of the term. His documentary can be said to give view to baseball as a significant feature on an American 'vernacular landscape'. Burns claims such like intention in the preface to the television series' accompanying book, by affirming the Barzun dictum, 'whoever wants to know the heart and mind of America had better learn baseball'. Burns (with Lyn Novick) elaborates:

> For both the book and the film series, it was our intention to pursue the game – and its memories and myths – across the expanse of American history. We quickly developed an abiding conviction that the game of baseball offered a unique prism through which one could see refracted much more than the history of games won and lost, teams rising and falling, rookies arriving and veterans saying farewell. The story of baseball is also the story of race in America, of immigration and assimilation, of the struggle between labour and management, of popular culture and advertising, of myth and the nature of heroes, villains, and buffoons; of the role of women and class and wealth in our society. The game is a repository of age-old American verities, of standards against which we continually measure ourselves, and yet at the same time a mirror of the present moment in our modern culture – including all of our most contemporary failings.[21]

Whether or not *Baseball* lives up to Burns's ambition is arguable. The predominant criticism made of the programme is that Burns invests it with a liberal optimism for baseball as a unifying force standing above the divisions and conflicts of American civilization. This criticism is elaborated as the essay proceeds, but to be clear at the outset, the position of this author is that *Baseball* largely fulfils Burns's Barzunian ambition, and in so doing presents an illuminating cultural history of its subject. Indeed, *Baseball* presents a history on the ground which makes the past audible via what Burns refers to as 'a chorus of first-person voices'.[22] Furthermore, imagery from period photography, artwork and newsreel footage gives 'authentic' view of baseball through the years, placing the sport within a vernacular landscape, as claimed for Burns above. The cumulative effect is an historical ethnography developed across the series. Thus *Baseball* presents not only a history from the ground but also a 'history from within', whereby genuine attempt is made to show baseball from the inside out, i.e. from the perspective of its collective heart and mind. Here, cultural history meets social history as *Baseball* addresses themes of race, gender and class. As the essay proceeds, these themes are discussed respectively in relation to key episodes in the history of baseball – the Negro Leagues; the All American Girls Baseball League; the Chicago Black Sox scandal – and in contrast to the representation of these episodes within the feature films *Soul of the Game*, *A League of Their Own* and *Eight Men Out*.

At this point it becomes appropriate to take up a general discussion of history within feature film before returning to sport and the particular examples of baseball-related films mentioned above and, where appropriate, their relationship to the documentary *Baseball*. The conventional historian's view of feature film dealing with historical episodes is one of scepticism. The position is aptly captured by Arthur Marwick's remark, 'a film is a film is a film'.[23] Unsurprisingly, Marwick goes on to endorse Carnes's claim that film does not 'provide a substitute for history that has been painstakingly assembled from the best available evidence and analysis'.[24] Yet, given the acknowledgement, 'more and more of the population learn smatterings of history from film', Marwick concedes that historians must be prepared to enter the public fray of films' discussion. The obligation of such engagement for the historian is the need to 'show exactly how films which appear to be based on real events in fact depart very seriously from these events'.[25] Accordingly, Marwick attacks the Hollywood film *U-571* (2000) for its distortion of events surrounding the capturing of the Enigma decoding machine from a German submarine in May 1941. While in reality the capture was made by the British navy, *U-571* reset the incident in April 1942 to conveniently allow the capture to be an act of American heroism. The director Jonathon Mostow dismissed obvious enough broadsides at the film's credibility by claiming its purpose to be 'entertainment not information'.[26] In common parlance such a response would be regarded as a cop-out. While the feature film may not be expected to follow the rigours of academic history, there is surely a responsibility to keep embellishment at remove from wilful distortion. In the case of *U-571* some British critics called for the film to carry an historical disclaimer. Given the film's very existence on the basis of historical pretension this request would not seem unreasonable.

Another film to rouse controversy, in terms of historical inaccuracy, is the Mel Gibson directed *Braveheart* (1995). Jeffrey Richards has accused the film of, *inter alia*, having the 'Scots wear woad a thousand years too late and clan tartan five hundred years too early'.[27] Inaccuracy abounds concerning locations of battles and the biographical details of historical figures. More alarming to Richards than the error in detail per se, is the subsequent bolstering within Scotland of an extremely crude nationalism based on the film's blatant Anglophobia. However, this is not to suggest that films of historical theme less prone to distortion than *Braveheart* do not have ideological implications. For example, and from the genre of sport films, the Disney production *Miracle* (2004) presents the story the US Men's Hockey team in preparation for the 1980 Winter Olympic Games. The film concludes with the US team overturning a previous defeat against the much-fancied Soviet Union team, winning the Olympic Final and claiming the Gold Medal. The actual occurrence of events may not be in dispute but the portrayal of the US team's triumph in *Miracle* can be seen as a thinly disguised glorification of American patriotism transpiring at the height of the Cold War. The film might also serve to rouse patriotism during the current period of scare over terrorism.[28]

Within some branches of contemporary scholarship on history and film, meticulousness of detail and accuracy in fact are not of paramount importance. According to Rosenstone:

> history film [may be seen] as part of a separate realm of representation and discourse, one not meant to provide literal truths about the past ... but metaphoric truths which work, to a large degree, as a kind of commentary on, and challenge to, traditional historical discourse.[29]

From this perspective might not *Braveheart* be doing history a favour by challenging the conventional telling of the William Wallace story that has been handed down over the years in history books? Some may believe so, but if a film is to be defended on the grounds of an entertainment as opposed to an information value, then surely it can offer little by way of historical lesson either literally or metaphorically. Rosenstone uses Barthes's term 'reality effects' to describe how filmic depictions of historical events can rouse strong feelings within the viewer. The elicitation of an immediate emotional impact is what distinguishes 'the history film from history on the page'. But, if we accept Natalie Zemon Davis's view that filmmakers are not reasonably expected to be official historians but 'artists for whom history matters', in tandem with Rosenstone's claim that history feature films and docudramas are becoming increasingly relied upon by a 'huge segment of the population' for historical knowledge, then filmmakers – at least those who make historically themed films – might well be regarded as artists burdened with considerable responsibility.[30] Obviously enough, the historical film will not be as complex and detailed as the written history. Rather than assessing the merits of a film by comparing it to the written historical record it is preferable to see it as a special and very pertinent type of cultural history. In that regard, the historical film's merits will have much to do with how it negotiates the 'experiential and emotional complexities' that arise in regard to its historical subject matter.[31]

Women in baseball: *A League of Their Own*

According to Pierre Sorlin, all historical films are imaginary reconstructions of the past, which 'combine actual events and completely fictitious individual episodes'.[32] He goes on to suggest that as a device to hold audience interest, the representation of history in film passes from the general to the particular and in so doing is inclined to narrow the viewing focus to personal situations. Some films more than others will justify Sorlin's contention. The 1992 film *A League of Their Own* certainly does so. *A League of Their Own* is a fictionalized account of the first year of the All-American Girl's Baseball League (AAGBL). The League commenced in 1943 at a time when the men's major league, and men's baseball in general, was threatened by the unavailability of personnel, given the large number of men involved in war service. While the film, directed by Penny Marshall, is rather obviously intended to be historically informative about this significant episode in American sporting history, it plays to the talents of its Hollywood ensemble (including Geena Davis, Tom Hanks, Madonna, Lori Petty and Rosie O'Donnell) who are cast into fictional composite roles to resemble stereotypes of characters associated with the AAGBL. The film is based on an eponymous television documentary from 1987.[33] The documentary features interviews with women who played in the AAGBL and it is apparent enough that characters in the film *A League of Their Own* have been framed in their image.

A number of possibilities have been put forward for the real life player on whom the Geena Davis character Dottie Hinson is based. As she shared the same first name, team and position, Dottie Green, catcher for the Rockford Peaches, has been prominently mentioned. More importantly, though, Davis's Hinson character is representative of the glamorous in appearance, yet athletically capable, young woman that was sought by the organizers of the AAGBL. Susan Cahn has noted the determination from the outset to construct a women's baseball league that was culturally distinct from women's softball.[34] While the latter sport carried a derided image of mannishness, the AAGBL was conceived as a bastion of ladylikeness. Accordingly, the young women recruited to the league were sent to etiquette classes and throughout gruelling road trips across the US Midwest teams were accompanied by female chaperons and the players were confined to their hotel rooms after dark. The chauvinistic intentions of the AAGBL owner – Philip K. Wrigley of chewing gum fame, depicted in the film as confectionary magnate Mr Harvey – and the resultant resentment of the players are clearly exposed in *A League of Their Own*. Players are shown mocking their compulsory attendance of a 'charm school', and as reluctant to wear mini-skirt type dresses that gave no protection against skin abrasion to the upper legs when sliding into base. Most impressively, in mark of historical respect to the women who played in the AAGBL, the film portrays the players as not only dedicated to baseball but as highly proficient sportspeople. This image is reinforced by coverage of the AAGBL in the 'Sixth Inning' of *Baseball*.

A League of Their Own is unarguably of the Hollywood blockbuster type. Yet, as one critic argues, 'despite creating some cliché sports movie team characters and predictable plot points, [the film offers] sassy dialogue and capture[s] well the prevailing social attitudes of the 1940s'.[35] Indeed, the fictionalization is developed in a way that enhances the film's depiction of the age and the AAGBL within it. For example the romantic tension that simmers between Hanks's Jimmy Dugan and Davis's Dottie Hinson would have been eventually consummated in most Hollywood films made in the last few decades. However, Dottie's primary source of identity remains being a housewife and she not only checks her attraction to Jimmy – who also acts honourably towards her – but quits baseball after one season to return to life on the farm with her husband upon his release from the army. This in itself is a romanticzed plotline that fits well within conventional desires of respectable womanhood, but, nevertheless, the tension that weighed on Dottie between obligation to domesticity and wanting to play baseball was surely experienced by women in the AAGBL.

The representation of Hanks's Dugan as a cantankerous, alcoholic former player, who initially resents being assigned the job of managing the Rockford Peaches, and does so only for the pay cheque, is also sociologically interesting. The real manager of the Rockford Peaches was former ballplayer Eddie Stumpf and there is no suggestion that he was anything like Hanks's Dugan in temperament and attitude. It seems more likely that the Dugan character was modelled on the reputedly alcoholic Jimmie Foxx, the former batting great who assented to manage the Fort Wayne Daisies in the AAGBL once unable to secure himself a playing contract in the majors. However, more important than the real life influence for the character is that Dugan symbolizes the prevailing male negativity about woman being able to play baseball. Dugan's initial view was little different from that of the male spectators in *A League of Their Own* who goaded AAGBL players from the bleachers. That the women were able to turn the opinion of the arch-critic Dugan around was further testament to their playing skills, and his character is again symbolic in this regard. While male chauvinism toward woman ballplayers was no doubt well entrenched, there must have been men who had their prejudices altered after watching the AAGBL in the 1940s.

The relevant listing in *Leonard Maltin's Film Guide* describes *A League of Their Own* as 'good natured fiction that sheds light on a neglected chapter of real-life sports history'.[36] The renowned film critic Roger Ebert gives a similar view with a personal twist. Ebert confesses that although being a devoted young baseball fan (12 years of age) in 1954 when the AAGBL folded, he had no idea about the flourishing existence of women's professional baseball in the

United States until he saw *A League of Their Own* upon its release in 1992.[37] Ebert's ignorance is likely to have been common. Gai Ingham Berlage notes in the conclusion to her book *Women in Baseball: the Forgotten History* that 'the biggest impact on the public awareness' of the history of women's baseball in the US has been *A League of Their Own*.[38] Berlage adds the qualifying concern that, while the film has served a positive purpose in bringing women's baseball to public attention, it can give the false impression that the AAGBL is the beginning and end of the story and that once the men returned from the war women stopped playing the sport altogether. This cautionary note notwithstanding, it can be reasonably concluded that *A League of Their Own* is a significant artefact of *popular history*, performing a valuable informational function. That the film is available in a DVD format also containing the 1987 documentary adds to this informational or educative value.

Gender is, of course, the key theme of social history interest in *A League of Their Own*, intertwined with other themes, especially regionalism – the farm-girls Dottie and her sister Kit being teased at the AAGBL trials in Chicago by the wisecracking urbanites Doris (Rosie O'Donnell) and May (Madonna). Race is another theme touched on in the film, but only fleetingly. During a Rockford Peaches warm-up session a wayward ball is retrieved by an African American woman in the crowd. Dottie moves part way towards the woman for the ball to be thrown to her but the woman throws it over her head to the player on base. Reinforced by a knowing look from Dottie, the point is clear enough – this woman would have found a place within the AAGBL if only it had been open to African American women. The inaugural year of the AAGBL was still some four in advance of Jackie Robinson's debut for the Brooklyn Dodgers in 1947. It is thus unsurprising in historical terms that the AAGBL was not open to African American women in 1943. Perhaps race could have been more thoroughly covered in *A League of Their Own* but the mere glimpse of the ball-throwing woman symbolizes the absence of African Americans from women's baseball and baseball in general at that point in American history.

Race in baseball: *Soul of the Game*

Race and baseball in the post-war 1940s is the central theme of another 1990s film, *Soul of the Game* (1996), directed by Kevin Rodney Sullivan. The film is set in 1945, the year that Jackie Robinson became a rookie for the Kansas City Monarchs in the Negro American League. The storyline of *Soul of the Game* focuses on the fortunes of three real life characters, Robinson, his team-mate Satchel Paige, and the big-hitting Josh Gibson of the Negro National League team the Homestead Grays. Paige and Gibson were the biggest stars in the Negro leagues and were anticipated to be the first African American players to join the Majors when rumblings about the integration of baseball stirred towards the end of the Second World War. *Soul of the Game* looks at the three players in relation to Branch Rickey's plan to sign a Negro league player to the Brooklyn Dodgers. The film offers a seemingly reliable account of how Rickey sent scouts to scrutinize leading 'Negro' players, with observation being made as much of their character and temperament as of playing ability. The film captures the sense of injustice felt by Paige and Gibson at being overlooked by Rickey for Robinson. It also addresses Gibson's apparent decline in mental health, attributable to a brain tumour that caused his death at the age of 36 in January 1947.

Soul of the Game importantly gives view to the showman-like style of the Negro Leagues as played out in the exchanges between Paige and Gibson. The 1976 film *The Bingo Long Travelling All-Stars and Motor Kings* (based on William Brashler's novel) went further in this regard, via the fictional depiction of a team that breaks away from the Negro leagues in 1939 to travel in circus fashion from town to town. This film has been criticized for its comedic celebration of a Stepnfetchit type 'Negro' baseball.[39] However, in its defence, *The Bingo Long Travelling All-Stars and Motor Kings* draws upon historical referents. Negro teams, especially when operating independently of the leagues, did at times resort to vaudevillian gimmickry to attract audiences. Even the Kansas City Monarchs spent a period barnstorming around the Midwest, playing exhibition games including a number against the sect-based House of David team. As Sobchack remarks, 'the film's humour is often pointed', the descent into farce forcing reflection upon the ludicrous circumstances into which the players were pushed to make a dollar from their sport.[40] The light-hearted invocation of W.E.B. Dubois in repartee between the lead characters Bingo Long and Leon Carter (the former claimed by Director John Badham to be loosely based on Satchel Paige, the latter on Josh Gibson, both of whom are shown in Newsreel footage at the commencement of the film), too, has serious intent. It is from Leon's mention of Dubois that Bingo derives inspiration to put his own team together in defiance of the exploitative Negro League managers.

The setting of *The Bingo Long Travelling All-Stars and Motor Kings* and *Soul of the Game* at either end of the Second World War, respectively, makes for interesting comparison. The hand-to-mouth existence of the 'All-Star' players in the late 1930s is not apparent with the elite Negro league players seen in *Soul of the Game*. These players enjoy affluent lifestyles by comparison, and as much as they would no doubt prosper further from entry to the Majors, their motivation to move beyond the Negro leagues appears more intrinsic than instrumental, being driven by a desire for ultimate recognition as ballplayers. However, *Soul of the Game*, from the outset, shows that the talents of Paige and Gibson were nurtured and developed within a sporting culture quite different from that of modern Major league baseball. Early in the film Jackie Robinson rebukes Paige during a game for showboating. This gives indication of what is to come; Robinson rather than Paige will be the first player to gain a Major league contract. Towards the end of the film Branch Rickey attends a game between the Kansas City Monarchs and the Homestead Grays, presumably to finalize his decision on the player to be signed by the Brooklyn Dodgers. Following a by-now familiar exchange of mock insults, Paige walks three batters to get Gibson to the plate and, although Paige strikes his adversary out, Rickey looks on suitably unimpressed by these antics. Even though Paige wants to curry favour with Rickey he is unable to play the game in a way acceptable to the Dodger's manager, the latter providing symbolic presence within the film of a white baseball audience.

Aaron Baker suggests that the Paige and Gibson characters personify the title of *Soul of the Game*. They do so by embodying a 'black style', typical of 'Negro' baseball.[41] Robinson's acceptance by Rickey does not indicate that he is devoid of this style but that he has not been enculturated into the 'Negro' game to the same extent as Paige and Gibson, after their many years of playing under segregation. Robinson's 'tricky baseball' was no doubt seen by white fans in racialised terms, but positively, without pejorative vaudevillian association. Robinson is portrayed in *Soul of the Game* as an individual socialized into the disciplinary ways of white organization. His background as an army lieutenant comes patronisingly to the fore in his interaction with fellow players, including Paige. For Baker, this portrayal sees 'Robinson as an Uncle Tom who has yet to learn about the soul of the game his teammates play'.[42] This characterization of Robinson serves to sharpen his distinction in the film from Paige and Gibson, but such cinematic simplification masks the complexity of the real Jackie Robinson and, in less heroic terms, builds on the one dimensional image that was created in *The Jackie Robinson Story* (1950), in which Robinson himself played the title role. *Soul of the Game* thankfully has no villains; even the temptation to so portray Rickey was avoided in favour of an ambiguous depiction of his motives. Yet, unintended or otherwise – and perhaps largely attributable to a superb acting performance by Delroy Lindo – Satchel Paige emerges as *Soul of the Game*'s ultimate hero. Given Paige's existence on the margins of American baseball's history this may be regarded as just reward and in keeping with the retrieval of Paige in historical work since the 1970s.[43]

Cinema's tendency to promote romantic heroism at the expense of historical sobriety comes as no surprise and it does not deter historians such as Rosenstone from arguing for the informative importance of film. After all, conventional history writing, in many cases, is hardly free of hero celebration. Within the filmic domain, documentary, as well as feature film, is prone to heroic promotion. A particularly interesting persona in regard to Negro baseball is the former Kansas City Monarch's player Buck O'Neil, who features at various points throughout Ken Burns's *Baseball*. O'Neil played for the Monarchs from the late 1930s until the mid-1950s, with an interruption for military service in the mid-1940s. O'Neil, drawing upon his own background in the Negro American League, provides interview-style commentary on various aspects of race in baseball. O'Neil reflects upon the demise of the Negro leagues without rancour. While remembering his playing experience with tremendous affection, he suggests the Negro leagues became a necessary casualty as baseball advanced towards its ongoing destiny as the 'American pastime'. A number of reviewers regard O'Neil's as the most important voice in *Baseball*, as he comments on race in a non-antagonistic tone tinted with stoic pride. One journalist describes O'Neil as, 'a man whose stories and comments you always wanted more of', while Ken Burns regards him as *Baseball*'s 'conscience'.[44]

Daniel A. Nathan has interestingly critiqued the iconographic status publicly conferred upon O'Neil since his appearance in *Baseball*. Nathan believes that O'Neil provides 'the preferred personification of the Negro leagues', his refusal to be bitter making comfortable viewing, especially for a white television audience.[45] According to Nathan, O'Neil is seen to epitomize the declining values of contemporary America – 'self-reliance, integrity and moral worth and resolve' – the kind of values that Jackie Robinson was accredited with tenaciously upholding during his first season with the Dodgers in 1947. Viewed against the loudness and ill-temperedness of rap culture, O'Neil offers the alternative of a soothing voice, delivering a homespun humanism of cross-race appeal. O'Neil's rejection of victimhood confers upon him, according to Nathan, a 'version of heroic masculinity' whereby his bravery allows something positive to be derived from an unfortunate episode in the nation's history.[46] But O'Neil's is a rare voice. Nathan shares with writer Daniel Okrent the view (expressed during the 'Fifth Inning' of *Baseball*), 'O'Neil has a generosity of spirit that perhaps goes above and beyond the call'.[47] Nathan is partially critical of O'Neil himself; 'the version of the past that he narrates usually lacks a biting social critique and is instead a "feel good" history', but the brunt of his criticism is with O'Neil's heroic portrayal in the media. 'O'Neil ... is often used to represent race and the past simplistically. By positing O'Neil as an American icon, as an example of how to succeed in America, the media have placed the burden of improved race relations on African Americans, rather than whites *and* blacks'.

While this accusation may pertain to some subsequent media representations of O'Neil, it would be inaccurate to suggest that he is used in such a way in *Baseball*. Indeed, the view is clearly enough expressed throughout *Baseball*, particularly in the 'Fifth Inning', covering the 1940s and featuring the majority of O'Neil's commentary, that the racial segregation of baseball is a stain on the nation's historical pretension to democracy, for which white America is responsible. Burns has, indeed, been criticized for spending too much time in *Baseball* concentrating on the issue of racism.[48] This criticism sits interestingly alongside another. McConnell claims that Burns shares with the early American filmmaker D.W. Griffith, 'a universalist compulsion to turn whatever he was filming into a Big Statement on Everything'.[49] It is doubtful that Burns would take either of these criticisms to heart as he unapologetically works with a very large canvas and interweaves race through his images of America.

Scandal in the American game: *Eight Men Out*(ed)

An insightful comparative discussion of the respective history telling merits of documentary and feature film is presented in Daniel A. Nathan's book *Saying It's So: a Cultural History of the Black Sox Scandal.*[50] Nathan considers representations of the scandal in *Baseball* and in the 1988 film *Eight Men Out. Eight Men Out* is based on Eliot Asinof's acclaimed book of the same name.[51] The film, directed by John Sayles, roughly follows the chronological chapter development of Asinof's book: the fix, the series, the exposure, the impact, the trial, the aftermath. This episodic flow appears as an attempt to give importance to events over characters. According to Nathan, a strength of *Eight Men Out* is that it avoids sentimentalizing the scandal by making heroes of key figures, as in the manner of *Field of Dreams*' (1989) retrieval of the batting legend 'Shoeless' Joe Jackson.[52] *Eight Men Out*, Nathan notes, 'resists providing a unified vision of the Black Sox scandal ... by offering multiple perspectives on the narrative's principal actors'. Compared to contemporaneous baseball films, such as *Field of Dreams* and *Bull Durham* (1989), *Eight Men Out* was not a box office success, and, as Nathan suggests, this is likely to do with the film not living up to the usual conventions of cinematic drama.[53] For some critics, the denial of a singular narrative voice made the film difficult to follow and to appear as a series of fragments rather than a dramatic whole.[54]

Sayles dismisses clear-cut conclusions, believing that facile resolution does not do justice to the messiness of historical reality. The 'big story', for Sayles, is a jumble of the 'different stories' that the key characters involved in the Black Sox scandal have told overtime, often at cross-purposes with each other.[55] With regard to historically themed films in general, Sayles insists that to provide audiences with simple endings is to treat them condescendingly.[56] Accordingly, Sayles credits filmgoers with the capacity to absorb complexity and expects them to do further homework on the historical episodes treated in the films they watch. Sayles went on to appear as an onscreen commentator in the 'Third Inning' of *Baseball*, which concludes with coverage of the Black Sox scandal. Sayles endorses the view that the collective resentment created by the White Sox owner Charles Comiskey's parsimonious treatment of players had led to the game-fixing bribes being accepted. This view confers the representation of Comiskey in *Eight Men Out*, where his accountability for the ensuing scandal is flagged almost at the outset of the film. On the one hand Sayles's appearance in *Baseball* might be regarded as an endorsement of his view on the need for different filmic treatment of historical episodes, less generously it might be seen as artistic collusion, whereby *Baseball* and *Eight Men Out* reinforce each other's historical authority. The apparentness of such collusion is compounded by character doubling. In *Baseball* the voiceover for quotes by Hugh Fullerton is provided by the writer Studs Terkel, and the actor John Cusack provides a similar function for 'Buck' Weaver (White Sox third baseman). In *Eight Men Out*, Terkel plays the role of Fullerton and Cusack the role of Weaver.

Nevertheless, there are interesting points of dissimilarity, if not discrepancy, to note between *Baseball* and *Eight Men Out*. Apportionment of blame is one such dissimilarity. As indicated above, Comiskey is portrayed negatively from early on in *Eight Men Out*, and although Sayles would disfavour the identification of villains as he does heroes, Comiskey fairs badly in contrast to the sympathetic portrayal of most of the indicted players, excluding perhaps the chief conspirators of the eight, 'Chick' Gandil and 'Swede' Risberg. Comiskey fairs little better in *Baseball*; however, even greater opprobrium is heaped on the organized crime boss Arnold Rothstein, who is alleged to have been the figurehead behind the bribery scam. The lengthy segment in *Baseball*'s 'Third Inning' on the Black Sox scandal opens with focus on a photographic image of Rothstein, accompanied by voiceover reading of a well-known passage from F. Scott Fitzgerald's *The Great Gatsby*, which substitutes the fictional character of Meyer Wolfsheim for Arnold Rothstein. Included in the passage is the line, 'It never occurred to me that one man could start to play with the faith of fifty million people – with the single mindedness of a burglar blowing a safe'.[57] The use of this quote is evocative and relevant, but in the flow of the documentary narrative a viewer could be forgiven for failing to comprehend its fictional source. A less subtle usage of Fitzgerald's line could have avoided the unequivocal indictment of Rothstein and the inevitable implication of his casting as 'principal villain' (to use Nathan's term) in *Baseball*'s telling of the Black Sox scandal.[58]

Nathan contends that the demonizing of Rothstein in *Baseball* allows for a simple rendering of the scandal's complex events; other parties – the players, the gambler intermediaries, Comiskey – are complicit, but at the bottom line of blame stands Arnold Rothstein.[59] There is credence to this criticism but Nathan's subsequent claim that Burns's intention is for the players to be pitied, '[he] apparently wants viewers to feel their pain' is questionable. An alternative explanation for the primary blame being pinned on Rothstein is that he is someone extraneous to the game of baseball. Rothstein is portrayed as a verminous interloper, who sullies baseball with corruption typical of the worst side of American life. There is no great pity in *Baseball* for the players who succumb to the dubious solicitations of Rothstein's sleazy operatives, but the poison that infects the players comes from without, and with this recognized the game's intrinsic virtues remain untainted.

Nathan is correct in suggesting that the Black Sox scandal presents an especially difficult moment for Burns, hopeless romantic of baseball such that he is. But rather than don a different cloak to deal with the difficulty, Burns romances his way through it. The residue of Rothstein's iniquitous intrusion into baseball is dealt with by an agent of good from the outside in the person of Kenesaw Mountain Landis, appointed as the game's first commissioner by the owners of the Major Leagues in 1920. Although acquitted of criminal wrongdoing by the courts, the Black Sox players were subsequently banned by Landis from ever playing in the Majors again. *Baseball* does not condemn the players but arguably gives the impression that their expulsion was warranted as the game must be above the type of moral wrongdoing they were complicit in bringing to it. Nor does the recognition of an important intervention propose reverence of its enactor Kenesaw Mountain Landis. To ensure otherwise, Landis's reputation for self-promotion is identified in *Baseball*, John Sayles referring to him as a 'showboat judge'. Furthermore, in the 'Sixth Inning' of the documentary, Landis, still commissioner of the Majors in the 1940s, is exposed for stonewalling initiatives to break the colour line. The depiction of Landis, as with that of other figures, follows the mood of the particular historical episodes represented in *Baseball*.

Baseball, documentary and 'popular history'

Gerald Early remarks in the opening episode of *Baseball*:

> I enjoy the game ... principally because it makes me feel American and I think there are only three things that America will be known for two-thousand years from now when they study this civilization: the Constitution, jazz music, and baseball. They're the three most beautifully designed things this culture has ever produced.

Burns's documentaries *Baseball* and *Jazz* (2001) are obviously enough dedicated to the study of two of these cultural forms and *The Civil War* (1990) and *Thomas Jefferson* (1997) are intrinsically concerned with the US Constitution. *Baseball* and *Jazz* are diametrically opposite in their respective audience ambitions. *Baseball* is intended to identity the deep cultural significance of the sport and, in this sense, to complicate something that is simple, while *Jazz* takes an arcane musical form and attempts to explain its broader significance within America, thus simplifying something that is complicated. Relatedly, Burns's associate Geoffrey C. Ward has remarked, 'jazz ... is primarily an African American creation but it belongs to all of us'.[60]

The racial dimension of the statement can be inverted and applied to baseball, it is a game primarily created by white Americans, but belonging to all.

Both jazz and baseball are thus identified in the respective documentaries as cultural repositories of democratic values, and it is more than coincidental that both *Jazz* and *Baseball* first screened on the public television network PBS. PBS was established in 1969 under the imprimatur of the Public Broadcasting Act of 1967.[61] This act followed the report of the Carnegie Commission on Educational Television, a key recommendation of which was that public television should 'help us see America whole, in all its diversity' and be the 'clearest expression of American diversity, and excellence within diversity'.[62] Ken Burns has been an advocate of this notion of public television throughout his documentary making career and adherence to it is apparent in *Jazz* and *Baseball*.

It is important also to reiterate that *Baseball* is very much about the collective aesthetic experience of that sport. In a further remark to Ken Burns, Geoffrey C. Ward claims, 'jazz is art, not sociology'.[63] This is to recognize that art exists within the realm of culture, not divorced from the reality of social relations, but existing essentially in aesthetic terms apart from the extraneous social circumstances that come to bear on culture. These circumstances necessarily create social relations of culture, but baseball, like jazz, although lived out in historical webs of social relations, is art, first and foremost. Accordingly, Burns sets out to capture the popular appreciation of baseball's aesthetic moments and, simultaneously, to portray the collective passions that have gone into the game's cultural making.

Such portrayal has not been to the liking of all. In *Saying It's So*, Nathan regards *Baseball* as 'superb infotainment and mediocre social history'.[64] Two points of qualification are made. Firstly, Nathan claims to use the term infotainment in a way 'only partly pejorative' and, secondly, he indicates that his criticism pertains especially to *Baseball*'s account of the Black Sox scandal. Although Nathan's book is subtitled 'a cultural history of the Black Sox scandal' his dissatisfaction with *Baseball* is expressed via reference to social history. Nathan sees fault with *Baseball*, 'because it is largely driven by nostalgic images, dramatizations, and sound bites rather than analysis, it implicitly argues that feeling is first, that the best way to know the past is emotionally'.[65] For Nathan, giving view to emotion clouds the analytical possibilities of 'social history'. Nathan's cultural history is thus limited, being restricted to the 'documentary' category identified by Raymond Williams. His study of the Black Sox scandal thus analyses the way that the human experience of the scandal, in its various facets, has been recorded since 1919. In itself this is fine, but Nathan tends to ignore the lived experience dimension of cultural history by identifying human practices exclusively in relation to social history. The imposition of this particular dichotomy sustains his critical view of *Baseball* being steeped in emotion. Nathan can, in turn, be criticized for reducing *Baseball* to mere cultural artefact existing in separation from the lived history that it seeks to portray.

Nathan further accuses Burns of being 'more interested in excavating and exhibiting the ways in which ordinary Americans felt about the [Black Sox] scandal than he is in trying to figure out what brought it about or what it meant and means'.[66] This again seems a harsh judgement in its assumption that an inquiry primarily into how Americans have felt about baseball over the years mutually excludes a factual and analytical treatment. The over 30 minutes devoted to the Black Sox scandal in *Baseball* appears well researched, quite detailed and not noticeably at odds with the historical literature. Nathan admits, '*Baseball* [is] an acutely visceral documentary', which reflects the twentieth-century development in American cultural life toward 'sentiment and style ... feeling and form'. This comment points to how the documentary might best be regarded now and in years to come, i.e. as a visual document in keeping with the spirit of its times and the century in covers, a significant cultural study giving view to a major component of the American 'vernacular landscape'. Jules Tygiel claims that in *Baseball*, Burns 'encapsulated the excessive idealization of the game'.[67] This may be so, but idealization is not idolatry, and, in this sense, *Baseball* does not glorify the game but attempts to reveal the collective emotional investment that has been put into it over time. By taking such an approach the documentary contributes to historical knowledge on the *making* of baseball by American people.

Like any documentary maker Burns stood between the 'two counterpoised tendencies' identified earlier in the chapter, actuality and creativity. How well the documentary maker negotiates this tension becomes a matter of debate within interlocutions about his/her work. In regard to historical documentaries for a general audience such as *Baseball*, opinion differs on the worthiness of the offering as an item of popular history.[68] The position of the present author is supportive of Burns, as I regard *Baseball* to be a fine filmic record of, and resultantly a contribution to, cultural history. I find the words of John Grierson pertinent to Burns's endeavour:

> realist documentary ... has given itself the job of making poetry where no poet has gone before it, and where no ends, sufficient for the purposes of art, are easily observed. It requires not only taste but also inspiration, which is to say a very laborious, deep-seeing, deep-sympathising creative effort needed.[69]

Other academic critics are less favourable, including Daniel A. Nathan, believing *Baseball* to be overly rhetorical at the expense of analysis. However, and importantly in conclusion, a key point of agreement between academics such as Nathan and the present author, who work at the disciplinary intersection of history and cultural studies, is that documentaries and feature films matter. As even the sceptical historian Arthur Marwick admits, the majority of people in the present day come to know history more through film than the written word. The sporting past is no exception. And as film and documentary makers increasingly connect sport to other cultural and social themes, related critical discussion becomes all the more necessary.

Notes

[1] Grierson, *Grierson on Documentary*, 179.
[2] Hardy, *John Grierson*, 48.
[3] Grierson, *Grierson on Documentary*, 180.
[4] Kilborn and Izod, *An Introduction to Television Documentary*, 12.
[5] Secrest, *Kenneth Clark*, 230.
[6] Clark, *Civilisation*, xv. Clark was also confident that attendance of art galleries could be encouraged upon the general public. Upon appointment as Director of the National Gallery, he opened doors at 8 a.m. on the days of two major soccer matches in London in the hope of attracting football supporters to the gallery before their afternoon on the terrace: Secrest, *Kenneth Clark*, 92.
[7] Clark, *The Other Half: A Self Portrait*, 137–8. The concept of public service broadcasting in Britain was framed by John Reith during his time as Managing Director and Director-General of the British Broadcasting Corporation in the 1920s and 1930s. See Scannell, 'Public Service Broadcasting'.
[8] Marwick, *The New Nature of History*, 237–9.
[9] Samuel, 'People's History', xvi.
[10] Hoskins, *The Making of the English Landscape*, 14.
[11] Hoskins also wrote and hosted a subsequent series of 25 minute television documentary programmes focussing on the landscapes of particular regions in England. Meinig, 'Reading Landscape', 200.
[12] Hoskins, *English Landscapes*, 6.
[13] Hoskins, *Fieldwork in Local History*, 184.
[14] Hoskins, *The Making of the English Landscape*, 222.
[15] Johnson, *Ideas on Landscape*, 40.
[16] Hoskins, *The Making of the English Landscape*, 17.
[17] Johnson, *Ideas on Landscape*, 168.
[18] Ibid., 20.
[19] Conzen, *The Making of an American Landscape*.
[20] Meinig, 'Reading Landscape', 228.

21 Ward and Burns, *Baseball*. The preface to the book, titled 'Where Memory Gathers' is written by Ken Burns and Lyn Novick, xvii–xviii.

22 Ibid., xviii.

23 Marwick, *The New Nature of History*, 239.

24 Ibid. The quote is taken from Carnes' introduction to *Past Imperfect*, 9–10.

25 Marwick, *The New Nature of History*, 238–9.

26 Ibid., 239.

27 Richards, *Films and British National Identity*, 185.

28 Silk, Schultz, and Bracey 'From Mice to Men'.

29 Rosenstone, *History on Film/Film on History*, 8–9.

30 Barthes and Davis cited in Ibid., 16.

31 Ibid., 159.

32 Sorlin, *The Film in History*, 21.

33 The 'original documentary that inspired the film' is included on the *A League of Their Own* DVD, produced by Columbia Pictures, 2000.

34 Cahn, *Coming on Strong*, 148.

35 Williams, *Sports Cinema 100 Movies*, 106.

36 *Leonard Maltin's 2003 Movie & Video Guide*, 783.

37 Ebert, 'A League of Their Own' (*Chicago Sun-Times*, July 1, 1992).

38 Berlage, *Women in Baseball*, 193.

39 Rogosin, *Invisible Men*, 149–50.

40 Sobchack, 'Baseball in the Post-American Cinema', 182.

41 Baker, 'Sports Films, History, and Identity', 228.

42 Ibid. For an alternative viewpoint see Ardolino, 'Soul of the Game: Film Review', 386. Ardolino regards the film as 'quite empathetic about the debt that Robinson owed to his Negro League predecessors'. Ardolino notes how the film establishes a lineage from Paige and Gibson to Robinson and on to Willie Mays, who features in the film as a young boy.

43 The noted breakthrough study is Peterson, *Only the Ball Was White*.

44 Edgerton, *Ken Burns's America*, 125.

45 Nathan, 'Bearing Witness to Blackball', 455–61.

46 Ibid., 463–4.

47 Ibid., 468.

48 Edgerton, *Ken Burns's America*, 122.

49 Cited in Ibid., 126.

50 Nathan, *Saying It's So*.

51 Asinof, *Eight Men Out*.

52 Nathan, *Saying It's So*, 178.

53 Ibid., 180–1.

54 For example Roger Ebert, as cited by Ardolino, 'Ceremonies of Innocence and Experience', 47.

55 Nathan, *Saying It's So*, 181.

56 'A Conversation Between Eric Froner and John Sayles', Carnes, *Past Imperfect*, 11–28 (28).

57 Fitzgerald, *The Great Gatsby*, 60–1. The line is spoken by the narrator Nick Carraway in conversation with Jay Gatsby, following a luncheon with Meyer Wolfsheim. Upon the gangster's departure from the table, Gatsby informs Carraway that Wolfsheim was responsible for the 1919 World Series fix. 'The Faith of Fifty Million People' is used as the title for the 'Third Inning' (1910–20) of *Baseball*.

58 *Baseball*'s villainous portrayal of Rothstein is also criticized by Riess, 'The Early Innings', 65.

59 Nathan, *Saying It's So*, 205.

60 Edgerton, *Ken Burns's America*, 181.

61 Aufderheide, 'Television Public Service Broadcasting', 48.

62 Poon, 'Making Money and Serving the Public Interest', 128.

63 Edgerton, *Ken Burns's America*, 181.

64 Nathan, *Saying It's So*, 206.

65 Ibid.

66 Ibid., 205.

67 Tygiel, *Past Time*, 220.

68 Edgerton, *Ken Burns's America*, 127, comments favourably in this regard: 'Ken Burns, the producer-director as popular historian, regularly presents both the myth and reality of *Baseball*'s

legendary figures and incidents, leaving it up to the audience to decide which version of events it wants to believe'.

[69] Grierson, *Grierson on Documentary*, 84.

References

Ardolino, F. 'Ceremonies of Innocence and Experience in *Bull Durham*, *Field of Dreams*, and *Eight Men Out*'. In *Journal of Popular Film and Television* 18, no. 2 (1990): 43–52.

Ardolino, F. 'Soul of the Game: Film Review'. *NINE: a Journal of Baseball History and Culture* 5, no. 2 (1997): 384–7.

Asinof, E. *Eight Men Out: The Black Sox and the 1919 World Series*. New York: Henry Holt, 1987.

Aufderheide, P. 'Television Public Service Broadcasting: Public Interest Mandates – US'. In *Television Industries*, edited by D. Gomery and L. Hockley, 45–8. London: British Film Institute, 2006.

Baker, A. 'Sports Films, History, and Identity'. *Journal of Sport History* 25, no. 2 (1998): 217–33.

Berlage, G.I. *Women in Baseball: The Forgotten History*. Westport, CT: Praeger, 1994.

Cahn, S.K. *Coming on Strong: Gender and Sexuality in Twentieth Century Women's Sport*. Cambridge, MA: Harvard University Press, 1994.

Carnes, M.C. (ed. with T. Mico, J. Miller-Monzon, and D. Rubel) *Past Imperfect: History According to the Movies*. New York: Henry Holt, 1995.

Clark, K. *Civilisation*. London: British Broadcasting Corporation, 1969.

Clark, K. *The Other Half: A Self Portrait*. London: Hamish Hamilton, 1977.

Conzen, M.P., ed. *The Making of an American Landscape*, 2nd ed. London: Routledge, 2007.

Edgerton, G.R. *Ken Burns's America*. New York: Palgrave for St Martin's Press, 2001.

Fitzgerald, F.S. *The Great Gatsby*. London: Everyman's Library, 1991.

Grierson, J. *Grierson on Documentary*, ed. and intro. by Forsyth Hardy. London: Collins, 1946.

Hardy, F. *John Grierson: A Documentary Biography*. London: Faber and Faber, 1979.

Hoskins, W.G. *The Making of the English Landscape*. Harmondsworth: Penguin, 1970.

Hoskins, W.G. *English Landscapes: How to Read the Man-made Scenery of England*. London: British Broadcasting Service, 1973.

Hoskins, W.G. *Fieldwork in Local History*, 2nd ed. London: Faber and Faber, 1982.

Johnson, M. *Ideas on Landscape*. Malden, MA: Blackwell, 2007.

Kilborn, R., and J. Izod. *An Introduction to Television Documentary: Confronting Reality*. Manchester: Manchester University Press, 1997.

Leonard Maltin's Movie & Video Guide. New York: Signet, 2002.

Marwick, A. *The New Nature of History: Knowledge, Evidence, Language*. Basingstoke: Palgrave, 2001.

Meinig, D.W. 'Reading Landscape: an Appreciation of W.G. Hoskins and J.B. Jackson'. In *The Interpretation of Ordinary Landscapes*, edited by D.W. Meinig, 195–244. New York: Oxford University Press, 1979.

Nathan, D.A. 'Bearing Witness to Blackball: Buck O'Neil, the Negro Leagues, and the Politics of the Past'. *Journal of American Studies* 35, no. 3 (2001): 453–69.

Nathan, D.A. *Saying It's So: a Cultural History of the Black Sox Scandal*. Urbana, IL: University of Illinois Press, 2003.

Peterson, R. *Only the Ball Was White: a History of Legendary Black Players and All-Black Professional Teams*. New York: Oxford University Press, 1992.

Poon, G.P. 'Making Money and Serving the Public Interest: Public Broadcasting Can and Should Do Both'. In *Public Broadcasting and the Public Interest*, edited by M.P. McCauley, E.E. Peterson, B.L. Artz, and D. Halleck, 127–38. Armonk, NY: M.E. Sharpe, 2003.

Richards, J. *Films and British National Identity: From Dickens to Dad's Army*. Manchester: Manchester University Press, 1997.

Riess, S.A. 'The Early Innings'. *Journal of Sport History* 23, no. 1 (1996): 63–8.

Rogosin, D. *Invisible Men: Life in Baseball's Negro Leagues*. New York: Atheneum, 1985.

Rosenstone, R.A. *History on Film/Film on History*. London: Pearson Longman, 2006.

Samuel, R. 'People's History (Editorial Preface)'. In *People's History and Socialist Theory*, edited by R. Samuel, xv–xxxix. London: Routledge and Kegan Paul, 1981.

Scannell, P. 'Public Service Broadcasting: the History of a Concept'. In *Understanding Television*, edited by A. Goodwin and G. Whannell, 11–29. London: Routledge, 1990.

Secrest, M. *Kenneth Clark: A Biography*. New York: Fromm, 1986.

Silk, M., J. Schultz, and B. Bracey. 'From Mice to Men: *Miracle*, Mythology and the "Magic Kingdom"'. *Sport in Society* 11, no. 2/3 (2008): 279–97.

Sobchack, V. 'Baseball in the Post-American Cinema, or Life in the Minor Leagues'. In *Out of Bounds: Sports, Media, and the Politics of Identity*, edited by A. Baker and T. Boyd, 173–97. Indianapolis, IN: University of Indiana Press, 1997.

Sorlin, P. *The Film in History: Restaging the Past*. Totowa, NJ: Barnes and Noble, 1980.

Tygiel, J. *Past Time: Baseball as History*. New York: Oxford University Press, 2000.

Ward, G.C., and K. Burns. *Baseball: An Illustrated History*. New York: Knopf, 1994.

Williams, Randy. *Sports Cinema 100 Movies: The Best of Hollywood's Athletic Heroes, Losers, Myths and Misfits*. Pompton Plains, NJ: Limelight Editions, 2006.

The 'global triumph' of sport

Globalization has, for a number of years now, been a buzzword within the humanities and social sciences. Usage of this term has been driven by an academic fascination with the world as an increasingly interconnected place, in which localized forms of culture have become increasingly subject to homogenizing global influences.[1] The immediacy of contact made possible by the developments in communication has thus given rise to the discussion of *global culture*. The term globalization tends to imply that culture is handed down and, by this understanding, poses challenge to a sustained view of cultural activities and practices being formed and shaped within particular urban, regional and national settings. Relatedly, globalization works against a continuation of the idea of culture being collectively *made* by people within contexts of lived experience. In short, the notion of globalization appears at odds with the position on cultural history advanced in this volume.

However, as Maguire suggests in his seminal book on globalization and sport, to submit to the intellectual discussion of global culture does not mean subscription to the view that such a culture has been set in stone.[2] Via Roland Robertson, Maguire points out that globalization is a process, which prompts consideration of the world as 'a single place' made up of interweaving cultural patterns.[3] In the final analysis there is no one global culture or cohesive system, but we can imagine a 'global field' where increasingly cultural interaction, mimesis and borrowing occur. Furthermore, Robertson uses the term 'glocalization' to convey the idea that homogenizing global influences are not customarily imposed onto local cultures.[4] The global cultural impulse is, in most cases, 'intertwined with forces of heterogenization'.[5] Such forces will apply differently in regard to different forms of culture. For example, global impulses will impact differently on music cultures than they will on sport cultures. Indeed, Rowe argues that sport tends to not only resist globalizing forces but to repudiate them.[6] His point is that some sports cultures – association football being a key example – are so strongly embedded with national allegiance that globalization as a concept bears little relevance to what goes on in the arena of global football and the national media that report on its tournaments.

Rowe's description of the media generated chauvinism in England during the 2002 FIFA World Cup brings to mind George Orwell's scathing criticism of the nationalist fervour roused in England during the visit of the Dynamo Moscow soccer team in the closing months of 1945.[7] Orwell's concern seemed to be that no sooner had the Second World War ended than emergent international tensions were flamed on the football field by club teams symbolic in their respective representations of Russia and England. Hence Orwell's famous characterization of sport as 'war minus the shooting'. Sport faired little better under the pen of novelist Alan Sillitoe. Writing shortly after the 1972 Olympic Games, Sillitoe lambasted the decision taken by the International Olympic Committee President Avery Brundage to allow the Games to continue following the deaths of 11 Israeli athletes in a hostage crisis involving Palestinian terrorists.[8] Sillitoe claimed that this 'indecent' decision – based he believed on national pride and avarice – showed not only that 'sporting spirit' had become a sham, but raised the question of whether it had ever existed at all.

Such scepticism would no doubt have vexed the founder of the modern Olympic Games Pierre de Coubertin. The French aristocrat was aware that the modern Games could not replicate those of Ancient Greece in practice but he sincerely believed in the continuation of the Hellenistic sporting spirit.[9] In keeping with the classical humanist dimension of the Greek legacy, Coubertin defined *Olympism* as a highpoint in the 'cult of humanity' where men strive to the limits of their imperfection. It is in this humanly based sense of excellence that they aspire to heroism.[10] Coubertin lived during an age of fractious national relations in Europe but, in unwitting anticipation of Orwell's distinction, he spoke of patriotism rather than nationalism as the ideational means best suited to mustering cross-national support for the Olympic Games at the twilight of the nineteenth-century. As MacAloon notes, Coubertin 'was no fool', he was aware of the practical difficulty of the task before him, yet as an 'irrefragable and aggressive optimist' he believed that the essential goodness of Olympism will prevail over the political pitfalls that no doubt hinder the conducting of the Games.[11] However, again according to MacAloon, what Coubertin never did realize 'was that the dramatization of evil and conflict at the Olympics would prove an essential component of their global triumph'.

Toward such realization we may turn to an unlikely source, the enigmatic Spanish artist Salvador Dali. Under commission from the Spanish Olympic Committee – presided over at the time by Juan Antonio Samaranch – Dali painted *Cosmic Athlete* for the Biennial Arts Festival to coincide with the 1968 Olympic Games in Mexico City.[12] One of Dali's least abstract paintings, *Cosmic Athlete* is a dreamlike adaptation of Myron's *Discobulus*. The message is debatable; indeed, in keeping with Dali's lingering commitment to surrealism, unknowable in certainty even to its creator. The amber glow that surrounds the coliseum-like building behind the discus thrower could envision either heaven or hell and related speculation pertains to the multitude of naked figures ascending a darkened cloud, some reaching for offshoots of the Olympic flame. However one chooses to interpret *Cosmic Athlete* the words of a popular art historian remain pertinent, '[Dali] painted unreality with meticulous realism, which is why [his work] is so disturbing'.[13] Dali gives us an image of the 'dramatization of evil and conflict at the Olympics', which Coubertin could not countenance. Yet how might this image be reconciled with the notion of 'global triumph'?

Herbert Read suggests that Dali's association with reactionary political forces in Spain since the 1940s was reflected in a retreat from humanistic values in his paintings.[14] Orwell was even harsher in his assessment of Dali, declaring that in Dali's outlook and character 'the bedrock decency of a human being does not exist'.[15] Be this as it may, Dali was not beyond evoking political criticism within his work. Important in this regard are his 1945 paintings *Atomica Melancholica* and the ironically titled *The Apotheosis of Homer*. Each of these works is said to be an expression of Dali's horror at the dropping of the first atomic bomb on Hiroshima.[16] Of particular interest is the symbolism of baseball apparent in both paintings. In *Atomica Melancholia* players slide into base as a distant umpire looks on and a faceless player and ghostly figure shape up to each other with baseball bats as weapons. *The Apotheosis of Homer* features a familiar Dali technique whereby a crutch-like object is used to prop up a large wilting mass, appearing with various degrees of clarity in different paintings as an atrophying bodily organ. The crutch in *The Apotheosis of Homer* is made up of a piece of dilapidated wood resembling an old baseball bat. In *Atomica Melancholia* in particular Dali rather clearly uses the imagery of baseball to suggest a relationship between American cultural imperialism and the vanquishing of Japan that occurred with the human annihilation caused by the bombing.[17]

This is not to suggest that Dali disliked baseball and its role within American cultural life. In the year following the end of the Second World War Dali commenced work with Walt Disney on a film, *Destiny*, which did not eventuate into production. Nevertheless, Dali's fascination with the liveliness of American popular culture, including baseball, had spurred his enthusiasm for such a project. Indeed, he prepared a sketch *Baseball Player* in association with the film.[18] As far back as 1928, Dali declared his interest in popular culture as the key signatory of the *Anti-Artistic Manifesto* (better known as the *Yellow Manifesto*). Sounding not unlike the Futurists before them, Dali and his Surrealist colleagues declared the contemporary art scene and its related areas such as theatre – at least within Dali's Catalonia – to be 'suffocating and crushingly boring'.[19] Supported 'in contrast' were the 'new phenomena full of an intense joy and joviality [which] hold the attention of today's youth'. Amongst the items of popular culture mentioned favourably by Dali and colleagues, 'there is ... the stadium, boxing, tennis and other sports'. Underlying Dali's promotion of sport was the humanistic belief, one not far from Coubertin's view little more than 20 years earlier, 'that sportsmen are closer to the spirit of Ancient Greece than our [contemporary] intellectuals'.

In 1986 Salvador Dali supported Barcelona's successful bid for the staging of the Olympic Games in 1992. In what might be read as a positive evocation of *Cosmic Athlete* Dali declared his support 'with all my energy and all the solar energy in the bronze muscles of the athletes'.[20] So irrespective of Dali's political affinities we can see via his attitude to sport the pervasiveness of a humanistic temperament over the years. Looking back to the *Manifesto*, Dali 'affirmed' not only the athlete but also the crowd. Dali's declaration that the anonymous crowd 'contributes with its daily effort and affirmation of the new era ... living in harmony with its own time' runs counter to the denigration of the mass mind, characteristic of intellectualism throughout the twentieth century. The 'global triumph' of the Olympic Games occurs via the unbridled desire of the universal crowd for a festival of sport in the 'spirit' of the Greeks irrespective of the 'evil and conflict' that frequently come to bear on the occasioning of the Games. But as ever Dali's messages were mixed and his enthusiasm for sport as a burgeoning area of popular culture was not unrelieved from surrealist nightmare. His 1943 painting *Poetry of America* offers an early criticism of forces of globalization within modern sport. By later giving the painting the alternative title *Cosmic Athletes* Dali may have been reintroducing it as a counter-aesthetic to *Cosmic Athlete*.[21]

Writing in 1960 Arthur Koestler used the term 'coca-colonization' to describe how Europe had consented to American cultural imperialism: 'The United States ... waged no Opium War against us to force their revolting "coke" down our throats. Europe bought the whole package because it wanted it. The Americans did not americanize us – they were merely one step ahead on the road towards a global civilization.'[22]

Koestler continues, in familiar cultural elitist fashion, that the emerging mass-culture is uniform, mechanized and vulgar, levelled-down 'to the lowest common denominator'.[23] Dali's *Poetry of America* provides a somewhat different take on 'coca-colonization'; his painting offers critical reflection upon the future rather than a tiresome rant about a past lost. According to Radford, *Poetry of America*, with its 'weeping map of Africa', highlights the exploitation of African-Americans.[24] The Coca-Cola bottle attached to the breast of one of the pirouetting football players oozes 'black blood' onto a symbolically white cloth. Descharnes and Neret note Dali's admission that *Poetry of America* was intended as a warning against race conflict in the United States, which became a portent given events in that country since the mid-1940s.[25] Nevertheless, Dali's ambivalence prevails in even this highly moralistic painting, its landscape representing Dali's 'New World', a welcomed Americanization of his own Catalonia.[26] The painting also depicts triumph as much as despair for 'Black America' in the form of a naked athlete (perhaps a basketball player) stemming from the upper-spine of a white football player and projecting upwards – 'the egg of the future world balanced on his forefinger'.[27]

Poetry of America shows that commercialization of culture has been part of an intra-colonizing process within the US, but that the vitality of cultural forms, especially sport, promise resistance to the shackles of social exploitation. Sport has never been the panacea wished by some social optimists, including Coubertin, but nor does it typify the descent into 'global civilization' as a current generation of pessimistic scholars are inclined to indicate. The artwork of Salvador Dali continues to provide us with an appreciation of the historical complexity of modern sport and that we do well to regard sport with ambivalence rather than either outright celebration or negativity.

In his book on the history of fame, *The Frenzy of Renown*, Leo Braudy contends that two of the best-known public figures of the post-First World War period, Ernest Hemingway and Charles Lindbergh, were famous for their 'exemplary solitude'.[28] As the spotlight of a nascent mass-media beckoned for would-be celebrities, these reluctant 'stars' shunned its glare. Not so their contemporary Salvador Dali whose genius for self-promotion made the most of the publicity opportunities offered by the age.[29] Dali also believed that as a great artist he was entitled to indulge his every whim, the 1920s providing an ideal time for the pursuit of gluttony – 'Dali gorged on chicken, champagne, and anything else he could "possess in the sacred tabernacle of the palate"'.[30] Another celebrity of the time, Babe Ruth did not share Dali's talent for self-promotion – he had no need to given the attention afforded him by the burgeoning 1920s media-industry – but the description of Dali's gluttony could almost be written for The Babe. As discussed in an earlier essay, Ruth's hedonism was part of his popularity. Ruth's story resonates with what Braudy refers to as the 'democratization of fame'; his lack of social graces and etiquette did not exclude Ruth from posh hotels and elite gatherings, and this was not missed by an attentive public. The 'average Joe' was able to live the grand lifestyle vicariously through adoration of the socially ordinary Ruth.

But contrary to the popular view – captured superbly in a 1922 photo of a boater and bow-tie clad Ruth shoulder deep within a high-spirited crowd of young men and boys[31] – Ruth was not as accessible as his public imagined him to be. Ruth's social ordinariness was checked by his cultural extraordinariness owing to his rare talent on the baseball diamond. Upon scrutiny, the clamour surrounding a star such as Ruth is built on an unwitting deceit. The imagining of him as one of the people was not really about wanting him to be like the people, but about people wanting to be like him – extraordinary rather than ordinary. The desire for immortality is at the heart of this wish. As Charles Lemert puts it: 'to encourage celebrity is to pretend that the deadliness of ordinary life is not as it is. We invent celebrities because, as recompense for our gifts to them, they encourage us to escape for a time from what is and must be.'[32]

Thankfully only the most hubristic of sport stars fail to appreciate the mortal limitation of their superlative talents. Their post-match aches and pains and ongoing battles against injury, fatigue and psychological meltdown no doubt serve as reminders of mortality. The extraordinariness of these mortals may be god-given but this does not make them god-like. No wonder so many sporting greats have shied from public expectation and its attendant scrutiny in preference for the 'exemplary solitude' of Hemingway and Lindberg, and that in the current day those who submit to the frenzy of renown do so in ways to merely enhance the mirage of accessibility. No better example is the appearance of the global soccer darling David Beckham in artist Sam Taylor-Wood's video portrait *David*, exhibited at London's National Portrait Gallery in 2004.

David, shown on a one metre-wide plasma screen, featured a 67 minute recording of David Beckham asleep in his Madrid hotel room, the camera gaze providing eyelevel view of the player's head and naked torso. Gallery visitor's – by most accounts *David* attracted an overwhelmingly female audience – were invited to take as much time as they pleased to experience virtual intimacy with Beckham, although few onlookers seem to have stayed longer than 20 minutes.[33] The title of Taylor-Wood's work suggests gleeful comparison to Michelangelo's famous statue, but more pertinent association is to be made with the viewing of a sleeping monarch by privileged courtesans in the seventeenth century. Yet, stripped of historical referent, is *David*, as claimed by art journalist Laura Barton, 'nothing more than an hour's footage of a really handsome, really famous footballer fast asleep'?[34]

Catherine Fowler argues that Taylor-Wood's *David* challenges the notion that intimacy with celebrity must remain at a 'discursive level'.[35] This is to say that Beckham's willingness to be filmed in the privacy of sleep and to have the resultant recording placed on public display appears to disrupt the distinction between a materially present and mediated present Beckham – being in the gallery with Beckham promises, as the title of Barton's article suggests, to be in bed with Beckham. However, the impression of greater intimacy with Beckham is, as Fowler concludes, just that: an impression. The closeness to Beckham in a darkened space gives an initial illusion of intimacy that is eventually broken once an awareness of the public context in which *David* is viewed returns to the onlooker. *David* may well be nothing more than a famous and handsome footballer asleep on film, but this is the trick of Taylor-Wood's art. The promise of intimacy is snatched by the realization of impersonality and the reminder that Beckham is after all a 'public man'.

Beckham's handsomeness and sexual attraction to people drawn to men is not in question, but upon stepping out of the National Portrait Gallery and back onto the streets of London, during the course of an afternoon, the viewers of *David* may well have seen in passing a number of young men whose looks could arguably rival those of David Beckham. Yet these men will at best receive a second glance and a lingering thought. The desire to be with Beckham is generated by his unattainability, an acknowledgement of his extraordinariness, which unlike the fame of someone like Paris Hilton – or even Beckham's former-pop-star wife Victoria – is based on his superlative talent. In 1961 Daniel Boorstin predicted that as we move into what we have now come to call the global age, the fabrication of fame will intensify. But then, as now, to use Boorstin's words, 'we can make a celebrity, but we can never make a hero … [as] heroes are self-made'.[36] Adoration for Beckham, even from those who know little or nothing about soccer, is ultimately attributable to his prowess heroism. This he shares with Ruth, and thus like the Babe, Beckham is a *cultural* icon with god-like allure. Wanting to be with Beckham and to be like Ruth are different expressions of the same underlying desire, to be close to superhumaness and within seeming reach of immortality.

However, the relationship between the sport hero and his/her public will not always be struck in these terms. While the celebration of celebrity involves self-deception,[37] honest confrontation of the human condition marks the relationship between the *sport* loving fan and the sport hero. Sport lovers appreciate not only the aesthetic dimension to sport performance, but also the moral dimension of the contest, which, for the hero, necessarily involves struggle – against opponents, against the clock, against pain, against oneself. With struggle comes suffering and the suffering metaphorically promoted by sport since gladiatorial times is the confrontation of death.[38] Engagement in forms of modern sport is not often life threatening, but all highly competitive sport involves confrontation of mortal being. Sport careers vary in length according to the sport and other factors, but the sporting life is a human life in microcosm and its expiration is all too quick – a consequence anxiously observed by both athlete and fan. The well-rehearsed suggestion that sport spectatorship and following is surrender to passivity bears no understanding of the communal relationship between sport hero, team and fan(s). The hero's suffering is shared by the fan, week in week out, tournament to tournament and it is through such preparedness to suffer that sporting cultures are made, not handed down. Such is the 'global triumph' of sport and such has been its historical existence – across different national, regional and local contexts – as not only a 'whole way of life' but, also, as a 'whole way of struggle'.

Notes

[1] Inglis and Hughson, *Confronting Culture*, 216.

[2] Maguire, *Global Sport*, 4.

[3] Robertson, *Globalization*.

4   Robertson, 'Glocalization'.

5   Inglis and Hughson, *Confronting Culture*, 224.

6   Rowe, 'Sport and the Repudiation of the Global', 282.

7   Orwell, 'The Sporting Spirit'.

8   Sillitoe, 'Sport and Nationalism'.

9   Finley and Pleket, *The Olympic Games*, 4.

10 MacAloon, *This Great Symbol*, 141 and 258. For a comprehensive primary source see de Coubertin, *Olympism*.

11 MacAloon, *This Great Symbol*, 181.

12 Juli, 'Salvador Dali's Surrealistic Sports'. For an image of *Cosmic Athlete* see Descharnes and Neret, *Salvador Dali: The Paintings*, Volume 2, 576.

13 Beckett, *The Story of Painting*, 674.

14 Read, *A Concise History of Modern Painting*, 141–2.

15 Orwell, 'Benefit of Clergy', 189.

16 Descharnes and Neret, *Dali*, 141. Images of these paintings can be seen in Descharnes and Neret, *Salvador Dali: The Paintings*, Volume I, *The Apotheosis of Homer*, 382; *Atomica Melancholica (Melancholy, Atomic, Uranic Idyll)*, 385.

17 A cultural history of baseball in Japan, in terms of the Japanese receiving the game from US visitors then *making* it their own is fascinatingly told in Whiting, *You Gotta Have Wa*.

18 Juli, 'Salvador Dali's Surrealistic Sports', 695.

19 'The Anti-Artistic Manifesto [1928]', in Descharnes, *Oui*, 46–50.

20 Juli, 'Salvador Dali's Surrealistic Sports', 694.

21 For an image of *Poetry of America* see Descharnes and Neret, *Salvador Dali: The Paintings*, Volume I, 364.

22 Koestler, *The Lotus and the Robot*, 277.

23 George Ritzer's subsequent discussion of the 'McDonaldization' of culture and society, although developed sociologically, retains elements of the alarmism sounded by Koestler. Ritzer, *The McDonaldization of Society*.

24 Radford, *Dali*, 202.

25 Descharnes and Neret, *Salvador Dali: The Paintings*, Volume I, 380.

26 Ibid., 374.

27 Ibid., 380.

28 Braudy, *The Frenzy of Renown*.

29 In an unheard of distinction for a painter Dali featured on the cover of *Time* magazine in 1936. Schiebler, *Dali*, 13.

30 Dali cited in Conrad, *Modern Times, Modern Places*, 193.

31 Ward and Burns, *Baseball*, 152–3.

32 Lemert, *Muhammad Ali*, 33.

33 Barton, 'In Bed with Beckham', 54; Fowler, 'Spending Time with (a) Celebrity'.

34 Barton, 'In Bed with Beckham'.

35 Fowler, 'Spending Time with (a) Celebrity'.

36 Boorstin, *The Image*, 58.

37 Lemert, *Muhammad Ali*, 34.

38 Cf. Gumbrecht, *In Praise of Athletic Beauty*, 158–9.

References

Barton, L. 'In Bed with Beckham'. *Time* (17 May 2004): 54.

Beckett, Sister W. *The Story of Painting*, enhanced and expanded edition. London: Ted Smart, 1994.

Boorstin, D.J. *The Image: or what Happend to the American Dream*. London: Penguin, 1963 [1961].

Braudy, L. *The Frenzy of Renown: Fame and Its History*. New York: Vintage, 1997.

Conrad, P. *Modern Times, Modern Places: How Life and Art, Were Transformed in a Century of Revolution, Innovation and Radical Change*. New York: Alfred A. Knopf, 1999.

de Coubertin, P. *Olympism: Selected Writings*. Lausanne: International Olympic Committee, 2000.

Descharnes, R., ed. *Oui: the Paranoid-Critical Revolution, Salvador Dali writings 1927–1933*. Boston, MA: Exact Change, 1998.

Descharnes, R., and G. Neret. *Dali*. Cologne: Taschen, 2006.

Descharnes, R., and G. Neret. *Salvador Dali: The Paintings*, in two volumes. Volume I, 1904–1946; Volume II, 1946–1989. Cologne: Taschen, 2007.

Finley, M. I., and H. W. Pleket. *The Olympic Games: The First Thousand Years*. London: Chatto and Windus, 1976.

Fowler, C. 'Spending Time with (a) Celebrity: Sam Taylor-Wood's Video Portrait of David Beckham'. In *Framing Celebrity: New Directions in Celebrity Culture*, edited by S. Holmes and S. Redmond, 241–52. London: Routledge, 2006.

Gumbrecht, H.U. *In Praise of Athletic Beauty*. Cambridge, MA: The Belknap Press of Harvard University, 2006.

Inglis, D., and J. Hughson. *Confronting Culture: Sociological Vistas*. Cambridge: Polity, 2003.

Juli, R.B. 'Salvador Dali's Surrealistic Sports'. *Olympic Review* 229–30 (1986): 694–6.

Koestler, A. *The Lotus and the Robot*. London: Hutchinson, 1960.

Lemert, C. *Muhammad Ali: Trickster in the Culture of Irony*. Cambridge: Polity Press, 2003.

MacAloon, J.J. *This Great Symbol: Pierre de Coubertin and the Origins of the Modern Olympic Games*. Chicago, IL: The University of Chicago Press, 1981.

Maguire, J. *Global Sport: Identities, Societies, Civilization*. Cambridge: Polity, 1999.

Orwell, G. 'Benefit of Clergy: Some Notes on Salvador Dali'. In *The Collected Essays, Journalism and Letters of George Orwell, volume III: As I Please (1943–1945)*, edited by S. Orwell and I. Angus, 185–95. Harmondsworth: Penguin, 1970.

Orwell, G. 'The Sporting Spirit'. In *Essays: George Orwell*, selected and intro. by John Carey, 967–70. New York: Knopf, 2002.

Radford, R. *Dali*. London: Phaidon, 1997.

Read, H. *A Concise History of Modern Painting*, new and augmented edition. London: Thames and Hudson, 1974.

Ritzer, G. *The McDonaldization of Society*. Thousand Oaks, CA: Pine Forge, 2000.

Robertson, R. *Globalization: Social Theory and Global Culture*. London: Sage, 1992.

Robertson, R. 'Glocalization: Time-Space and Homogeneity-Heterogeneity'. In *Global Modernities*, edited by M. Featherstone, S. Lash, and R. Robertson, 25–44. London: Sage, 1995.

Rowe, D. 'Sport and the Repudiation of the Global'. *International Review for the Sociology of Sport* 38, no. 3 (2003): 281–94.

Schiebler, R. *Dali: The Reality of Dreams*. Munich: Prestel, 2005.

Sillitoe, A. 'Sport and Nationalism'. In *Mountains and Caverns*, 84–8. London: W.H. Allen, 1975.

Ward, G.C., and K. Burns. *Baseball: An Illustrated History*. New York: Knopf, 1994.

Whiting, R. *You Gotta Have Wa: When Two Cultures Collide on the Baseball Diamond*. New York: Macmillan, 1989.

Index

Works of art (in italics) refer to books except where otherwise specified
Locators for headings which also have subheadings refer to general aspects of that topic